Cephale
et
Procris

Recent Researches in Music

A-R Editions publishes seven series of critical editions, spanning the history of Western music, American music, and oral traditions.

Recent Researches in the Music of the Middle Ages and Early Renaissance
    Charles M. Atkinson, general editor

Recent Researches in the Music of the Renaissance
    James Haar, general editor

Recent Researches in the Music of the Baroque Era
    Christoph Wolff, general editor

Recent Researches in the Music of the Classical Era
    Eugene K. Wolf, general editor

Recent Researches in the Music of the Nineteenth and Early Twentieth Centuries
    Rufus Hallmark, general editor

Recent Researches in American Music
    John M. Graziano, general editor

Recent Researches in the Oral Traditions of Music
    Philip V. Bohlman, general editor

Each edition in *Recent Researches* is devoted to works by a single composer or to a single genre. The content is chosen for its high quality and historical importance, and each edition includes a substantial introduction and critical report. The music is engraved according to the highest standards of production using our own proprietary software called MusE.

For information on establishing a standing order to any of our series, or for editorial guidelines on submitting proposals, please contact:

A-R Editions, Inc.
801 Deming Way
Madison, Wisconsin 53717

800 736-0070 (U.S. book orders)
608 836-9000 (phone)
608 831-8200 (fax)
http://www.areditions.com

RECENT RESEARCHES IN THE MUSIC OF THE BAROQUE ERA, 88

Elisabeth-Claude
Jacquet de La Guerre

Cephale et Procris

Edited by Wanda R. Griffiths

A-R Editions, Inc.
Madison

A-R Editions, Inc., Madison, Wisconsin 53717
© 1998 by A-R Editions, Inc.

All rights reserved. No part of this book may be reproduced or transmitted in any form by any electronic or mechanical means (including photocopying, recording, or information storage and retrieval) without permission in writing from the publisher.

The purchase of this work does not convey the right to perform it in public, nor to make a recording of it for any purpose. Such permission must be obtained in advance from the publisher.

A-R Editions is pleased to support scholars and performers in their use of *Recent Researches* material for study or performance. Subscribers to any of the *Recent Researches* series, as well as patrons of subscribing institutions, are invited to apply for information about our "Copyright Sharing Policy."

Printed in the United States of America

ISBN 0-89579-404-7
ISSN 0484-0828

∞ The paper used in this publication meets the minimum requirements of the American National Standard for Information Sciences—Permanence of Paper for Printed Library Materials, ANSI Z39.48-1984.

Contents

Acknowledgments vii

Introduction ix
   The Composer ix
   Text and Author x
   The Music of the Edition x
   The Reception of the Opera xii
   Notes on Performance xiii
   Notes xvii

Text and Translation xx
   Personnages du Prologue / Characters of the Prologue xx
   Prologue xxi
   Acteurs de la tragédie / Actors of the Tragedy xxiv
   Acte I / Act 1 xxiv
   Acte II / Act 2 xxix
   Acte III / Act 3 xxxv
   Acte IV / Act 4 xl
   Acte V / Act 5 xlv

Plates li

Cephale et Procris

Prologue 3

Acte I
   Scène première. *Procris, Borée* 72
   Scène seconde. *Procris, Dorine* 75
   Scène troisième. *Procris, Arcas* 79
   Scène quatrième. *Arcas, Dorine* 80
   Scène cinquième. *Dorine, Arcas, Troupe d'Athéniens et d'Athéniennes* 86
   Scène sixième. *Tous les acteurs de la scène précédente. Le Roi, Cephale* 109
   Scène septième. *Tous les acteurs de la scène précédente. Le Roi, La Prêtresse* 113
   Entr'acte: Second Air [pour les Athéniens] 110

Acte II
   Scène première. *Procris* 116
   Scène seconde. *Procris, Cephale* 121
   Scène troisième. *Cephale* 127
   Scène quatrième. *Borée, Troupe de Thraces de la suite de Borée, Cephale retiré à l'écart* 131

Scène cinquième. *Tous les acteurs de la scène précédente. Troupe de pâtres et de bergères* 146
Scène sixième. *Cephale, Borée* 153
Scène septième. *L'Aurore, Cephale, Iphis* 154
Scène huitième. *L'Aurore, Iphis* 160
Entr'acte: Bourée 151

Acte III

Scène première. *Cephale* 164
Scène seconde. *Cephale, Iphis* 167
Scène troisième. *Cephale, Iphis, La Volupté, Suite de la Volupté, Troupe de Plaisirs, de Graces, et quatres Amours* 170
Scène quatrième. *L'Aurore, Iphis, Cephale, La Volupté, Les Plaisirs, et Les Graces* 186
Scène cinquième. *L'Aurore, Iphis* 192

Acte IV

Scène première. *Dorine, Arcas* 194
Scène seconde. *L'Aurore, Iphis, Dorine, Arcas* 198
Scène troisième. *Procris* 205
Scène quatrième. *Procris, La Jalousie, La Rage, Le Désespoir* 210
Scène cinquième. *Procris, La Jalousie, La Rage, Le Désespoir* 211
Scène sixième. *La Jalousie, La Rage, Le Désespoir, Troupe de Démons, Procris* 214
Scène septième. *Procris, Cephale, Dorine* 229

Acte V

Scène première. *Procris, Dorine* 232
Scène seconde. *Borée, Procris, Dorine, Troupe de Thraces et d'Athénians* 237
Scène troisième. *Procris, Dorine* 261
Scène quatrième. *L'Aurore, Procris, Dorine* 261
Scène cinquième. *L'Aurore* 264
Scène sixième. *L'Aurore, Iphis* 265
Scène septième. *Cephale, Arcas* 267
Scène dernière. *Procris, Dorine, Cephale* 268

Critical Report 275

Sources 275
Editorial Methods 276
Critical Notes 279

Acknowledgments

The assistance and support of many people are necessary in order to complete a project of this size. I greatly appreciate the support which Roland Jackson has showed for this project over the years, particularly in its initial phase while I was still working on my doctorate at the Claremont Graduate School. Catherine Massip of the Bibliothèque Nationale was extremely helpful, always responding promptly to my requests for microfilm or information. I am grateful to Marie N. Deseilligny of Suzzallo Reference (University of Washington) for her help in tracking down English translations for the characters in the opera. Ann Therkelsen generously assisted me in translating some of the especially tricky passages of the *livret*. Rebecca Rollins provided invaluable assistance by reading the prefatory material with fresh eyes and providing me with very helpful comments. Both Rebecca and Diane Johnson have provided a great deal of moral support over the years, patiently talking me through whatever the current crisis might be and offering words of encouragement and support.

The biggest expression of gratitude goes to my husband Glenn Nestlerode, who has always supported my work both through his willingness to listen to me talk about the project, and by quietly taking over tasks and duties which I would otherwise be handling so that I could have more time to work on the edition. I am also grateful to my daughter Elizabeth, who calls me back from the seventeenth century when I am in danger of getting lost in my work, and reminds me to appreciate dandelions and playing games and being alive.

Introduction

The Composer

Elisabeth-Claude Jacquet was born in 1665 to Claude Jacquet and Anne de La Touche.[1] The family members were artisans and therefore part of the emerging middle class, not part of the nobility. Her father was an organist and harpsichord builder, her mother was related to the Daquin family.[2] Elisabeth was a child prodigy, making her first documented appearance at court at the age of twelve in July of 1677. The description of her performance states that she had been appearing there for four years.[3] It was apparently at this performance that Louis XIV decided to take her into the court so that she would receive an appropriate education. Although we know nothing regarding her musical education, we do know that Louis XIV's offspring by his mistresses, who were also reared at court, received music instruction from some of the best musicians of the day: Jean-Henri d'Anglebert, Michel Richard de Lalande, and François Couperin.[4]

In 1684 at the age of nineteen Jacquet married Marin de La Guerre, the son of the well-known organist and composer Michel de La Guerre.[5] Marin was an organist, harpsichord teacher, and composer, although none of his compositions are known to have survived. Just one year after her marriage, Jacquet is reported to have had her first stage work, a pastorale (now lost), performed at court in the Dauphin's apartment.[6] Her first extant work was published three years later, the 1687 *Pièces de clavessin*, followed around 1691 or 1692 by her (unpublished) ballet *Jeux à l'honneur de la victoire*,[7] and in 1694 by her opera *Cephale et Procris*.[8] Jacquet's trio sonatas were completed by 1695. Sébastien Brossard borrowed them in that year so that he could make a copy,[9] thus making them among the earliest sonatas by a French composer to circulate in France.[10]

At some point in the first years of their marriage, a son was born to Elisabeth and Marin. The only thing we know of this son is what Titon du Tillet tells us in his entry on Jacquet in his *Parnasse français*: "She had an only son, who at eight years of age surprised those who heard him play the Harpsichord, whether in performance of pieces, or in accompaniment; but death carried him off in his tenth year."[11]

By the time her opera was performed at the Paris Opéra (Académie Royale de musique) in 1694, Jacquet was at a high point in her career and life. She had composed works for the stage, published a set of harpsichord pieces, and was well known as a performer and improviser on the harpsichord. She was married to a fellow musician who appeared to be supportive of her musical endeavors, had a musically gifted son, and had the attention of the king, as the dedications to him appearing in her publications attest.

We know nothing of Jacquet's musical endeavors in the years between the performance of her opera and the appearance of her 1707 publication *Sonates pour le violon et pour le clavecin*. This apparent lack of musical productivity may perhaps be explained by five painful losses she suffered during this time: her son, who probably died between 1695 and 1700, assuming he was born within the first five years of her marriage, her mother in 1698, her father in 1702, her husband in 1704, and her older brother Nicolas in 1707.[12]

From 1707 Jacquet was actively involved in the musical life of Paris. During this time she was among the first in France to publish books of cantatas, and she ran a musical salon out of her home, where she gave a series of popular recitals. She also performed at, and composed music for, the fair theaters (Théâtres de la Foire) between about 1708 and 1715.[13] Her last major work was a Te Deum, composed in 1721 to celebrate the recovery of young Louis XV from smallpox and sung in the chapel at the Louvre.[14] Little is known of Jacquet's musical activities during the 1720s, although a few songs by her were published by Christoph Ballard in some of the *Receuil d'airs sérieux et à boire*.[15] She died on 27 June 1729, and was buried at her parish church (Saint-Eustache) in Paris. According to Titon du Tillet, Jacquet's "last compositions" passed into the hands of her heirs upon her death and, although they had not yet been printed as of 1732, he fully expected them to be published.[16] They have never been found.

Jacquet was recognized by her contemporaries and in the years following her death as a composer of significant stature. Titon du Tillet's entry concerning Jacquet in his *Parnasse français* (1732) is quite long and includes an engraving of her likeness taken from a medal struck in her honor following her death. Only four other musicians received such a distinction in Tillet's work.[17]

Text and Author

The *livret* for *Cephale et Procris* was written by Joseph-François Duché de Vancy (1668–1704),[18] a poet considered to be a protégé of Louis XIV's wife, Madame de Maintenon. Duché was secretary to the Duc de Noailles and taught at Saint-Cyr, Madame de Maintenon's school for girls established in 1686 near Versailles.[19] It is generally agreed that Duché was not an especially gifted poet. His *livrets* have a reputation for confusing story lines and poor poetry.[20] In an age when the *tragédie lyrique* was considered as much a poetic art form as a musical work of art, the impact of a poor libretto on the opera's reception should not be underestimated.

The elements found in Duché's *livret* are quite typical for the time.[21] The prologue contains the characteristic allusions to Louis XIV's greatness, glory, and successes, despite the fact that by the early 1690s France was beginning to experience military reversals and economic distress. One of the characters in the prologue (the sea god Nerée) points the way to the story of Procris and her tragic love, another common feature of seventeenth-century prologues, proclaiming that it will be fortunate if the tale of her sorrows helps the listeners resolve to "flee a thralldom / Ever disastrous to the peace" of their days. In the main story many typical elements are present, elements such as the mixing of gods in the affairs of mortals, lovers thwarted by fate or the gods, opportunities for scenes involving fantastic elements (*les merveilleux*) such as casting spells or calling up creatures from the underworld, and opportunities for large celebrations enacted on stage with much singing and dancing. This latter is known as the *divertissement* and there is usually one in each act.

Acts 1 through 5 recount the story of Cephale and Procris, originally found in Ovid's *Metamorphoses*, but with significant changes, as is typical in *tragédie lyrique*. In the original, for example, Cephale and Procris are already married, and the only rival is L'Aurore who wants Cephale for herself. Besides adding a rival for Procris' affections (Borée), Duché also adds confidants for all the characters and changes many plot details to adapt the story for the expectations of the Parisian public.

The story as told by Duché is set in Athens and centers on the love triangle involving Cephale (a military hero who has just subdued Thrace), Procris (daughter of King Erictée of Athens), and Borée (the prince of Thrace and Cephale's military rival). A secondary love interest, which bears no relation to the main plot, involves the confidants of Procris and Cephale, Dorine and Arcas. The plot involves the thwarting of Cephale and Procris' hope of marriage to each other by the intervention of the gods, who dictate that Procris and Borée must be married instead. L'Aurore (Dawn) wants Cephale for herself and so tries to comfort him when he finds out that he will not be allowed to marry Procris, presumably so he will then be more receptive to her own advances. L'Aurore soon confesses her love for Cephale, but he is obviously stunned by her confession, a reaction that she interprets as rejection, and she becomes furious. Wishing to cause Cephale the same pain of rejection she has experienced, L'Aurore calls up demons to cast a spell on Procris causing Procris to believe Cephale has been unfaithful to her. L'Aurore wants Procris to hurt Cephale by rejecting him, thereby getting revenge on Cephale. The spell is successful and Procris vehemently scorns Cephale at their next encounter.

In a rather unexpected plot twist, L'Aurore has a change of heart and takes pity on the mortals. She breaks the spell on Procris and convinces her that Cephale has not been untrue, telling her only that a jealous deity had cast a spell on her. At L'Aurore's urging, Procris goes off in search of her love in order to renew their mutual passion. She encounters him involved in a fight with Borée, and tries to intervene. In doing so, she is accidentally struck by an arrow from Cephale's bow. In the final scenes, Procris and Cephale bid each other farewell and she dies, leaving Cephale to bewail his fate and grieve for his beloved.

Although Duché wrote the poetry, which was then set to music by Jacquet, it was normal for poets and composers to collaborate.[22] No correspondence has come to light concerning whatever contact Duché and Jacquet may have had during the preparation of the *livret* for *Cephale et Procris*, but it is reasonable to assume that there is some joint responsibility for larger elements of the story as well as for smaller details.

The fact that Duché and Jacquet included a secondary love interest between the confidants, Arcas and Dorine, is somewhat surprising. While the presence of confidants is typical throughout this period, by 1694 it was not typical to involve these characters in a secondary plot, as the presence of these secondary intrigues confused the main plot, thereby disrupting unity of action, one of the primary aesthetic tenets of French drama. In a further departure from the Lullian norm, Duché and Jacquet used humor in the first of two scenes centering on this secondary love interest (1.4 and 4.1). This humor, as well as a confusing plot, complicated by the presence of a secondary intrigue, may have been among the factors contributing to the opera's lack of success.

The Music of the Edition

Jacquet's opera follows the formula established by Lully in many ways.[23] This is not surprising in a work appearing so soon after Lully's death, and yet Jacquet's approach to *tragédie lyrique* exhibits some significant stylistic departures. Perhaps the most striking difference involves the opera's conclusion. Whereas Lully provided a large choral or instrumental apotheosis at the end of all of his *tragédies lyriques*, both those with happy endings and those with tragic, Jacquet gives her opera a quiet, poignant ending. In the penultimate scene of the opera, Procris dies on stage of a wound accidentally inflicted by her lover Cephale's hand. During her final moments she sings an accompanied recitative, and when she begins to describe her feelings and visions as death overtakes her, Jacquet specifies in the score two moments of absolute silence.

Jacquet's use of silence for dramatic effect is a unique feature for this genre.[24] Music was continuous during the *tragédie lyrique* from the opening notes of the *ouverture* to the end of the final scene. This constant flow of music was interrupted by silence not once, but twice, during Procris' accompanied recitative "Non, vivez." Since no eyewitness reports have come to light, we cannot know for certain how the audience reacted to Jacquet's novel use of this device. We know, however, that the French opera-going public was notorious for their loud behavior at performances,[25] and when the full five-part string ensemble accompanying Procris ceased playing for two (rather slow) beats, it is likely that most of the spectators would have turned their attention away from their socializing and toward what was happening in the drama.

In the final scene, Cephale grieves for his love and berates the heavens for their cruelty. His last note dies away and the opera is over, with no instrumental postlude or final chorus to comment on the tragic events.

In another departure from Lullian convention, Jacquet rejects the use of choral interjections at points of dramatic impact. Lully frequently employed the large group of singers present on stage to punctuate dramatic moments through choral exclamations such as "O ciel!" The result of Jacquet's exclusion of the chorus from such moments is an intensified focus on the reaction of the character who is most affected by whatever dramatic event is taking place. Thus in act 1, scene 7, when Cephale hears the proclamation by the priestess of Minerva that King Erictée must give his daughter Procris to Borée in marriage, rather than to Cephale, we see the immediate and intense reaction by Cephale. He attempts to assimilate this most distressing news and turns to the king to beg for mercy, but quickly moves to rage as he reflects on what the gods have done. Throughout this dramatic scene, the chorus remains a passive observer, instead of actively making exclamations or comments on the distressing decree handed down by the gods.

Jacquet's opera shows her to be a fine dramatist, her music supporting the drama in several ways. In act 1, scene 4, Jacquet uses music to heighten the effect of the humor in the interchange between two secondary characters, Dorine and Arcas. At the beginning of this scene we learn that Arcas has been unsuccessfully pursuing Dorine for quite some time. Arcas' tone throughout this scene alternates between vexation and coaxing. Dorine's quite consistent response is a matter-of-fact rejection of her suitor's advances, but she occasionally teases and frequently offers advice to the lovesick Arcas. The scene is comprised of a series of recitative and air combinations, closing with a duo. Jacquet's musical settings for this scene illustrate some of the devices at her command for underlining the dramatic meaning of the text.

Dorine's response to Arcas' proclamation that her beauty draws him to her and that her harshness cannot counteract that attraction takes the form of advice: "Tâche à vaincre un amour qui te rend misérable" (Seek to conquer a love who makes you miserable). Dorine goes on to say that she wishes to spare him some unnecessary sighs and to bring benevolent aid to his distress. Arcas is thus set up to believe that Dorine is about to relent and submit to his advances. In Dorine's next line of text, she proposes a solution other than the one Arcas is expecting: "Arcas, je ne te verrai plus" (Arcas, I will see you no more).

In this exchange, we can see how Jacquet's music assists in setting up expectations for this long-awaited confession of Dorine's love. The first two lines of text, "Je veux, pour t'épargner des soupirs superflus, / Préter à ton dépit un secours favorable" (I desire, in order to spare you needless sighs, / To bring benevolent aid to your distress) are set to a flowing melody which gracefully ascends and descends primarily by conjunct motion. The listener begins to get the sense that something is about to happen at the point where the first of the above two phrases ends and the second begins, as there is no pause or even hesitation between the phrases. The last syllable of the first line falls on an eighth note (*-flus* of *superflus*) on the downbeat of measure 8 and the first syllable of the next phrase enters on the eighth note immediately following. The phrase continues with a descending scale passage, coming to rest briefly on the second syllable of *dépit* (distress). Jacquet continues to raise expectations of what is to follow by setting the word *Arcas* with a tonic to subdominant harmonic progression (D minor), and pausing for an entire measure (three beats) on the second syllable of *Arcas*. No other note in this section receives such a long durational value. The listener is thus waiting for Dorine to finally relieve Arcas' suffering and give in to his persistent wooing.

Jacquet underlines the element of surprise contained in the text which follows, "je ne te verrai plus" (I will see you no more), by using syncopation and employing rapid note values for both voice and basse continue. The off-beat entrance and rapid delivery catch Arcas, as well as the audience, by surprise. Dorine's unexpected response to Arcas' suffering is announced so quickly that we hardly realize it has happened before it is over. A perfect cadence on the last two syllables (*-rai plus*) emphasizes the finality of Dorine's decision.

Another example of Jacquet's skill as a dramatist can be found in the *divertissement* of act 4, where she uses the music accompanying La Jalousie to set up an ironic undertone. In this scene, the furies have come at L'Aurore's request to cast a spell on Procris. La Jalousie sings the air "Pour calmer" (4.5), in which she claims to have been sent by the heavens to calm Procris' anxieties. The basse continue, however, makes it clear that La Jalousie has come to upset Procris instead. Jacquet uses running eighth notes, a technique that always conveys agitation in the music of this time. The bass line in "Pour calmer" is particularly agitated in that it does not pause or cease at any of the cadence points, coming to rest only at the end of the air. As the air draws to its conclusion we find out

La Jalousie's true purpose—to make Procris more susceptible to the spell the demons will cast. This is accomplished when La Jalousie tells Procris that her love (Cephale) has a new love, and then encourages Procris not to cling to her affection for such a flighty person. Shocked by this (false) revelation concerning Cephale, Procris quickly falls unconscious.

There are several beautiful airs that powerfully convey the character's depth of emotion at that moment, airs such as Procris' "Lieux écartés" (2.1) and "Funeste mort" (4.3). Another deeply expressive piece is her duet with Cephale, "Le Ciel m'avait flatté" (2.2), in which the two thwarted lovers communicate their grief and longing for each other through musical sighs and expressive harmonies. There is very little in the seventeenth-century *tragédie lyrique* repertoire that can rival the touching scene near the end of the final act in which Procris dies. As the scene opens, she sings a beautiful accompanied recitative, "Non, vivez," in which she declares her love for Cephale and commands him to forget her so that he will be happy. She abruptly feels the effects of her mortal wounds, and in passages punctuated by moments of dramatic silence, poignantly describes the darkness beginning to descend on her, then the transporting light as death approaches.

The Reception of the Opera

Cephale et Procris opened at the Paris Opéra on 17 March 1694.[26] It received only five or six performances and was never revived in Paris.[27] It is difficult to analyze the various elements that may have caused this work to fail. An important contributing factor appears to have been the high expectations of the Parisian opera-going public for a *tragédie lyrique* by the celebrated composer Jacquet de La Guerre. While a few works performed at the Opéra in the years following Lully's death were well received, most were not. Once the word was out that Jacquet was composing an opera, people eagerly awaited this new work, touting Jacquet as the composer most capable of carrying on the Lullian tradition of *tragédie lyrique*.

In December 1691 a letter addressed to Jacquet appeared in the *Mercure galant*, supposedly from Lully's ghost, praising her and her "opéra nouveau."

Qu'on vantait à la Cour, de même qu'à la Ville,
Un Opéra nouveau, que vous avez donné,
Et quoiqu'on vous connut pour femme très habile,
Que d'un si grand travail on était étonné.

L'entreprise, il est vrai, n'eut jamais de pareille.
C'est ce qu'en votre Sexe aucun Siècle n'a vu,
Et puis qu'il devait naître une telle Merveille,
Au Règne de LOUIS ce prodige était dû.

How people praise at court, as well as in the city, A new work that you have given, And although everyone knew you to be a very clever woman, They were surprised at such a grand piece of work.

The enterprise, it is true, never had any equal. It is something that no other century has seen in your sex, And then that such a marvel was to be born, It is to the reign of Louis we are indebted for this prodigy.[28]

We cannot know for certain to which of Jacquet's compositions the writer was referring. Was it perhaps her ballet *Jeux à l'honneur de la victoire*, composed in 1691? Or was she already working on *Cephale et Procris*, a project that her friends and supporters had already made known around Paris? Whichever work the poem refers to, it is clear that as early as 1691 expectations for Jacquet's music loomed large.

In the next stanza, "Lully" transfers to Jacquet the responsibility for providing the king with musical entertainment:

A ce fameux Héros j'eu le bonheur de plaire.
Il daigna de tout temps écouter mes Concerts.
Ce que j'ai fait pour lui, c'est à vous de le faire.
Vous devez succéder à l'honneur que je perds.

To this famous hero [Louis XIV] I had the good fortune of giving pleasure. He always deigned to hear my music. That which I did for him, now is up to you to do. You must inherit the honor of which I am deprived.

The Parfaict brothers, in their "Histoire de l'Académie Royale de Musique,"[29] tell us that the names of Jacquet and the librettist Duché de Vancy were heard all over Paris, as people could talk of nothing else but the upcoming production of *Cephale et Procris*. Since there is no other account of the reception of *Cephale et Procris*, it is worth quoting the relevant passage from the Parfaict brothers' history in full:

If advance praise could assure the success of a work, never before had an opera seemed more likely to succeed. The names of Duché and Mlle de La Guerre echoed throughout Paris. People fell into ecstasy at rehearsals of this poem [i.e., the opera], and unfortunate were those who would dare to say that one must await the judgment of the public. The day arrived, what a change! It was a complete reversal [of public opinion], and the opera expired at its fifth or sixth performance.[30]

An interesting anecdote, which has only received attention in Catherine Cessac's recent book, is included in the Parfaict brothers' "Histoire." In it we find another hint concerning the intense level of advance praise preceding the first performance of *Cephale et Procris*, thereby greatly raising expectations for the work. We are also given a rare glimpse into the relationship of Elisabeth and her husband Marin:

The day after the première, M. de La Guerre, who loved and tenderly esteemed his wife, found himself with several people who were criticizing the new opera, imposed silence on them, telling them, Messieurs, I assure you that my wife's opera is very good, it is only your overture that is excessive.[31]

There may be other reasons besides the high expectations caused by advance praise contributing to the poor reception of *Cephale et Procris*. The plot was complicated and contained confusing twists, and comic intrigue had been intentionally excluded from the *tragédie lyrique* for nearly twenty years.[32] Also, late in 1693, just a few months before Jacquet's opera was performed, the church increased its attack on the theater, and specifically on operas, labeling them sensuous and inappropriate forms of entertainment.[33]

Whatever the causes for its poor reception, Jacquet's opera was certainly not alone in its failure. Very few *tragédies lyriques* performed in the 1690s met with success. These were turbulent years for the Opéra. By the 1690s, Louis XIV had ceased expressing an interest in opera, a change usually attributed to the religious conservatism of his wife, Madame de Maintenon.[34] The king's lack of interest in productions at the Opéra caused problems for Parisian audiences, who were accustomed to looking to the king's taste to direct them to the best in entertainment. It was also a very difficult time for France in general. The financial difficulties brought on by Louis XIV continuing to pour the country's resources into his military endeavors had begun to have a negative effect on all levels of French society. The country's morale was also suffering, since the king's previously successful military forces were now meeting with devastating defeats.

Notes on Performance

Tempo

Only one or two tempo indications appear in the published score of *Cephale et Procris*. Several are found in the prologue section of the basse continue partbook and in the set of manuscript parts comprising Brossard's arrangement of the prologue (see the section in the critical report concerning "Sources"). Although some pieces have an Italian tempo in one part and French in another, these terms generally agree with each other.[35] *Vite* and *presto* are given at the beginning of the *ouverture*'s second movement, for example. *Fort vite* and *prestissimo* are indicated for the "Passepied pour les Violons." Occasionally, however, the tempo words do not quite agree. Both *prestissimo* and *presto* are indicated, for example, for the gigue, as well as for the prologue's concluding chorus, "Volez, volez."

One surprising contradiction occurs in the "Marche pour Nerée." The word *gravement* appears in the fagotto ou basse de violon part, while the word *presto* appears in the basse de viole part. These two words clearly convey two different tempos. The basse continue partbook indicates only the word *staccato* at this point. Besides the word *gravement*, the fagotto ou basse de violon part indicates *picqué*, the French equivalent of *staccato*.[36] There are no other clues in the sources that can help us to determine which of these two tempo indications was intended. Marches such as this one, however, were often used to move large groups of singers and dancers on or off stage and tended to be performed at a stately tempo. This suggests that the appropriate tempo for this piece would be *gravement*, rather than *presto*.

Meter

One of the primary performance concerns surrounding French baroque recitative is the interpretation of the meter signatures. Meters are constantly shifting in order to allow the caesura and rhyme of the French *vers*[37] to receive metrical accents, while still setting the text to music that highlights the long and short syllables of French speech patterns. Scholars have attempted to reconstruct the relationship of these meters to each other based on the writings of late seventeenth- and early eighteenth-century theorists.[38]

In *Cephale et Procris* Jacquet is quite consistent in her use of meters in dialogue recitative. She uses predominantly 2 and 3/2 in her declamatory passages; C and ₵ appear only occasionally, for a few measures at a time, and they tend to be the first measure in a character's speech, or else they are found in the last measure or two at the end of a speech. There are a few points in Jacquet's opera where she employs C or ₵ for a slightly longer passage. These passages are usually transitional in nature, such as Borée's eight measures at the beginning of act 2, scene 4.

Jacquet uses the meter signature 3 only for airs, or air-like passages of measured recitative interspersed throughout dialogue scenes. It is never incorporated into recitative as a single measure, a practice that differs distinctly from that of Lully. Not all of Jacquet's airs carry 3 as a time signature, however. Some are in 2 or ₵, and some employ more than one time signature. All four of Jacquet's monologue airs employ 2 as the meter signature with occasional measures in 3/2 ("Lieux écartés" [2.1], "Dieux cruels" [2.3], "Amour, que sous tes loix cruelles" [3.1], and "Funeste mort" [4.3]).

Particularly interesting is Jacquet's designation of the meter signature 3/2 for one of her dialogue airs. It is the only dialogue air in the opera with this meter signature throughout. The reason for Jacquet's choice of this meter (which was usually defined by theorists as a slow triple meter)[39] may perhaps be found in the text. Procris is admitting her love for Cephale, but this is not a happy moment, since they already know the gods will not allow them to be wed. The choice of 3/2 rather than 3 presumably ensures a slow performance, one more in keeping with the poignant nature of this encounter.

Jacquet's use of 2 and 3/2 as the primary meter signatures in her recitative avoids the problem of shifting between quarter-note and half-note beats, since both of these meters use the half note for the beat. Loulié's doctrine of beat equivalence appears, therefore, to work well throughout Jacquet's passages of recitative. Jacquet usually uses shorter note values in measures with a meter signature of C (eighths and sixteenths) while employing longer note values in ₵ (quarters and eighths).

The time signatures 2 and ₵ appear side by side so rarely in Jacquet's opera that it is difficult to discern whether or not any difference in tempo might be intended. When they do appear in consecutive measures, one is usually found in the last measure in one section and the other appears in the first measure of a new section.

Instrumental Forces

Published scores from the seventeenth century provide only a few clues as to intended instrumentation since these scores were not destined for use in mounting a production.

Rather, they were meant to provide amateur musicians with music so that they could play through their favorite pieces at home. Some of Lully's stage works were printed in "full score," meaning that all the lines of music were present, including internal choral and instrumental parts. Many other works, especially during the *préramiste* period, were printed in a reduced score (*parties réduits*) showing only the outer two parts (*dessus* and *basse*). Christoph Ballard used this latter format when he published the memorial score for Jacquet's *Cephale et Procris*, although he chose to print it in folio as opposed to quarto (roughly one-fourth the size of a folio score), which was used for many *préramiste* scores. Plate 1 shows the opening measures of Procris' monologue air "Lieux écartés" (2.1) as found in the published score: three systems containing two, three, and three staves respectively. The only scoring indication is found in the second system where the word "Accompagnement" seems to indicate a reduction of orchestral forces.

Even Lully's "full scores" did not specify an intended instrument for each line of music, only the occasional word "Violons" or "Flûtes" or "Hautbois." Scholars have determined that these terms usually specify larger categories of instruments: "Violons," for example, indicates the full five-part string ensemble (plus the wind players for large instrumental numbers and choruses), and "Hautbois" indicates both hautbois and bassons. When seventeenth-century scores call for *flûtes*, recorders usually are intended, as the designation *flûte d'Allemagne* is used to specify the transverse flute.[40]

The hautbois used in the orchestra for *Cephale et Procris* would have been the true baroque oboe, which had largely completed its transition from shawm to oboe by the end of Lully's life in 1687.[41] Passages scored for trompettes were played on an instrument that had remained basically unchanged since the end of the sixteenth century.[42] In the seventeenth century only trumpets in C and D were known. While sacred music from the late seventeenth century calls for trumpets in C or in D, never employing both types of trumpet in the same work, dramatic works do sometimes call for trumpet in C in one piece and then trumpet in D later in the opera. In such cases, the trumpeter probably added (or removed) a supplementary tube, which could change the instrument's pitch from D to C or vice versa.[43] Only two pieces in *Cephale et Procris* call for trompettes: the march and chorus "Célébrons d'un héros" (1.5). Both pieces are in D major.

We know that the typical orchestral texture included five string parts: the outer two parts (*dessus* and *basse de violon*) plus the three internal parts, known as the *parties* (*haute-contre*, *taille* and *quinte de violon*). All of the *dessus* players played the same part, except in passages in trio texture when they divided into *premier* and *second dessus*. Trio passages are usually intended for the smaller group of instrumentalists, known as the *petit choeur*.[44] The sound contrast between *grand* and *petit choeur* is thus created in two ways: by changing the texture from five parts to three, and by having this reduced number of parts played by fewer instrumentalists. The internal string parts were played on instruments roughly equivalent to the modern viola that were tuned the same, but each notated on a different clef: C1 for the haute-contre, C2 for the taille, and C3 for the quinte.[45]

The term *basse de violon* has been used to describe different instruments at different times. By the middle of the eighteenth century, it essentially indicates a cello.[46] In the seventeenth century, however, it was applied to several different instruments, each with a different size and tuning, but all belonging to the violin family. The oldest and most common basse de violon was a four-stringed instrument tuned a tone lower than normal cello tuning (B♭'–F–c–g). Another instrument to which this term was applied was a five-stringed instrument similar to a cello, but slightly larger. It was tuned C–G–d–a–d' and the fifth string allowed this instrument a wider range than the earlier basse de violon. This instrument was probably used in the orchestra at the Paris Opéra because Theobaldo di Gatti is reported to have played it in Lully's orchestra. He arrived in Paris in 1675 or 1676, and remained in that post until his death in 1727.[47]

The *basse de viole* (or *viole de gambe*) remained an important member of the opera orchestra throughout this period, although this instrument is rarely specified in the scores, probably because its presence is simply taken for granted. Its presence seems to have been quite ubiquitous, playing recitatives and airs as well as doubling the basse de violon in choruses, dances, and instrumental numbers.[48]

In the published scores of Lully's *tragédies lyriques*, figures in the basse continue are absent from the *airs de ballet* and most other independent *symphonies*. Figures are present, however, in choruses and instrumental movements labeled *ritournelles*, the latter being typically in trio texture. Figures gradually disappeared from the choruses during the *préramiste* era. They are never present in Rameau's operas. Graham Sadler noticed that in Lully's published scores when the words basse continue appear in the score, the bass line is figured. When the words basse continue do not appear, no figures are present.[49]

While this pattern is more or less consistent in the published score of *Cephale et Procris*, it is not entirely so. Thus, "Basse continue" has been included in the score below the bottom staff at the beginning of each piece in which the continuo is to play. If the indication does not appear, the harpsichord does not play for that piece, generally these are large choruses and instrumental numbers.

The number of instrumentalists performing in the 1694 production of *Cephale et Procris* was likely similar to those listed in 1704, the earliest year for which we have records concerning instrumental performing forces at the Opéra:[50]

grand choeur
12 dessus de violon
3 hautes-contre
3 tailles
2 quintes

petit choeur
2 dessus de violon

10 basses de violon, violon-   2 basses de violon or
   celles, or contrebasses[51]   violoncelles
4 flûtes and hautbois
4 bassons
1 clavecin   1 clavecin
2 théorbes   2 théorbes
2 basses de viole   2 basses de viole

The total number of players in the *grand choeur* was thus approximately 43, and in the *petit choeur* approximately nine.

One question that arises from studying the above list concerns what instrument plays the lowest part in *petit choeur* passages that have a high bass part, usually notated in alto clef. Was the lowest part in trio passages played by the basse de violon in a high register, or was it doubled by an haute-contre de violon? There is conflicting evidence from Lully's day concerning which instruments played during choral *petit choeur* passages. Some published scores indicate rests for all instrumentalists except the basse continue in such passages, while a few extant violon parts indicate that the instruments doubled the choral *petit choeur*. Lois Rosow has found some instances in the eighteenth century where all three *parties* contain the high bass line in trio passages.[52] In Brossard's prologue arrangement of *Cephale et Procris*, whenever the orchestral *petit choeur* accompanies the choral *petit choeur*, Brossard included the lowest part in his *3e dessus ou haute-contre de violon* part. Following Brossard's lead, this high bass part for trio passages is included in the haute-contre de violon part throughout the opera, without taking it away from the basse de violon where it always appears notated in a C clef in the manuscript partbook.

The number of musicians listed above as playing flûtes and hautbois should be interpreted as four instrumentalists prepared to play either instrument. At this time, wind players were expected to be able to play instruments from both the flûte and hautbois families (including bassons), as evidenced both by payment records and by written directives occasionally found in the parts which tell the wind players to "turn [the page] and prepare your flutes."[53] The sources never specify both flûtes and hautbois at the same time. These instruments are usually called for in passages in trio texture, so there would have been two players on each part.

Vocal Forces

Lully and his immediate successors scored their full choruses for four parts: dessus, haute-contre, taille, and basse. Women usually sang only the dessus, while the lower three parts were sung by men.[54] Passages in trio texture for the *petit choeur* are comprised of the dessus singers divided into two parts plus the haute-contre. Evidence from the eighteenth century suggests that there would have been approximately five to eight singers on a part, with the outside two voices (dessus and basse) more heavily weighted than the haute-contre and taille.[55]

Vocal Ornamentation

Both the printed score of Jacquet's opera (Ballard) and the manuscript partbooks contain only one ornament sign, the "+." In Ballard this occurs a total of only fifteen times in solo vocal or choral music. A few small grace notes are present in both Ballard and the manuscript partbooks. These are found in act 1, scene 3 (Procris: "Je n'ose attendre"), act 1, scene 4 (Dorine: "L'amour n'est point charmante"), and act 2, scene 2 (Procris: "En vain vous flattez mes douleurs"). In his *Eléments ou principes de musique* (1696) Loulié defined *agréments* such as these as *petits sons*, explaining that they were inserted between regular tones "to render the melody more agreeable."[56] According to Loulié, these *petits sons* were shorter or weaker notes tied to one of the regular notes and were to be executed lightly. In most cases, they should be performed with the value of the small note taken away from the note to which it is tied.

Ornamentation indications occur much more frequently in the manuscript partbooks, particularly at cadences. Shown below is a typical cadence indicating an ornament.

In most cases, such cadences would be realized as shown below:

Ornamentation indications can be found at one time or another in all the vocal parts, but not necessarily at the same time. This raises some interesting questions. Sometimes there is an ornament in the seconde dessus recitante part but not in the premier dessus even though these two parts are singing in unison at that point. Does that mean that only some of the dessus singers were supposed to ornament that particular note, or is this merely the product of a careless copyist? Where ornaments appear in different parts at slightly different times, does Jacquet intend for the dessus singers, for example, to ornament beat one while the taille and dessus instrumentalists place an ornament on beat two? It makes sense that an ornament found in the second but not in the first dessus part should be extended to both parts. Ornaments that occur in one of the internal parts, but not in the dessus, may very well be intended to be performed as such.

The most interesting examples of ornamentation are the performance versions of a few prologue pieces found in the basse recitante partbook. These are especially enlightening because no other late-seventeenth-century sources containing written-out graces and rhythmic alterations have come to light.[57] The music has been altered in two airs sung by Pan, a performance version of Pan's part of the duo with Flore, which occurs in between these two solo airs, and in a brief double recitative for Pan and Flore, "Quelle divinité."

These alterations were probably made by Brossard in preparation for his performance of the Prologue in Strasbourg. A comparison of the music for "Il est temps" in the edition with plate 4 quickly reveals the extensive nature of Brossard's alterations. Pan's music also reveals many types of alterations, including *port de voix, tierce de coulée,* and *notes inégales*.[58] The only music for Pan that does not show similar changes is "A l'abri du fracas des armes," possibly explained by the fact that this is a double continuo air, and so the bass vocal line and the basse continue line must be closely unified.

Another alteration apparently made by Brossard to the dessus recitante partbook is the addition of breath marks. These are found only in the prologue, and only in this one partbook. In the original, they look like upside-down sixes and their placement gives us insight into the rather short-breathed phrases that were apparently the norm at this time.[59]

Altered Notes

The practice of slightly lengthening the first note of a pair of notes while shortening the second dates back to the sixteenth century. At this earlier time it was not associated with French practice, but was instead one of the freedoms musicians routinely employed when ornamenting or improvising. The association of this technique with French practice, known as *notes inégales*, began around 1650.[60]

Many theorists stress that certain passages are played as *notes inégales* even when they are notated as equal. This has perhaps led to the assumption that such passages are always written as equal, an assumption that is not borne out by a careful examination of the evidence. David Fuller notes that

> The careful composer who wished to ensure inequality or equality in doubtful situations used symbols or written directions. The dot of addition was the usual sign for inequality; very occasionally there was no compensatory shortening of the second note of the pair.[61]

In *Cephale et Procris*, a clear example of *notes inégales* appears in the premier dessus de violon partbook in the final section of the *ouverture*'s second movement (see plate 2). The meter signature in this section is **3** and the music consists primarily of eighth notes with conjunct motion predominating. The published score does not indicate dotted rhythms at this point (see plate 3). Several of the instrumental parts and partbooks for the Prologue, however, contain at least some indications for *notes inégales* performance in this section. The *notes inégales* notation present in the instrumental parts is an example of what Fuller described as "no compensatory shortening of the second note of the pair."[62]

Brossard clearly believed that the eighth notes in this section of the *ouverture* should be performed as *notes inégales*. Whether Jacquet intended for this particular passage to be performed in this way cannot be known for certain, but the passages where Brossard has indicated a *notes inégales* performance fit well with theorists' descriptions for such passages.

The presence of dots to indicate *notes inégales* in this one section actually raises more questions than it answers. Why are the dots notated only in this one passage and nowhere else in the prologue instrumental pieces? (Brossard was of course only concerned with the Prologue and so would not have made any alterations to pieces in the main body of the opera.) Given the widespread use of *notes inégales* during this period, it seems likely that the other prologue instrumental pieces should be played in the same manner. Since this is the first instrumental piece in the opera, Brossard perhaps intended this passage as a type of case study which he used to illustrate to his Strasbourg musicians how similar passages should be performed in the French style.

Staging

While no drawings or other materials relative to the staging of *Cephale et Procris* have survived, many drawings and paintings representing scenery for various ballet and opera performances in late-seventeenth- and early-eighteenth-century France exist.[63] The majority of these designs were by Jean Berain, who from 1674 until his death in 1711 designed costumes and scenery for productions mounted both in Paris for the Opéra and for court opera performances. Set changes were done before the audience's eyes using large machinery to move the biggest set pieces. The resulting noise was (somewhat) covered by instrumental pieces performed between the acts.[64]

Machines were also used to create special effects. The entrance of gods or goddesses was made much more dramatic, for example, by having them appear in the air above the stage in a chariot drawn by flying dragons. In *Cephale et Procris*, L'Aurore appears to Cephale descending in a *machine brillante* (3.6). Since L'Aurore represents the Dawn, the machine was likely painted gold and may have been covered with some material that sparkled, suggesting rays of the sun.

Notes

1. *New Grove Dictionary of Music and Musicians*, s.v. "Jacquet de la Guerre, Elisabeth-Claude," by Edith Borroff; Edith Borroff, *An Introduction to Elisabeth-Claude Jacquet de La Guerre* (Brooklyn: Institute of Mediaeval Music, 1966), 5–20; Barbara Garvey Jackson, "Musical Women of the 17th and 18th Centuries," in *Women & Music: A History*, ed. Karin Pendle (Bloomington and Indianapolis: Indiana University Press, 1991), 54–94; Catherine Cessac, *Elisabeth Jacquet de La Guerre: une femme compositeur sous le règne de Louis XIV* (Arles: Actes Sud, 1995). Cessac found Jacquet's baptism record, dated 17 March 1665, finally putting to rest the question of her year of birth, previously thought to be sometime between 1664 and 1667; see Cessac, "Les *Jeux à l'honneur de la victoire* d'Elisabeth Jacquet de La Guerre: premier opéra-ballet?" *Revue de musicologie* 81 (1995): 236, note 5.
2. Borroff, *An Introduction*, 5.
3. Ibid., 6. The description appeared in the *Mercure galant* (a Paris monthly) in July 1677. This passage is also quoted in Carol Neuls-Bates, *Women in Music: An Anthology of Source Readings from the Middle Ages to the Present* (New York: Harper & Rowe, 1982); rev. ed. (Boston: Northeastern University Press, 1996), 62.
4. Julie Ann Sadie, "*Musiciennes* of the Ancien Régime," in *Women Making Music: The Western Art Tradition, 1150–1950*, ed. Jane Bowers and Judith Tick (Urbana and Chicago: University of Illinois Press, 1986), 197.
5. Borroff, *An Introduction*, 10–11. Michel de La Guerre is credited with composing the first "comédie française en musique," entitled *Le Triumphe de l'Amour sur des bergers et bergères*. He died in 1679, five years before Elisabeth and Marin were married.
6. Ibid., 12.
7. For an analysis and discussion of the surviving *livret* for this work, see Cessac, "Les *Jeux à l'honneur de la victoire*," 235–47.
8. See Wanda R. Griffiths, "Jacquet de La Guerre's *Cephale et Procris*: Style and Performance," Ph.D. diss., Claremont Graduate School, 1992; Borroff, *An Introduction*, 21–44; and Catherine Cessac, *Elisabeth Jacquet*, 67–80.
9. Brossard mentions this in the "Catalogue des livres de musique," (Bibliothèque Nationale, Rés. Vm^{8}21) which he submitted to the king along with his collection of music and books on music. The manuscript copy of Jacquet's sonatas, which was deposited in the royal library as part of Brossard's collection, is the only extant copy of these pieces. Jacquet's sonatas are among the first to appear in France so we are fortunate indeed that Brossard took such a great interest in Jacquet's music, thereby preserving scores that might otherwise have been lost.
10. Sonatas composed by Italians had been circulating in France for several years, although none were published there until after 1700. François Couperin is usually credited with composing the first trio sonatas in France, circulating them under an Italian pseudonym as early as 1692.
11. Borroff, *An Introduction*, 19. See also Titon du Tillet, *Le Parnasse français* (Paris, 1732), 635–36.
12. Cessac, *Elisabeth Jacquet*, 107, 110.
13. Ibid., 164–68.
14. Borroff, *An Introduction*, 15.
15. May 1721, January 1724, and February 1724. See the "Liste Chronologique des oeuvres" in Cessac, *Elisabeth Jacquet*, 190–91.
16. "Ses derniers ouvrages n'ont point été encore imprimés, et sont entre les mains de ses héritiers." Quoted in Borroff, *An Introduction*, 19.
17. Ibid., 17. For more on Titon du Tillet, see Julie Anne Sadie, "Parnassus Revisited: The Musical Vantage Point of Titon du Tillet," in *Jean-Baptiste Lully and the Music of the French Baroque: Essays in Honor of James R. Anthony*, ed. John Hajdu Heyer (Cambridge: Cambridge University Press, 1989), 131–57.
18. Besides *Cephale et Procris*, Duché de Vancy wrote *livrets* for *Théagènie et Chariclée* (a *tragédie lyrique*) and *Les Amours de Momus* (a ballet), both performed in 1695 with music by Demarest; the 1698 ballet *Les Fêtes galantes* (Destouches); and the *tragédie lyrique Scylla* (Théobaldo di Gatti, 1701). He also collaborated with Danchet on *Iphigénie en Tauride* (Desmarest and Campra, 1704).
19. Borroff, *An Introduction*, 23.
20. Maurice Barthélemy points this out in his article "Theobaldo di Gatti et la tragédie en musique 'Scylla'," *Recherches sur la musique française classique* 9 (1969): 56–66, (hereafter *RMFC*), going so far as to say that the entire merit of *Scylla* is due to the composer, di Gatti (58). Barthélemy cites Michel Antoine's study *Henri Desmarest* (Paris, 1965) in footnote 2 on p. 58, stating that Antoine demonstrates the unwieldy and complicated nature of the *livrets* Duché de Vancy wrote for Desmarest.
21. For background concerning the seventeenth-century French *livret*, see Patrick J. Smith, *The Tenth Muse* (New York: Alfred A. Knopf, 1970), 42–62.
22. Quinault, Lully's most frequently used librettist, after submitting a list of potential opera plots to the king who then selected one, would submit a copy of the overall plan for the opera to Lully, who then decided where elements such as duos, choruses, dances, and spectacle scenes would take place. After Quinault completed the full text and submitted it to the members of the Académie des Inscriptions, who made changes, Lully would then set the text to music, feeling free to make further changes as it suited him. See Norman Demuth, *French Opera: Its Development to the Revolution* (Sussex: The Artemis Press, 1969), 147.
23. The best background in English concerning both the Lullian and *préramiste tragédie lyrique* can be found in James R. Anthony's *French Baroque Music from Beaujoyeulx to Rameau*, revised and expanded ed., (Portland, Oregon: Amadeus Press, 1997), 93–164. Concerning innovations by other *préramiste* composers, see Leslie Ellen Brown, "Departures from Lullian Convention in the *tragédie lyrique* of the *préramiste* Era," *RMFC* 22 (1984): 59–78. For a discussion of the differences and similarities between Jacquet's opera and other *préramistes tragédies lyriques*, see Wanda R. Griffiths, "Jacquet de La Guerre's *Cephale et Procris*: Style and Drama," in *Music in Performance and Society: Essays in Honor of Roland Jackson*, ed. Malcolm Cole and John Keogel (Warren, Michigan: Harmonie Park Press, 1997), 250–68.
24. Concerning the probable impact of Jacquet's use of silence for dramatic effect on André Campra, who was in Paris in March 1694, see Griffiths, "Jacquet de La Guerre's *Cephale et Procris*," 265–68.
25. See Lois Rosow, "Performing a Choral Dialogue by Lully," *Early Music* 15 (1987): 334. Also, Jérôme de La Gorce, "L'Opéra et son public au temps de Louis XIV," *Bulletin de la Société de Paris et de l'Ile-en-France* 108 (1981): 45.
26. Coincidentally, this date was within a day or two of Jacquet's twenty-ninth birthday. For information on the theatre in the Palais Royale, which was home to the Académie Royal de Musique (Paris Opéra) at this time, see Barbara Coeyman, "Theatres for Opera and Ballet During the Reigns of Louis XIV and Louis XV," *Early Music* 18 (1990): 22–37.
27. The only other known performance of *Cephale et Procris* was a performance of the Prologue in 1696 by Sébastien Brossard with his Académie de Musique in Strasbourg.

28. *Mercure galant*, December 1691, 233–42. Quoted in Cessac, *Elisabeth Jacquet*, 64. The English translation is my own here as elsewhere in this edition, unless otherwise noted.

29. Claude and François Parfaict's "Histoire" remains in manuscript and is housed at the Bibliothèque Nationale (n.a.fr. 6532).

30. "Si les louanges prématurées assuroient le succès d'une pièce jamais opera n'en aurait eu un semblable. Les noms de Duché et de Mlle de La Guerre retentissoient par tout Paris. On tombait en extase aux répétitions de ce Poème, et malheur à ceux qui auroient osé dire qu'il fallait attendre le jugement du public. Ce jour arriva; quel changement! Il fut total, et l'opera expira à sa cinquième, ou sixième représentation." Parfaict, "Histoire," 81; quoted in Cessac, *Elisabeth Jacquet*, 68.

31. "Le lendemain de la première, Mr de La Guerre, qui aimait et estimait tendrement son épouse, se trouvant avec plusieurs personnes qui critiquoient l'opera nouveau, leur imposa silence, en leur disant, Messieurs, je vous assure que l'opera de ma femme est fort bon, il n'y a que son ouverture qui est trop grande." Parfaict, "Histoire," 80; quoted in Cessac, *Elisabeth Jacquet*, 68.

32. Lully and Quinault only used humor in their first three *tragédies lyriques* (*Cadmus et Hermione*, *Alceste*, and *Thésée*). They discontinued this practice after 1675 because the academicians objected to mixing tragedy and humor in the same genre.

33. Robert M. Isherwood, *Music in the Service of the King: France in the Seventeenth Century* (Ithaca: Cornell University Press, 1973), 320 and 328–32.

34. Louis XIV and Mme de Maintenon were married most probably in the fall of 1683, but the marriage was never announced or acknowledged publicly. Although Mme de Maintenon was part of the nobility, she was not royalty and therefore not eligible to become queen. Their relationship, as well as Mme de Maintenon's position as de facto queen, was taken for granted at court. She had a tremendous influence over Louis XIV and is usually blamed for the dramatic decrease in the gaiety of court life in the last twenty years of Louis' reign (d. 1715).

35. These terms tend to be consistent throughout a particular part, probably reflecting the nationality of the instrumentalist for whom Brossard intended the part. The *fagotto ou basse de violon* part uses only French, for example, while the first violin uses only Italian.

36. Brossard equates these two terms in his *Dictionnaire* (1703).

37. The caesura was the syllable falling approximately at the midpoint of the line, usually the sixth syllable in a twelve-syllable line, and the fourth, or occasionally the sixth, in a ten-syllable line. The rhyme was the last counted syllable in the line. A *vers* is a single line of poetry.

38. George Houle, *Meter in Music, 1600–1800: Performance, Perception and Notation* (Bloomington: Indiana University Press, 1987); Irmgard Herrmann-Bengen, *Tempobezeichnungen: Ursprung, Wandel im 17. und 18. Jahrhundert* (Tutzing: Hans Schneider, 1959); Putnam Aldrich, *Rhythm in Seventeenth-Century Italian Monody* (New York: W. W. Norton, 1966). Also, see the section marked "Tempo" in each chapter of Roland Jackson's *Performance Practice, Medieval to Contemporary: A Bibliographic Guide* (New York: Garland, 1988). See also the updates to that guide which appear in the fall issue each year of *Performance Practice Review* (1988–97). For articles relating directly to meter in the seventeenth- and eighteenth-century *tragédie lyrique*, see David Tunley, "The Union of Words and Music in Seventeenth-Century French Song—The Long and the Short of It," *Australian Journal of French Studies* 21 (1984): 281–307, and Tunley, "Grimarest's *Traité du Récitatif*: Glimpses of Performance Practice in Lully's Operas," *Early Music* 15 (1987): 361–64; Lois Rosow, "French Baroque Recitative as an Expression of Tragic Declamation," *Early Music* 11 (1983): 468–79; and Rosow, "The Metrical Notation of Lully's Recitative," in *Jean-Baptiste Lully, Actes du colloque/Kongressbericht, Saint-Germain-en-Laye—Heidelberg 1987*, ed. Jérôme de La Gorce and Herbert Schneider (Laaber: Laaber-Verlag, 1990), 405–22.

39. Rosow, "The Metrical Notation of Lully's Recitative," 408.

40. The most complete study of Lully's orchestration practices is Jürgen Eppelsheim, *Das Orchester in den Werken Jean-Baptiste Lullys* (Tutzing: Hans Schneider, 1961). See also Edmond LeMaître, "L'orchestre dans le théâtre lyrique français chez les continuateurs de Lully 1687–1715," *RMFC* 26 (1988–90): 83–131.

41. Bruce Haynes, "Lully and the Rise of the Oboe as Seen in Works of Art," *Early Music* 16 (1988), 336.

42. Michel Morisset, "Etude sur la musique française pour trompette de Lully à Rameau," *RMFC* 13 (1973), 36.

43. Ibid., 39–40.

44. It should be noted that this means that, besides interludes in trio textures which occur in choruses, the *petit choeur* alone should accompany the bass soloist in double continuo airs, which are always in trio texture. See Rosow, "Performing a Choral Dialogue," 333.

45. Concerning some conflicting evidence from late-seventeenth- and early-eighteenth-century scores about what instruments were intended for the *parties*, see Jean Duron, "L'orchestre à cordes Français avant 1715, nouveaux problèmes: les quintes de violon," *Revue de musicologie* 70 (1984): 260–69.

46. Mary Cyr, "*Basses* and *basse continue* in the orchestra of the Paris Opéra, 1700–1764," *Early Music* 10 (1982): 158.

47. Ibid.

48. Sylvette Milliot, "Réflexions et recherches sur la Viole de gambe et le Violoncelle en France," *RMFC* 4 (1964), 220.

49. Graham Sadler, "The Role of the Keyboard Continuo in French Opera, 1673–1776," *Early Music* 8 (1980): 153. Figures are of course present for all recitatives and dialogue airs.

50. The information is taken from tables found in Jérôme de La Gorce, "L'Orchestre de l'Opéra et son évolution de Campra à Rameau," *Revue de musicologie* 76 (1990): 25–26.

51. Neither the *violoncelle* nor the *contrebasse* would have been present in the Opéra orchestra as early as 1694. See Cyr, "*Basses* and *basse continue*," 155–58.

52. Rosow, "Performing a Choral Dialogue," 333.

53. Jérôme de La Gorce, "L'Académie Royale de Musique en 1704, d'après des documents inédits conservés dans les archives notariales," *Révue de musicologie* 65 (1979): 183.

54. On the *haute-contre* voice, see Frances Killingley, "'Haute-contre'—Alto or Tenor?" *Music and Letters* 54 (1973): 256–57; Frances Killingley, "The Haute-contre," *Musical Times* 115 (1974): 217; Neal Zaslaw, "The Enigma of the Haute-contre," *Musical Times* 115 (1974): 939–41; Mary Cyr, "On Performing 18th-Century Haute-contre Roles," *Musical Times* 118 (1977): 291–95; Lionel Sawkins, "For and Against the Order of Nature: Who Sang the Soprano?" *Early Music* 15 (1987): 315–24.

55. See Rosow, "Performing a Choral Dialogue," 327.

56. Loulié, *Elements*, 66. English translation taken from Frederick Neumann, *Ornamentation in Baroque and Post-Baroque Music with Special Emphasis on J. S. Bach* (Princeton: Princeton University Press, 1978), 62.

57. Concerning embellished arias in the eighteenth century, however, see John Spitzer, "Improvised Ornamentation in a Handel Aria with Obbligato Wind Accompaniment," *Early Music* 16 (1988): 514–22.

58. See Wanda R. Griffiths, "Brossard and the Performance of Jacquet de La Guerre's *Cephale et Procris*," *Performance Practice Review* 8 (1995): 28–53.

59. These have been included in the present edition transcribed as commas. For more information, see ibid., 39–44.

60. Houle, *Meter in Music*, 86.

61. *The New Grove Dictionary of Music and Musicians*, s. v. "notes inégales," by David Fuller.

62. Except for adding the sixteenth-note flag to indicate a shorter note value for the second note of each pair in these pas-

sages, I made no attempt in the present edition to interpret the *notes inégales* indications either through applying them in a more consistent manner or through applying them to other pieces in the opera.

63. See François Lesure, *L'opéra classique français, XVIIe et XVIIe siècles,* Iconographie Musicale, vol. I (Genève: Editions Minkoff, 1972), and Jérôme de La Gorce, "Aux sources de l'opéra français," *Conaissance des arts* 389–9 (1984): 28–35.

64. Concerning the importance of these entr'actes to Lully's productions, see Lois Rosow, "Making Connections: Thoughts on Lully's Entr'actes," *Early Music* 21 (1993): 231–38.

Text and Translation

The source for the text is *Receuil général des opéra représentez par l'Académie Royale de musique, depuis son établissement* (Paris, 1703–46; reprint ed., Geneva: Slatkine Reprints, 1971). The orthography of the original has been modified to reflect modern spellings and accents, and errors have been tacitly corrected. Text printed in parentheses indicates text found in the *livret,* but not set to music in the score. Bracketed text indicates text set to music in both Ballard's published score and the manuscript sources, but not found in the published *livret.*

The translation is by the editor. I have attempted to make the translation as literal as possible, while still retaining some of the feel of the poetic original. In the translation, capitalization and the use of commas to set off phrases reflect modern English usage. Punctuation at the ends of lines follows the *livret.*

In the context of the seventeenth-century *livret,* the word "*Entrée*" may be translated in two different ways, depending on its context. Sometimes the word indicates an opening dance by a particular group. An example may be found in the prologue, following the chorus "Chantons sa valeur immortelle," where the *livret* indicates "Dance (*Entrée*) of the Nymphs from the retinue of Flora." In other instances, the word simply indicates a dance, as in the prologue, following the solo "L'Amour soumet tout le monde," sung by A Sea God, where the staging description states: "The gods in Nereus' following begin their dances (*leurs danses*) again. Flora's nymphs join in, and together they dance the last dance (*la dernière entrée*)."

Cephale et Procris
Tragédie

Personnages du Prologue

Flore
Pan
Neree
Troupe de Nymphes de la suite de Flore
Troupe de Faunes et de Divinités des Bois
Troupe de Tritons et de Dieux de la Mer

Cephalus and Procris
Tragedy

Characters of the Prologue

Flora
Pan
Nereus
Band of Nymphs from the retinue of Flora
Band of Fauns and Forest Divinities
Band of Tritons and Sea Gods

Prologue

Le théâtre représente un bois. La mer paraît dans le fonds.

FLORE ET PAN
Il est temps que chacun se rassemble en ces lieux,
    Déja l'Aurore vigilante,
    Commençant sa route brillante,
Précède le soleil qui monte dans les cieux.

FLORE
On voit dans ces plaines fleuries
Le dieu des jours et des saisons
    Mêler l'or de ses rayons
    A l'émail de nos prairies.
Par tout mille oiseaux divers
Célébrent le retour de ce flambeau du monde,
    Et par les plus tendres concerts,
Accordent leurs chansons au murmure de l'onde,
    Que le zéphire emporte dans les airs.

PAN
    Rien ne doit retarder nos fêtes.
Le désir de chanter le plus puissant des rois,
    Nous fit assembler dans ces bois;
Si l'on voit s'élever d'effroyables tempêtes,
Vains ennemis, tremblez pour vos superbes têtes;
    La Gloire, asservie à ses loix,
    Va couronner ses dernières conquêtes
    Par de nouveaux exploits.

TOUS DEUX
Rien ne peut échapper à sa sagesse extrême,
Le vice est pour jamais à ses pieds abbatu.

PAN
    Ce n'est point de son diadème
Qu'il emprunte l'éclat dont il est revêtu.

FLORE
Toujours plus noble, et plus grand par lui-même,
    Sa gloire, sa grandeur suprême,
    Sont au-dessous de sa vertu.

TOUS DEUX
Chantons sa valeur immortelle.
Publions ses faits glorieux;
Que sa gloire soit éternelle,
Qu'elle dure autant que les dieux.

CHOEUR DE NYMPHES ET DE FAUNES
Chantons sa valeur immortelle.
Publions ses faits glorieux;
Que sa gloire soit éternelle,
Qu'elle dure autant que les dieux.

Prologue

The scene is a forest. The sea appears in the background.

FLORA AND PAN
It is time that everyone assembles in this place,
    Already the vigilant Aurora,
    Beginning her brilliant path,
Precedes the sun rising in the heavens.

FLORA
One sees in these flowery plains
The god of days and of seasons
    Blending the gold of his rays
    With the brilliancy of our meadows.
Everywhere a thousand diverse birds
Celebrate the return of this light of the world,
    And by the most delicate concerts,
Add their songs to the murmur of the sea,
    Which the breeze carries in the air.

PAN
    Nothing must deter our celebrations.
The desire to sing of the most powerful of kings,
    Makes us assemble in these woods;
If you see frightening tempests arising,
Presumptuous enemies, tremble for your arrogant heads;
    Glory, submitting to his laws,
    Is going to honor these recent conquests
    With new achievements.

BOTH
Nothing can escape his extreme wisdom,
Vice is forever humbled at his feet.

PAN
    It is not only from his crown
That he borrows the brilliance with which he is clothed.

FLORA
Always more noble and more grand by himself,
    His glory, his supreme grandeur,
    Are inferior to his virtue.

BOTH
Let us sing of his immortal valor.
Let us proclaim his glorious deeds;
Let his glory be eternal,
Let it endure as long as the gods.

CHORUS OF NYMPHS AND FAUNS
Let us sing of his immortal valor.
Let us proclaim his glorious deeds;
Let his glory be eternal,
Let it endure as long as the gods.

Entrée des Nymphes de la suite de Flore	*Opening dance of the Nymphs from the retinue of Flora*

DEUX NYMPHES / TWO NYMPHS

Qu'un coeur est heureux	How happy is the heart
Dans un doux esclavage!	In a sweet thraldom!
Qu'un coeur est heureux	How happy is the heart
Dans l'empire amoureux!	In the amorous empire!
Dans la vive ardeur qu'inspire le bel âge,	In the intense life that inspires youth,
Quand mille plaisirs peuvent combler ses voeux,	When a thousand pleasures can fulfill his desires,
Qu'un coeur est heureux	How happy is the heart
Dans un doux esclavage!	In a sweet thraldom!
Qu'un coeur est heureux	How happy is the heart
Sous l'empire amoureux!	Under the amorous empire!
Les tendres oiseaux de ce charmant boccage,	The tender birds of this charming grove,
Semblent nous chanter, en exprimant leurs feux;	Seem to sing to us, expressing their ardor;
Qu'un coeur est heureux	How happy is the heart
Dans un doux esclavage!	In a sweet thraldom!
Qu'un coeur est heureux	How happy is the heart
Sous l'empire amoureux!	Under the amorous empire!

Les Nymphes recommencent leurs danses, après lesquelles Nerée paraît sur la mer dans un char conduit par des tritons. Il est accompagné de huit dieux de la mer.	*The Nymphs begin their dances again, after which Nereus appears on the sea in a chariot drawn by tritons. He is accompanied by eight sea gods.*

FLORE ET PAN / FLORA AND PAN

Quelle divinité se présente à nos yeux?	What divinity appears before our eyes?
Nerée avance dans ces lieux.	Nereus is arriving in this place.

NEREE / NEREUS

Je sors de l'empire de l'onde	I leave the empire of the sea
Pour prendre part à vos concerts.	In order to take part in your concert.
L'Envie agite l'univers,	Jealousy disrupts the universe,
Et veut de sa fureur embraser tout le monde;	And wishes by his fury to enflame the entire world;
Mais sa jalouse rage en vain veut éclater,	But his jealous rage desires in vain to break forth,
Quels projets odieux pourront executer	What odious projects can be carried out
Des ennemis tremblants au seul nom de la France?	By enemies trembling even at the name of France?
Et qui craindraient de rien tenter,	And who would hold nothing in awe,
S'ils ne connaissaient la clémence	If they did not know the mercy
Du héros glorieux qu'ils osent irriter?	Of the glorious hero that they dare to provoke?

FLORE / FLORA

O vous! qu'un sort heureux sous ses loix a fait naître,	Oh you who are fortunate to be born under his laws,
Que le ciel à jamais protège votre maître!	Let the heavens forever protect your master!
Que de ses ans rien n'arrête le cours!	Let nothing stop the course of his years!
Ne demandez ni grandeur, ni victoire.	Ask neither glory, nor victory.
Pour vous combler de bonheur et de gloire,	In order to heap success and glory upon you,
C'est assez que les dieux prennent soin de ses jours.	It is enough that the gods are concerned with his life.

LE CHOEUR / CHORUS

Cherchons à satisfaire	Let us seek to satisfy
Les plus doux de nos voeux;	The sweetest of our desires;
Présentons-lui nos concerts, et nos jeux,	Let us present to him our concerts and our games,
Heureux! si nous pouvons lui plaire.	How happy we are if we are able to please him!

Entrée des dieux de la mer.

UN DIEU DE LA MER
L'Amour soumet tout le monde,
   Et jusques dans l'onde
   Tous sent ses feux;
Profitons de notre jeunesse,
   Suivons la tendresse;
   Le trait qui nous blesse
   N'est point dangereux.
   Profitons de notre jeunesse,
   Suivons la tendresse;
   Le trait qui nous blesse
   Doit nous rendre heureux.

Les dieux de la suite de Nerée recommencent leurs danses. Les nymphes de Flore s'y joignent, et forment avec eux la dernière entrée.

NEREE
Dans des lieux que le ciel garantit de l'orage,
Retraçons de Procris les tragiques amours.
Heureux! si de ses maux la vive et triste image

Peut nous résoudre à fuir un esclavage
Toujours funeste au repos de nos jours!

PAN
   A l'abri du fracas des armes,
Allons à nos concerts mêler des chants nouveaux;
   A l'honneur de tant de héros,
   Qui vont au milieu des alarmes
   Nous assurer un doux repos.

LE CHOEUR
   Volez, volez, ô guerriers invincibles!
Etendez vos exploits au bout de l'univers:
   Nous allons en des lieux paisibles
Célébrer par nos chants vos triomphes divers.
   Volez, volez, ô guerriers invincibles!
Etendez vos exploits au bout de l'univers.

Fin du Prologue.

Opening dance of the sea gods.

A SEA GOD
Love conquers the entire world,
   And even in the waves
   All feel his fire;
Let us take advantage of our youth,
   Let us indulge in tenderness;
   The arrow that wounds us
   Is hardly dangerous.
   Let us take advantage of our youth,
   Let us indulge in tenderness;
   The arrow that wounds us
   Might make us happy.

The gods in Nereus' following begin their dances again. Flora's nymphs join in, and together they dance the last dance.

NEREUS
In this place which the heavens shield from the tempest,
Let us recount again Procris' tragic loves.
How fortunate, if the violent and painful description of her sorrows
Is able to make us resolve to flee a thraldom
Ever disastrous to the peace of our days!

PAN
   Sheltered from the noise of weapons,
Let us blend new songs into our concerts;
   To the honor of such a hero,
   Who goes to the center of danger
   To secure our pleasant repose.

CHORUS
   Fly, fly, oh invincible warriors!
Spread your exploits to the edge of the universe:
   We are going in this peaceful place
To celebrate by our songs your diverse triumphs.
   Fly, fly, oh invincible warriors!
Spread your exploits to the edge of the universe.

End of the Prologue.

Acteurs de la Tragédie

L'Aurore
Procris, Fille d'Erictée, aimée de Cephale
Cephale, Amant de Procris
Borée, Prince de Thrace, Rival de Cephale
Erictée, Roi d'Athenes
Iphis, Nymphe, Confidente de l'Aurore
Dorine, Confidente de Procris
Arcas, Ami de Cephale, Amant de Dorine
La Pretesse de Minerve
Troupe d'Athéniens et d'Athéniennes
Troupe de Thraces de la suite de Borée
Troupe de Pâtres, et de Bergères
La Volupté
Troupe d'Amours, de Jeux et de Suivants de la Volupté
Dieux Zephires
La Jalousie
La Rage
Le Desespoir
Troupe de Démons

Characters of the Tragedy

Aurora
Procris, Daughter of [King] Erechtheus, in love with Cephalus
Cephalus, passionate admirer of Procris
Boreas, Prince of Thrace, Cephalus' rival
Erechtheus, King of Athens
Iphis, Nymph, Aurora's Confidante
Dorine, Procris' Confidante
Arcas, Cephalus' friend, enamoured of Dorine
Minerva's Priestess
Band of Athenien men and women
Band of people from Thrace from Boreas' retinue
Band of Shepherds and Shepherdesses
Voluptuousness
Band of Loves, Players and attendants to Voluptuousness
Zephyr gods
Jealousy
Rage
Despair
Band of Demons

Acte I

Le théâtre représente une place de la ville d'Athènes, ornée pour les jeux. Le temple de Minerve paraît dans le fonds.

Act 1

The scene is a place in the town of Athens, decorated for a celebration. The temple of Minerva appears in the background.

Scène première

Procris, Borée

BOREE
Me fuirez-vous toujours? Arrêtez, Inhumaine,
Votre injuste courroux ne peut-il se calmer?
   Ah! pour mériter votre haine,
Quel crime ai-je commis que de vous trop aimer?

   Vos mépris, votre indifférence,
   Sont-ils le prix de ma constance?

Un seul de vos regards pourrait charmer les dieux,
Part tout vous allumez une secrète flamme:
Ne pourra-t'on jamais faire naître en votre âme
   L'amour que l'on prend dans vos yeux?

PROCRIS
Malheureux qui ressent l'amoureuse puissance!
Il ne goûte en aimant que des biens imparfaits;
   Pour rendre deux coeurs satisfaits,
Il faudrait que l'amour, la paix, et l'innocence
   Fussent toujours d'intelligence,
Et c'est ce qui ne fût jamais.

BOREE
Vous tâchez vainement de paraître invincible,
Je sais ce qui vous porte à mépriser mes soins,

Scene 1

Procris, Boreas

BOREAS
Will you flee from me always? Stop, cruel one,
Cannot your unjust wrath be calmed?
   Oh! To deserve your hatred,
What crime have I committed other than to love you too much?

   Your disdain, your indifference,
   Are these the reward for my perseverance?

A single one of your glances was able to charm the gods,
Everywhere you incite a secret passion;
Can one never call into existence in your soul
   The love your eyes inspire?

PROCRIS
Unhappy are those who experience love's power!
In loving, one only delights in sweet imperfections;
   In order to gratify two hearts,
Love, peace, and innocence must
   Always be combined with understanding,
   And this never happens.

BOREAS
In vain you seek to appear unconquerable,
I know who persuades you to despise my attentions,

Cruelle, hélas! vous me haïriez moins
   Si vous étiez insensible.
Cephale va bientôt paraître dans ces lieux.
Sa valeur a domptée les peuples de la Thrace;
De vos fiers ennemis il a puni l'audace,
Philomèle est vengée, il est victorieux.
 	
   Vous aimerez, dans ce haut rang de gloire,
   Un jeune amant que vos yeux ont charmé;
Mais, s'il prétend sur moi remporter la victoire,
Vous pourrez quelque jour, sensible à sa mémoire,
   Vous repentir de l'avoir trop aimé.
	Cruel one, alas! You would loathe me less
	   If you were unfeeling.
	Cephalus will soon appear in this place.
	His valor subdued the people of Thrace;
	He has punished the audacity of your fierce enemies,
	Philomela is avenged, he is victorious.
	
	   You shall love, in this high, glorious rank,
	   A young lover whom your eyes have charmed;
	But, if he intends to win the victory over me,
	You may someday, sensitive to his memory,
	   Repent of having loved him too much.

Scène seconde / Scene 2

Procris, Dorine

DORINE
Vous méprisez la jalousie.
 	
   Que votre sort a d'appas!
Rien ne saurait troubler votre paisible vie.
Vous passez vos beaux jours sans crainte, sans envie.
   On vous aime, et vous n'aimez pas.
   Que votre sort a d'appas!
 	
PROCRIS
Hélas!
 	
DORINE
Vous soupirez? d'où vient cette tristesse?
 	
PROCRIS
   C'est trop déguiser ma faiblesse;
L'Amour m'a su lier du plus doux de ses noeuds;
Pardonne, si j'ai pu te cacher ma tendresse,
Suis-je la seule, hélas! qui feint d'être maîtresse
D'un coeur soumis aux loix de l'empire amoureux.
J'aime, il faut l'avouer, il ne m'est pas possible
   De fuir un doux engagement:
   Mais le seul nom de mon amant
   M'excuse assez d'être sensible.
 	
DORINE
   Cephale a-t'il su vous charmer?
Chacun sait que pour vous son ardeur est extrême.
 	
PROCRIS
Tu le connais; crois-tu que quand il aime,
   On puisse ne le pas aimer?
 	
DORINE
Aux plus tendres douceurs votre amour vous prépare;
Le Roi doit, en ce jour, vous donner un époux;
En faveur de Cephale on dit qu'il se déclare.
 	
PROCRIS
Je n'ose attendre un sort qui me paraît trop doux.
	DORINE
	You disdain jealousy.
	
	   How appealing is your lot!
	Nothing will trouble your peaceful life.
	You spend your lovely days without fear, without longing.
	   Somebody loves you, and you love not.
	   How appealing is your lot!
	
	PROCRIS
	Alas!
	
	DORINE
	You sigh? From where does this sadness come?
	
	PROCRIS
	   It is too much to hide my weakness;
	Love knows how to bind me with the sweetest of his bonds;
	Forgive me, if I have been able to hide from you my fondness,
	Am I the only one, alas, who pretends to be the mistress
	Of a heart subject to the laws of the amorous empire.
	I love, it must be confessed, it is not possible for me
	   To fly from a sweet bond:
	   But simply the name of my beloved
	   Excuses me sufficiently from being sensible.
	
	DORINE
	   Does Cephalus know how to charm you?
	Everyone knows that his passion for you is extreme.
	
	PROCRIS
	You know him; do you believe that when he loves,
	   One is able not to love him?
	
	DORINE
	Your love prepares you for the most tender sweetness;
	The king must, on this day, present to you a husband;
	People say he will declare himself in favor of Cephalus.
	
	PROCRIS
	I dare not expect a destiny that seems so pleasant to me.

On voit les ardeurs les plus belles
   Eprouver un sort rigoureux;
Et les coeurs qui pourraient être les plus fidèles,
   Sont souvent les plus malheureux.

Scène troisième

Procris, Arcas

ARCAS
Le devoir de Cephale auprès du Roi l'appelle.
Doit-il apprehender encore votre rigueur?
   Il vous conserve dans son coeur
   Une flamme immortelle.

Après avoir vaincu nos ennemis jaloux,
Et porté son courage au comble de la gloire,
   Vous l'allez voir à vos genoux,
Moins content des honneurs d'une illustre victoire,
   Que d'avoir combattu pour vous.
En cet heureux état, que faut-il qu'il espère?

PROCRIS
Mes désirs sont soumis aux ordres de mon père,
   C'est à lui de regler mes voeux.
Cephale, aux yeux du Roi, peut découvrir son âme,
S'il ne trouve que moi qui s'oppose à sa flamme,
   Il peut s'assurer d'être heureux.

Scène quatrième

Arcas, Dorine

ARCAS
   Seras-tu toujours inflexible?
   Je languis pour toi vainement.
   Les pleurs d'un malheureux amant
   N'ont pu rendre ton coeur sensible.
En vain le changement s'offre à me soulager,
   Je ne saurais être volage;
   Ingrate, ta beauté m'engage,
Et ta rigueur ne me peut dégager.

DORINE
Tâche à vaincre un amour, qui te rend misérable:
Je veux, pour t'épargner des soupirs superflus,
Prêter à ton dépit un secours favourable;
   Arcas, je ne te verrai plus.

ARCAS
Cruelle, il te sied bien de braver ma colère,
Tu sais que tes mépris servent à m'enflamer.

DORINE
Que ne sais-tu te faire aimer?

One sees the most noble passions
   Tested by a harsh fate;
And the hearts who would be able to be the most faithful,
   Are often the most unhappy.

Scene 3

Procris, Arcas

ARCAS
Cephalus' duty in the service of the king calls him.
Must he still fear your harshness?
   He preserves for you in his heart
   An everlasting flame.

After having vanquished our jealous enemies,
And having carried his courage to everflowing glory,
   You are going to see him at your knees,
Less content from the honors of an illustrious victory,
   Than from having engaged in combat for you.
In this happy state, what must he expect?

PROCRIS
My desires are subject to my father's orders,
   It is up to him to rule my wishes.
Cephalus can expose his soul to the eyes of the king,
If he finds only me who is opposed to his passion,
   He may be confident of being happy.

Scene 4

Arcas, Dorine

ARCAS
   Will you always be unyielding?
   I long for you in vain.
   The tears of an unhappy lover
   Have not been able to render your heart sympathetic.
In vain, change offers me relief,
   But I could not be fickle;
   Ungrateful one, your beauty engages me,
And your harshness cannot release me.

DORINE
Seek to conquer a love who makes you miserable:
I desire, in order to spare you needless sighs,
To bring benevolent aid to your distress;
   Arcas, I will see you no more.

ARCAS
Cruel one, it suits you well to defy my anger,
You know that your disdain serves to incite my passion.

DORINE
How is it that you can't make yourself loveable?

ARCAS
Apprends-moi donc le secret de te plaire!

DORINE
L'amour n'est point charmant, s'il n'offre des plaisirs,
Et tu portes partout le chagrin, la tristesse:
Penses-tu, pour charmer une jeune maîtresse,
   Qu'il n'en coûte que des soupirs?

ARCAS
  Promets-moi de m'aimer sans cesse,
De mes cruels ennuis tu finiras le cours.

DORINE
Je t'aime, cher Arcas, j'approuve ta tendresse,
Mais peut-on s'assurer qu'on aimera toujours?

ARCAS
Quoi? tu crois donc changer? Cruelle, quel outrage!

DORINE
  Pourquoi veux-tu que je m'engage
De ne cesser jamais de répondre à tes feux?
    Crois-tu qu'un serment amoureux
    M'empêcherait d'être volage?
Suis mes conseils, Arcas, vivons toujours en paix.
Un long engagement rarement a des charmes.

ARCAS
Que pour les tendres coeurs la constance a d'attraits!

ENSEMBLE
Pour vivre, sans chagrin, sans trouble, sans alarmes,

DORINE
Il faut ne s'engager jamais.

ARCAS
Aimons et ne changeons jamais.

Scène cinquième

Dorine, Arcas, Troupe d'Athéniens, et d'Athéniennes

LE CHOEUR
Célébrons d'un héros la valeur triomphante,
   Nos ennemis sont soumis à ses loix.
   Unissons nos coeurs et nos voix,
   Chantons sa victoire éclatante,
   Chantons ses glorieux exploits.

Première Entrée

ARCAS
Teach me then the secret of how to please you!

DORINE
Love is not at all charming, if it offers only pleasure,
And everywhere you spread vexation, sadness:
Do you think, in order to captivate a young mistress,
   That it only costs a few sighs?

ARCAS
  Promise to love me without ceasing,
You will end the course of my cruel vexation.

DORINE
I love you, dear Arcas, I approve of your affections,
But can one be assured that one will love always?

ARCAS
What? You believe then you will change? Cruel one, what an outrage!

DORINE
  Why do you want me to bind myself
To never stop responding to your passion?
    Do you believe that an amorous declaration
    Will prevent me from being inconstant?
Take my advice, Arcas, let us live always in peace.
A long involvement rarely has any appeal.

ARCAS
Faithfulness is attractive to loving hearts!

TOGETHER
In order to live without grief, without trouble, without affright,

DORINE
It is necessary never to become entangled.

ARCAS
Let us love and never change.

Scene 5

Dorine, Arcas, Band of Athenien men and women

CHORUS
Let us celebrate the triumphant courage of a Hero,
   Our enemies have submitted to his laws.
   Let us unite our hearts and our voices,
   Let us sing of his brilliant victory.
   Let us sing of his glorious exploits.

First Dance

Scène sixième

Tous les acteurs de la scène précédente.
Le Roi, Cephale

LE ROI
Redoublez vos chants d'allegresse,
　Formez les concerts les plus doux.
Mes armes ont rendu le repos à la Grèce,
　Et Cephale est l'heureux époux
　Que je destine à la Princesse.
Redoublez vos chants d'allegresse,
　Formez les concerts les plus doux.

Seconde Entrée

(LE CHOEUR)
(Célébrons d'un héros la valeur triomphante,
　Nos ennemis sont soumis à ses loix.
　Unissons nos coeurs et nos voix,
　Chantons sa victoire éclatante,
　Chantons ses glorieux exploits.)

[DEUX ATHENIENNES]
[Rendons-nous, cédons à la tendresse,
Du dieu des amours doit-on fuir les faveurs:
Les transports d'une heureuse faiblesse
Passent les douceurs d'une vaine sagesse,
Les ardeurs,
Les langueurs,
Sont des plaisirs faits pour les jeunes coeurs.]

Le temple de Minerve s'ouvre, et la grande prêtresse en sort.

Scène septième

Tous les acteurs de la scène précédente.
Le Roi, La Prêtresse

LE ROI
Que vois-je? de Pallas j'apperçois la prêtresse.

LA PRETRESSE
Prince, que faites-vous? quel hymen odieux
Osez-vous arrêter sans consulter les dieux?
　Ecoutez ce qu'une déesse
　Veut bien vous dire par ma voix.
　Le ciel désapprouve le choix
　Que vous faites pour la Princesse.
Si vous voulez qu'une profonde paix
Forme les noeuds sacrés d'une auguste hymenée,
　Accordez Procris à Borée,
Et condamnez Cephale à ne l'avoir jamais.

Elle se retire.

Scene 6

All the characters from the preceding scene.
The King, Cephalus

THE KING
Increase your songs of joy,
　Make your harmony the most sweet.
My weapons have returned peace to Greece,
　And Cephalus is the happy husband
　That I intend for the Princess.
Increase your songs of joy,
　Make your harmony the most sweet.

Second Dance

(CHORUS)
(Let us celebrate the triumphant courage of a hero.
　Our enemies have submitted to his laws.
　Let us unite our hearts and our voices,
　Let us sing of his brilliant victory.
　Let us sing of his glorious exploits.)

[TWO ATHENIAN WOMEN]
[Let us surrender ourselves, let us give way to tenderness,
Should one shun the kindnesses of the god of love:
The transports of a pleasing weakness
Surpass the sweetness of a hollow prudence,
Ardor,
Dreaminess,
Are pleasures suited for young hearts.]

The temple of Minerva opens, and the grand priestess comes out.

Scene 7

All the characters from the preceding scene.
The King, The Priestess

THE KING
What do I see? From Pallas I perceive the priestess.

THE PRIESTESS
Prince, what are you doing? What odious marriage
Do you dare to arrange without consulting the gods?
　Listen to what a goddess
　Wishes to tell you with my voice.
　The heavens disapprove of the choice
　You have made for the princess.
If you desire that a deep peace
Form the holy bonds of an august marriage,
　Grant Procris to Boreas,
And condemn Cephalus never to have her.

She withdraws.

CEPHALE
Qu'entends-je? Juste ciel! Seigneur, pourrez-vous croire
Que les dieux inhumains . . .

LE ROI
Je conçois vos douleurs.
Cet oracle est pour vous le plus grand des malheurs,
Mais l'amour au devoir doit céder la victoire.
Révérons les arrêts que les dieux ont dictés;
   Un héros doit trouver sa gloire,
A soumettre à leurs loix toutes ses volontés.

CEPHALE
Un rival, pour m'ôter la beauté que j'adore,
Pourrait . . .

LE ROI
Je vous entends; consultons les encore.
Puissiez-vous, à nos yeux, apaiser leur courroux!

CEPHALE
Ah! dieux cruels! où me réduisez-vous?

Ils entrent tous deux dans le temple.

Acte II

Le théâtre représente un lieu solitaire au pied du Mont Hymette. On voit quelques hameaux dans l'éloignement.

Scène première

PROCRIS
   Lieux écartés, paisible solitude,
Soyez seuls les témoins de ma vive douleur.
Des peines des amants je souffre la plus rude;
   Lieux écartés, paisible solitude,
Cachez le désespoir, qui regne dans mon coeur.

Hélas! quand j'ignorais la fatale puissance
   Du dieu qui m'a ravi la paix,
Contente des plaisirs qu'offre l'indifférence,
   Que mon sort était plein d'attraits!
Pourquoi, cruel Amour, par d'invincibles traits,
   As-tu dompté ma résistance?
Ah! j'aimerais encore les maux que tu m'as faits!

Mais les dieux inhumains m'ôtent toute espérance;
J'aime un jeune héros, il m'aime avec constance,
Et le ciel nous condamne à ne nous voir jamais.
   Lieux écartés, paisible solitude,
Soyez seuls les témoins de ma vive douleur.
Des peines des amants je souffre la plus rude;
   Lieux écartés, paisible solitude,
Cachez le désespoir, qui regne dans mon coeur.

CEPHALUS
What do I hear? Just heaven! Lord, can you believe
That the inhuman gods . . .

THE KING
I understand your distress.
This oracle is for you the greatest misery,
But love must cede victory to duty.
Let us honor the decree that the gods have imposed;
   A hero must find his glory,
By submitting his will to their rule.

CEPHALUS
A rival, to deprive me of the beauty whom I adore,
Could . . .

THE KING
I understand you; let us consult them again.
Would that you could appease their wrath in our regard!

CEPHALUS
Ah! Cruel gods! Why do you diminish me?

They both enter the temple.

Act 2

The scene is a secluded place at the foot of Mount Hymette. There are some hamlets in the distance.

Scene 1

PROCRIS
   Secluded place, peaceful solitude,
Be the sole witnesses of my intense grief.
Of the pains of lovers I suffer the most unkind;
   Secluded place, peaceful solitude.
Hide the despair that rules in my heart.

Alas! When I would ignore the ineluctable power
   Of the god who has carried away my peace,
Happy with the pleasures indifference offers,
   How my destiny was full of charms!
Why, cruel Love, by some insurmountable blows,
   Have you broken my resistance?
Ah! I would delight still in the troubles that you have caused me!

But the inhuman gods deprive me of all hope;
I love a young hero, he loves me faithfully,
And the heavens condemn us never to see each other.
   Secluded place, peaceful solitude
Be the sole witnesses of my intense grief.
Of the pains of lovers I suffer the most unkind;
   Secluded place, peaceful solitude,
Hide the despair that rules in my heart.

Cephale vient; hélas! tout redouble ma peine. Ne puis-je, sans le voir, abandonner ce lieu? Mes pleurs vont me trahir! quel tourment! quelle gêne!	Cephalus is coming. Alas! Everything increases my pain. Can I not, without seeing him, leave this place? My tears will betray me! What torment! What trouble!

Scène seconde / Scene 2

Procris, Cephale / *Procris, Cephalus*

CEPHALE / CEPHALUS

L'amour, belle Procris, près de vous me ramène, / Beloved, beautiful Procris, near you I return,
Je viens vous dire un éternel adieu. / I come to bid you an eternal farewell.
    Ma mort va contenter la haine /   My death will satisfy the hatred
    Des dieux inhumains et jaloux. /   Of the inhuman and jealous gods.

PROCRIS

Ce n'est point votre mort qu'exige leur courroux. / It is not your death at all that is called for by their wrath.

CEPHALE / CEPHALUS

N'est-ce pas me livrer à la Parque inhumaine, / Isn't it true that I must submit to inhuman Fate,
Que de me condamner à vivre loin de vous? / Which condemns me to live far from you?
Vous soupirez! vous me cachez vos larmes! / You are sighing! You hide your tears from me!
Quoi? seriez-vous sensible à mes cruels ennuis? / What? Could you be sensitive to my cruel anxieties?
Dieux! que mes maux auraient de charmes! / Gods! How my troubles would be appealing!

PROCRIS

Vous voyez malgré moi le désordre où je suis. / You see despite myself the disorder I am in.

[Un coeur trop sévère / [A heart too repressed
Fait un vain mystère / Makes a vain secret
Des maux que son amour le contraint de souffrir: / Of the troubles which his love compels him to suffer:
Ses soins et ses peines / His cares and his pains
Pour cacher ses chaînes / To hide his shackles
Ne servent qu'à les découvrir. / Serve only to expose them.
Ses soins et ses peines / His cares and his pains
Pour cacher ses chaînes / To hide his shackles
Ne servent qu'à les découvrir.] / Serve only to expose them.]

Vous payerez bien cher un aveu trop sincère! / You will pay dearly for too honest a confession!
Vous avez trouvé seul le secret de me plaire, / You alone have found the secret of pleasing me.
    Je n'ai plus rien à vous celer; /   I have nothing more to conceal from you;
    Mais, malgré toute ma faiblesse, /   But, despite all my weakness,
Aux volontés des dieux mon coeur doit immoler / To the will of the gods my heart must sacrifice
    Sa fatale tendresse, /   Its disastrous fondness.
Ne me reprochez point les maux que je vous fais, / Reproach me not the ills I cause you,
Laissez-moi remporter cette triste victoire . . . / Let me win this sad victory . . .
    Si vous avez soin de ma gloire, /   If you care about my pride,
    Prince, ne me voyez jamais. /   Prince, never see me again.

CEPHALE / CEPHALUS

Ah! puisque vous m'aimez, permettez que j'espère. / Ah! Seeing that you love me, permit me to hope.
Vous savez qu'Eole est mon père. / You know that Eolus is my father.
Je puis l'armer . . . / I am able to equip him with weapons . . .

PROCRIS

    En vain vous flattez mes douleurs; /   In vain you soothe my sorrow;
Il faut briser les noeuds d'une chaîne si belle; / It is necessary to break the bonds of so beautiful a chain;
Les dieux m'ont condamnée à d'éternelles pleurs; / The gods have condemned me to eternal tears;

Non, ce n'est plus que la Parque cruelle,
    Qui peut terminer mes malheurs.
	No, it is only cruel Fate
	    Who can end my unhappiness.

ENSEMBLE / TOGETHER

Le ciel m'avait flatté de la vaine espérance
    Que tout seconderait nos voeux;
    Hélas! un sort si rigoureux,
 Doit-il de tant d'amour être la récompense?
	The heavens have flattered me with the false hope
	    That all would further our wishes;
	    Alas! A destiny so harsh,
	 Must it be the reward of so much love?

PROCRIS

Adieu, Prince, je fuis, nos pleurs sont superflus.	Farewell, prince, I slip away, our tears are superfluous.

CEPHALE / CEPHALUS

Cruel destin! — Cruel destiny!

PROCRIS

O sort barbare! — O barbarous fortune!

ENSEMBLE / TOGETHER

Faut-il que le sort nous sépare? — Must fortune separate us?

PROCRIS

Adieu. — Farewell.

CEPHALE / CEPHALUS

Belle Procris, ne vous verrai-je plus? — Beautiful Procris, will I see you no more?

Scène troisième / Scene 3

CEPHALE

Dieux cruels, dieux impitoyables!
 Suis-je assez malheureux au gré de vos désirs?
    Vous m'enlevez tous mes plaisirs,
 Mon coeur désespéré vous trouve inexorables.
    Dieux cruels, dieux impitoyables,
 Suis-je assez malheureux au gré de vos desirs?
    (Lancez sur moi votre tonnerre,
 Sous vos injustes coups je demande à mourir.
 Mes cris vous font en vain une impuissante guerre,
 Vous me haïrez trop, pour me faire périr! . . .
 Que dis-je? . . . hélas! mes maux ont lassé ma constance.
 	
 Ah! pardonnez, grands dieux! si dans ce triste jour,
    Mon désespoir vous offense:
    Quels crimes sont plus dignes de clémence,
 Que ceux qu'aux tendres coeurs fait commettre l'amour?)
	Cruel gods, pitiless gods!
	 Am I unhappy enough to satisfy your desires?
	    You take away from me all my pleasures,
	 My despairing heart finds you inexorable.
	    Cruel gods, pitiless gods,
	 Am I unhappy enough to satisfy your desires?
	    (Hurl down on me your thunder,
	 Under your unjust blows I demand to die.
	 My vain cries to you have been an impotent struggle,
	 You hate me too much to put me to death! . . .
	 What am I saying? . . . Alas! My troubles have worn out my perseverance.
	
	 Oh! forgive, grand gods, if on this sad day,
	    My despair offends you:
	    What crimes are more worthy of clemency,
	 Than those that love makes tender hearts commit?)

On entend un bruit de symphonie. / *The sound of instruments is heard.*

Mon rival ici va paraître.
 Un bruit confus s'élève dans les airs,
    Sachons, sans nous faire connaître,
    Le sujet de ces concerts.
	My rival is going to appear here.
	 A confused noise rises through the air.
	    Let us find out, without being detected,
	    The reason for these sounds.

Cephale se retire à l'écart. / *Cephalus withdraws to the side.*

Scène quatrième

Borée, Troupe de Thraces de la suite de Borée, Cephale retiré à l'écart

BOREE
Les dieux m'ont, à la fin accordé la victoire.
  Mon amour est comblé de gloire,
Cet heureux jour va finir nos malheurs;

  Quel plaisir pour les coeurs fidèles!
Quand un heureux succès couronne leurs ardeurs,
  Et qu'après des peines cruelles,
Il est doux de chanter l'amour, et ses douceurs.

LE CHOEUR
  Quel plaisir pour les coeurs fidèles!
Quand un heureux succès couronne leurs ardeurs,
  Et qu'après des peines cruelles,
Il est doux de chanter l'amour, et ses douceurs.

UN THRACE
Paisibles habitants de ces douces retraites,
  Venez prendre part à nos jeux:
Cet ombre, ces gazons, ces demeures secrètes,
Tout y semble être fait pour les amants heureux.

Scène cinquième

*Tous les acteurs de la scène précédente.
Troupe de pâtres et de bergères.*

Première Entrée

UN PATRE ET UNE BERGERE
Les rossignols, dès que le jour commence,
  Chantent l'amour qui les anime tous,
Si les oiseaux cèdent à sa puissance,
  Quel mal faisons-nous
  D'aimer à sentir ses coups?
Si leur instinct est rempli d'innocence,
  Quel mal faisons-nous
  De suivre un penchant si doux?

Les pâtres et les bergères recommencent leurs danses; après quoi le même pâtre et la même bergère qui ont chanté le dernier Air, chantent le second couplet.

(Heureux troupeaux, paissez sur la verdure,
Pour vous l'Amour prodigue ses faveurs;
Vous n'avez point de loix que la nature,
  Les biens, les grandeurs
  Ne sauraient troubler vos coeurs:
Jamais chez vous la raison ne murmure,
  Les biens, les grandeurs
Ne valent pas vos douceurs.)

Scene 4

Boreas, Band of people from Thrace from Boreas' retinue, Cephalus withdrawn to the side

BOREAS
The gods have, in the end, accorded me victory.
  My love is crowned with glory,
This happy day will end our troubles;

  What a delight for faithful hearts!
When a fortunate success crowns their passions,
  And after cruel pains,
It is sweet to sing of love and its delights.

CHORUS
  What a delight for faithful hearts!
When a fortunate success crowns their passions,
  And after cruel pains,
It is sweet to sing of love and its delights.

A THRACIAN MAN
Peaceful dwellers of this pleasant retreat,
  Come take part in our games:
This shade, this grass, these hidden abodes,
All seem to be made for the happy lovers.

Scene 5

*All the characters from the preceding scene.
Band of shepherds and shepherdesses.*

First Dance

A SHEPHERD AND A SHEPHERDESS
The nightingales, as soon as the day begins,
  Sing of the love that enlivens them all,
If birds give in to her power,
  What harm can it do
  To savor her blows?
If their instinct is full of innocence,
  What harm can it do
  To follow such a sweet inclination?

The shepherds and shepherdesses begin their dances again; after which the same shepherd and the same shepherdess who sang the last Air sing the second verse.

(Happy band, tending your flocks on the greenery,
For you Love squanders his flavors;
You have no laws except those of nature,
  Wealth, titles
  Cannot trouble your hearts:
Reason never whispers where you live,
  Wealth, titles
Are not as valuable as your gentleness.)

Les danses des bergers continuent; quand elles sont finies, Cephale sort du lieu où il s'était retiré, et s'adresse à Borée.

Scène sixième

Cephale, Borée

CEPHALE
Vous n'êtes pas encore sûr de votre conquête.
Craignez du sort volage un dangereux retour.
Dussé-je voir la foudre à tomber toute prête,
Ma mort seule pourra m'arracher mon amour.

BOREE
Je souffre d'un jaloux l'impuissante colère,
  Ton amour te rend téméraire,
  Tu suis une aveugle fureur;
Mais mon coeur généreux veut bien te faire grace:
  Pour te punir de ton audace,
C'est assez que tu sois témoin de mon bonheur.

L'Aurore descend dans une machine brillante.

CEPHALE *sans voir* L'AURORE
Le traître à me braver porte son insolence?
Courons à la vengeance,
N'écoutons que l'ardeur dont je suis animé!

Scène septième

L'Aurore, Cephale, Iphis

L'AURORE
Cephale, où courez-vous? quelle fureur vous guide?

CEPHALE
  Je vais me venger d'un perfide,
Ou mourir pour l'objet dont mon coeur est charmé.

L'AURORE
Suspendez les transports d'un généreux courage
  De la beauté qui vous engage.
  Etes-vous tendrement aimé?

CEPHALE
  Nous ressentons des ardeurs mutuelles,
Nos tendres coeurs forment les mêmes voeux;
Jamais le ciel ne vit deux amants plus fidèles,
  Et n'en fit de plus malheureux.

L'AURORE
Procris peut vous tromper; peut-être que l'ingrate
N'aime qu'un vain honneur dont le charme la flatte,

The shepherd dances continue; when they are finished, Cephalus comes out of the place where he was hiding and speaks to Boreas.

Scene 6

Cephalus, Boreas

CEPHALUS
You are still not sure of your conquest.
Fear a dangerous reversal from inconstant fate.
Were I to see divine anger ready to fall,
Only my death would be able to tear my love for me.

BOREAS
I am enduring from a jealous one an impotent wrath,
  Your love renders you reckless,
  You follow a blind fury;
But my generous heart wishes to grant you forgiveness:
  In order to punish you for your impudence,
It is enough that you witness my victory.

Aurora descends in a sparkling machine.

CEPHALUS *without seeing* AURORA
The traitor shows his insolence to defy me?
Let us hasten to vengeance,
Let us harken only to the ardor which emboldens me!

Scene 7

Aurora, Cephalus, Iphis

AURORA
Cephalus, to where are you running? What fury guides you?

CEPHALUS
  I am going to avenge myself of a treacherous one,
Or die for the object that charms my heart.

AURORA
Withdraw the enthusiasm of a generous heart.
  From the beauty who engages you.
  Are you loved tenderly?

CEPHALUS
  We feel a mutual passion,
Our tender hearts form the same vows;
Never have the heavens seen two lovers more faithful,
  And by that made more unhappy.

AURORA
Procris is able to deceive you; perhaps the ingrate
Loving nothing but a false honor, the charms of which flatter her,

Elle cède à Borée, il triomphe à vos yeux;
    Commencez à mieux la connaître;
    Rarement l'Amour est le maître
    D'un coeur ambitieux,
J'ouvre au père du jour la céleste barrière.
Je précéde en tous lieux le dieu de la lumière;
La terre, à mon aspect, fait éclore ses fleurs;
    Je suis cette Aurore charmante,
    Dont la clarté toujours naissante,
    Peint l'univers des plus vives couleurs,
Et qui même, au milieu de mes tendres douleurs,
Toujours aimable, et toujours bienfaisante,
Enrichit si souvent la terre de mes pleurs.
    Suivez un conseil salutaire,
Vous souffrez pour Procris, elle a trop su vous plaire:
 	
    Guerissez-vous en la quittant;
    C'est être sage,
    Quand une maîtresse est volage,
    Que d'être inconstant.
	She yields to Boreas, he triumphs before your eyes;
	    Begin to understand her better;
	    Rarely is Love the master
	    Of an ambitious heart.
	I open to the father of the day the heavenly gateway.
	I precede in all places the god of light;
	The earth, at my countenance, makes the flowers bloom;
	    I am that charming Dawn.
	    Who every day gives birth to clarity,
	    Painting the universe in the most vivid colors,
	And the same who, in the midst of my tender sorrow,
	Always loveable, and always beneficent,
	So often enriches the earth with my tears.
	    Follow some beneficial advice,
	You suffer for Procris, she has known too well how to please you:
	    Heal yourself by giving her up;
	    This is being wise,
	    When a lady is fickle,
	    To be fickle oneself.

<div align="center">CEPHALE</div>Quoi! l'objet charmant que j'adore Aurait feint de répondre à mes tendres amours? Ciel! quel nouveau chagrin m'agite, et me dévore! Ah! je ne sais si Procris m'aime encore; Mais, hélas! je sens bien que je l'aime toujours.	<div align="center">CEPHALUS</div>What! The charming object of my affections Was pretending to respond to my tender love? Heavens! What new sorrow disturbs and consumes me! Oh! I know not if Procris still loves me; But, alas! I know well that I will love her always.
<div align="center">L'AURORE</div>Je vais tout employer, pour contenter votre âme; Ne craignez rien d'un rival odieux; Pour mieux cacher le feu qui vous enflamme, Ne paraissez point en ces lieux; Allez, reposez-vous sur ces guides fidèles. Avant que de suivre vos pas, Je veux, pour terminer tant de peines cruelles, Vous assurer un destin plein d'appas. Volez, charmants zéphires, accompagnez Cephale, Aux honneurs les plus grands ses jours sont destinés. Est-il un mortel qui l'égale? Volez, je vais le suivre, en des lieux fortunés. *Les zéphires enlevent Cephale.*	<div align="center">AURORA</div>I am going to employ everything in order to comfort your spirit; Fear nothing from a loathsome rival; To better conceal the fire that enflames you, Do not appear in this place; Go, rest yourself on these faithful guides. Before following in your steps, I wish, in order to end such cruel pains, To assure for you a destiny full of appeal. Fly, charming zephyrs, accompany Cephalus, His days are destined for the most grand honors. Is he a mortal without equal? Fly, I will follow him, in this fortunate place. *The zephyrs carry Cephalus away.*

Scène huitième

L'Aurore, Iphis

IPHIS

Pour rendre un amant volage,
Vous mettez tout en usage;
Pourquoi prendre tant de soins?
Je crois qu'il en coûte moins
Pour rendre un amant volage.

Scene 8

Aurora, Iphis

IPHIS

In order to make a lover inconstant,
You are using all your powers;
Why take so much care?
I believe that it would cost less
To make a lover inconstant.

L'AURORE

Je connais ce jeune héros.
Je sais quelle est sa constance, et sa flamme;
Tu te souviens du jour qu'il troubla mon repos,
Il venait en ces lieux confier aux échos
    Les tendres secrets de son âme:
    Mon coeur se sentit enflammé,
Rien n'a pu jusqu'ici dissiper ma faiblesse;

    De Pallas j'ai vu la prêtresse,
J'ai fait rompre un hymen, qu'elle allait confirmer;

Hé! que ne fait-on point, lorsque l'Amour nous blesse,
    Pour tâcher de se faire aimer?

IPHIS

Laissez-vous occuper d'une douce espérance,
Cephale, par vos soins, peut changer en ce jour.
    La plus longue persévérance
    Doit enfin cesser à son tour;
S'il est un temps marqué pour se rendre à l'Amour,
    Il en est un pour l'inconstance.

L'AURORE

    C'est trop demeurer dans ces lieux,
Allons trouver l'objet de mon amour extrême;
Avec plaisir j'abandonne les cieux,
L'endroit où l'on voit ce qu'on aime,
Vaut bien le séjour des dieux.

Acte III

Le théâtre représente les lieux où la Volupté fait son séjour; cette déesse paraît dans le fonds du théâtre couchée sur un lit de fleurs.

Scène première

CEPHALE

    Amour, que sous tes loix cruelles
    On souffre des maux rigoureux!
Par un espoir trompeur tu sais flatter nos voeux,
Pour nous livrer à des peines mortelles.
    Amour, que sous tes loix cruelles
    On souffre des maux rigoureux!
Quand tu contrains deux coeurs à ressentir tes feux,
    Dois-tu laisser rompre des noeuds
Qui devraient leur former des chaînes éternelles?
    Amour, que sous tes loix cruelles
    Les coeurs constants sont malheureux!
    Et qu'il en est peu de fidèles!
    Amour, que sous tes loix cruelles
    On souffre des maux rigoureux!

AURORA

    I know this young hero.
I know his loyalty, and his passion;
You remember the day when he began troubling my peace,
He came to this place to confide to the echoes
    The tender secrets of his soul:
    My heart felt enflamed,
Nothing even until now has been able to diminish my partiality;
    From Pallas I saw the priestess,
I caused a break in the marriage which she was going to sanction;
Well! What would we not do, when Love wounds us,
    To seek to be loved?

IPHIS

Let yourself be occupied with a sweet hope,
Cephalus, because of your pains, may change on this day.
    The longest perseverance
    Must finally cease in its turn;
If there is a correct time to surrender to Love,
    There is also a correct time for inconstancy.

AURORA

    It is too much to remain in this place,
Let us go find the object of my excessive love;
With pleasure I abandon the heavens,
The place where one sees that which one loves,
Is better than the dwelling place of the gods.

Act 3

The scene is the place where Voluptuousness makes her home. This goddess appears in the background inclining on a bed of flowers.

Scene 1

CEPHALUS

    Love, how under your cruel laws
    One endures harsh pains!
With a false hope you know how to build up our desires,
In order to betray us to grievous sorrows.
    Love, how under your cruel laws
    One endures harsh pains!
When you compel two hearts to feel your burning,
    Must you sever the knot
Which would have formed their everlasting bonds?
    Love, how under your cruel laws
    Faithful hearts are unhappy!
    And how few of them are faithful!
    Love, how under your cruel laws
    One endures harsh pains!

Scène seconde

Cephale, Iphis

IPHIS
Rien ne peut-il apaiser vos alarmes?
Quoi? Cephale, en ces lieux charmants,
Vous soupirez, vous répandez des larmes?

CEPHALE
Ah! pour les malheureux amants,
Est-il quelque séjour qui puisse avoir des charmes?

IPHIS
Vous devez espérer la fin de vos malheurs.
   Tôt ou tard l'Amour répare
Les maux qu'il fait aux tendres coeurs.
Et c'est souvent par d'extrêmes rigueurs
   Qu'il nous prépare
   A ses plus charmantes faveurs.
   Tôt ou tard l'Amour répare
Les maux qu'il fait aux tendres coeurs.

Parlant à la Volupté

Déesse dont toujours on aima la puissance,
   Vous, qui par d'agréables loix,
Rendez, quand il vous plaît, les héros et les rois,
Esclaves des plaisirs que votre main dispense;
Tranquille Volupté, venez, avec les jeux,
D'un trop fidèle amant apaiser le martyre.
   Vous pouvez combler tous nos voeux,
   Tout rit, tout plaît sous votre empire;
Et si quelqu'un se plaint du pouvoir amoureux,
   C'est moins de peine qu'il soupire,
Que du plaisir qui le rend trop heureux.

Scène troisième

Cephale, Iphis, La Volupté, Troupe de Jeux, de Plaisirs, et de Suivantes de la Volupté.

La Volupté et sa suite forment une entrée de ballet.

LA VOLUPTE
Tendres amants, bravez vos peines.
Le dieu qui vous donne des chaînes,
Doit à la fin vous secourir;
   La moindre grace
   Que l'Amour fasse,
Sait nous payer des maux qu'il fait souffrir.

LE CHOEUR
Tendres amants, bravez vos peines.
Le dieu qui vous donne des chaînes,
Doit à la fin vous secourir;

Scene 2

Cephalus, Iphis

IPHIS
Can nothing ease your distress?
What? Cephalus, in this charming place,
You sigh, you shed tears?

CEPHALUS
Oh! for unhappy lovers,
Is there any place that can hold some charm?

IPHIS
You must look forward to the end of your troubles.
   Sooner or later Love repairs
The pain that he causes tender hearts.
And often it is by extreme difficulties
   That he prepares us
   For his most pleasing favors.
   Sooner or later Love repairs
The pain that he causes tender hearts.

Speaking to Voluptuousness

Goddess whose power people always admired,
   You, who by pleasing laws,
Render, when it pleases you, both heroes and kings,
Slaves of the pleasures your hand dispenses;
Tranquil Voluptuousness, come, with your players,
Ease the torment of a too-faithful lover.
   You are able to gratify all our desires,
   All laugh, all are satisfied under your reign;
And if someone complains of love's power,
   It is less from pain that he sighs,
Then from the pleasures which makes him too happy.

Scene 3

Cephalus, Iphis, Voluptuousness, Band of Players, Pleasures, and followers of Voluptuousness.

Voluptuousness and her followers perform a dance.

VOLUPTUOUSNESS
Tender lovers, bravely face your suffering.
The god who gives you these bonds,
Must come to your aid in the end;
   The least favor
   That Love provides,
Is able to atone for the troubles that he makes us suffer.

CHORUS
Tender lovers, bravely face your suffering.
The god who gives you these bonds,
Must come to your aid in the end;

La moindre grace
    Que l'Amour fasse,
Sait nous payer des maux qu'il fait souffrir.

LA VOLUPTE

Loin de ces lieux, triste sagesse,
Doit-on défendre à la jeunesse
De se former des noeuds charmants?

(Dans le bel âge,
    Est-ce être sage
De fuir un sort qui peut nous rendre heureux?)

[Quelle folie,
    Quand de sa vie
Un jeune coeur perd les plus doux moments!]

La Volupté et sa suite recommencent leurs danses.

[UNE SUIVANTE DE LA VOLUPTE]
[La douce folie
    Que celle d'aimer!
    L'Amour doit former
Les beaux jours de la vie;
    La douce folie,
    Que celle d'aimer!
Plus ce dieu nous lie,
Plus il sait charmer,
Tout doit s'enflammer,
Le printemps y convie;
    La douce folie
    Que celle d'aimer!
    La douce folie
    Que celle d'aimer!]

[CHOEUR]
[La douce folie
    Que celle d'aimer!
    L'Amour doit former
Les beaux jours de la vie;
    La douce folie,
    Que celle d'aimer!
Plus ce dieu nous lie,
Plus il sait charmer,
Tout doit s'enflammer,
Le printemps y convie;
    La douce folie
    Que celle d'aimer!
    La douce folie
    Que celle d'aimer!]

The least favor
    That love provides,
Is able to atone for the troubles that he makes us suffer.

VOLUPTUOUSNESS

Far from this place, sad wisdom,
Should one forbid youth
Forming these delightful bonds?

(During youth,
    Is it being wise
To flee a destiny that can make us happy?)

[What madness,
    When from its life
A young heart loses its sweetest moments!]

Voluptuousness and her followers begin their dances again.

[A FOLLOWER OF VOLUPTUOUSNESS]
[The sweet madness
    Of loving!
    Love must form
Life's beautiful days;
    The sweet madness,
    Of loving!
The more this god binds us,
The more he knows how to delight,
All should be inflamed,
Spring invites us there;
    The sweet madness
    Of loving!
    The sweet madness
    Of loving!]

[CHORUS]
[The sweet madness
    Of loving!
    Love must form
Life's beautiful days;
    The sweet madness,
    Of loving!
The more this god binds us,
The more he knows how to delight,
All should be inflamed,
Spring invites us there;
    The sweet madness
    Of loving!
    The sweet madness
    Of loving!]

Scène quatrième

L'Aurore, Iphis, Cephale, La Volupté

L'AURORE
Pour dissiper votre tristesse,
   Vous voyez les soins que j'ai pris:
Tâchez de surmonter une indigne faiblesse;
La volage beauté, dont vous êtes épris,
   Est plus digne de vos mépris,
Qu'elle ne fus d'avoir votre tendresse.

CEPHALE
De mon funeste sort, ciel! quelle est la rigueur?

L'AURORE
Vous soupirez encore pour elle?

CEPHALE
J'ai honte d'être trop fidèle,
Mais, hélas! le dépit qui déchire mon coeur,
   Redouble ma peine cruelle,
   Et n'affaiblit point mon ardeur.

L'AURORE
Cessez d'être sensible aux beautés des mortelles;
Cherchez un sort dont les dieux soient jaloux,
De tant de déités qui brillent parmi nous,
   Les plus fières, les plus rebelles,
   Ces seront de l'être pour vous.

J'en dis peut-être trop; vous allez me connaître,

Cephale, il ne faut plus vous rien dissimuler,

   En vain j'ai voulu vous celer
Que de mon faible coeur l'Amour s'est rendu maître;
Mes soins pour le cacher ont été superflus,
Contre lui la fierté n'est qu'un faible remède,
   Hélas! quand ce dieu nous possède,
Les dieux les plus puissants ne se possèdent plus.
Vous voyez mon ardeur, parlez sans vous contraindre.

CEPHALE
De vos bienfaits mon coeur se sent comblé,
Mais . . . dieux!

L'AURORE
Que dites-vous?

CEPHALE
   Que mon sort est à plaindre!
Indigne des honneurs dont je suis accablé . . .

L'AURORE
N'achève pas, Ingrat, je prévois quel outrage
Tes injustes mépris seraient à mes ardeurs!

Scene 4

Aurora, Iphis, Cephalus, Voluptuousness

AURORA
To diminish your sadness,
   You see the cares I have taken:
Try to rise above an unworthy weakness;
The fickle beauty, with whom you are smitten,
   Is more worthy of your contempt,
Than of having had your affections.

CEPHALUS
Concerning my dreadful fate, heaven! How long must this go on?

AURORA
You still sigh for her?

CEPHALUS
I am ashamed of being too faithful,
But, alas! The vexation torturing my heart
   Increases my cruel pain,
   And weakens my passion not at all.

AURORA
Cease being sensitive to the beauty of these mortals;
Look for a type of whom the gods would be jealous,
Of all the gods who shine among us,
   The most stunning, the most rebellious,
   These are going to be the type for you.

Perhaps I have said too much; you are going to understand me,
Cephalus, it's no longer necessary to hide anything from you,
   In vain I have desired to conceal from you
That Love has made itself the master of my feeble heart;
My cares to hide it have been ineffective,
Against him pride is nothing but a weak remedy,
   Alas! When this god possesses us,
The most powerful gods no longer possess themselves.
You see my ardor, speak without restraining yourself.

CEPHALUS
My heart is overflowing from your kindnesses,
But . . . Oh gods!

AURORA
What are you saying?

CEPHALUS
   How my lot is to be pitied!
Unworthy of the honors with which I am overwhelmed . . .

AURORA
Don't finish, you ingrate, I see already what a gross insult
Your unfair contempt will be to my passion!

Va languir pour une volage?
Va te livrer à d'éternels malheurs?
Je ne serai pas seule à répandre des pleurs . . .
Il fuit . . . il m'abandonne à ma honte, et ma rage. . . .
Cephale, tu te perds, cesse de m'irriter:
Tu te repentirais d'avoir su me déplaire.

CEPHALE
Je n'ai rien fait pour mériter
Ni vos soins, ni votre colère.

Vous me faites voir en ce jour
Un barbare courroux, une rage inhumaine;
Je ne croyais pas que l'amour
Dût tant ressemble à la haine.

L'AURORE
Vous me bravez, Cruel, vous connaissez mon coeur,
Je vous ai fait voir sa faiblesse;
Vous ne savez que trop, que toute ma fureur
Ne peut égaler ma tendresse.

CEPHALE
De votre bonté interrompez le cours.
Votre amour outragé demande une victime,
Faites finir mes tristes jours,
Punissez-moi, suivez un courroux légitime.

L'AURORE
Je ne vous punirai qu'en vous aimant toujours.
Aimez qui vous méprise, et fuyez qui vous aime:

Vous serez le témoin de mes tendres ardeurs;
A vos yeux chaque jour j'offrirai mes douleurs,
Et jusques dans votre coeur même,
Mes maux, et mon amour trouverons des vengeurs.
Partez, c'est trop gêner votre âme impatiente;
Allez offrir à des trompeurs appas
L'hommage généreux d'une flamme constante.
Zéphires, accompagnez, et conduisez ses pas.

Scène cinquième

L'Aurore, Iphis

L'AURORE
Tu vois ma honte et mon supplice.

IPHIS
Vengez-vous de l'Ingrat qui cause vos ennuis.

L'AURORE
Quel triomphe pour lui! en l'état où je suis,
S'il savait que forcée à lui rendre justice,
Ma raison me contraint d'approuver ses mépris!

IPHIS Que dites-vous?	IPHIS What are you saying?

L'AURORE
Apprends quelle est mon infortune:
    Jamais je ne l'ai tant aimé,
Mon coeur malgré, lui-même, est surpris et charmé
    D'une vertu si peu commune. . . .
	AURORA
	Learn what is my unfortunate situation:
	    Never have I loved anyone so much,
	My heart is surprised in spite of itself and charmed
	    By so uncommon a virtue. . . .

(columns continue)

IPHIS
Que dites-vous?

L'AURORE
Apprends quelle est mon infortune:
    Jamais je ne l'ai tant aimé,
Mon coeur malgré, lui-même, est surpris et charmé
    D'une vertu si peu commune. . . .

Ah! c'est de quoi mon coeur doit encore le punir;
Il me quitte . . . il me hait . . . et sait toujours me plaire!

Vengeons-nous; je le puis. . . . qui peut me retenir? . . .

A mon juste courroux ma tendresse est contraire,
    Et je crains bien que ma colère
N'augmente mon amour, au lieu de le bannir.

Acte IV

Le théâtre représente les jardins du palais d'Erictée.

Scène première

Dorine, Arcas

ARCAS
    Borée épouse la Princesse.
Je dois avec Cephale abandonner ces lieux,
    Veux-tu répondre à ma tendresse,
    Ou pour jamais recevoir mes adieux?
Tu peux rendre aujourd'hui mon âme satisfaite,
    A m'épouser voudras-tu consentir?

DORINE
Le feu de ton amour pourrait se ralentir,
    S'il avait tout ce qu'il souhaite;
    Quelques plaisirs qu'on se promette,
Il n'est depuis l'hymen qu'un pas au repentir.

ARCAS
A d'éternels refus dois-je toujours m'attendre?

DORINE
N'espèrez pas que je me rende un jour,
Mon coeur de s'engager saura bien se défendre:

    Trop souvent l'hymen le plus tendre
    Eteint le flambeau de l'amour.

ARCAS
    Les mépris d'une cruelle
    Rendent le calme à mon coeur.
Malheureux qui s'obstine à souffrir la rigueur
    D'une beauté rebelle.
Dans l'empire amoureux le coeur le moins constant
    Est bien souvent le plus content.

IPHIS
What are you saying?

AURORA
Learn what is my unfortunate situation:
    Never have I loved anyone so much,
My heart is surprised in spite of itself and charmed
    By so uncommon a virtue. . . .

Oh! This is why my heart must yet punish him;
He abandons me . . . he hates me . . . and always knows how to please me!

Let us take revenge; I have the power . . . who can stop me? . . .

To my justifiable wrath my tenderness is contrary,
    And I fear greatly that my anger
Only increases my love, instead of banishing it.

Act 4

The setting is the gardens of Erechtheus' palace.

Scene 1

Dorine, Arcas

ARCAS
    Boreas is marrying the princess.
I must leave this place with Cephalus,
    Do you wish to respond to my tenderness,
    Or forever receive my farewell?
You can give my soul satisfaction today,
    Will you consent to marry me?

DORINE
The fire of your love may lessen,
    If it has all that it desires;
    Whatever pleasures we may anticipate,
After marriage it is only one step to regret.

ARCAS
Must I always look forward to your endless refusals?

DORINE
Do not hope that I will give up one day,
My heart will know well how to defend itself from entanglements:

    Too often the most affectionate wedlock
    Extinguishes the flame of love.

ARCAS
    The scorn of a cruel one
    Brings calm to my heart.
Unhappy is the obstinate one who suffers harshness
    From a stubborn beauty.
In the empire of love the heart the least constant
    Is very often the most content.

ENSEMBLE
Vivons toujours sans tristesse,
N'aimons qu'à rire et chanter.
    Quand l'amour nous blesse,
S'il offre un doux moment, tâchons d'en profiter;
Mais regardons un excès de tendresse
    Comme un faiblesse
    Qu'on doit éviter.
	TOGETHER
	Let us live always without sadness,
	Let us love only to laugh and sing.
	    When love strikes us,
	If it offers a sweet moment, let us seek to profit by it;
	But let us regard an excess of tenderness
	    As a weakness
	    That one must avoid.

Scène seconde

L'Aurore, Iphis, Dorine, Arcas

Scene 2

Aurora, Iphis, Dorine, Arcas

L'AURORE
Sur d'autres que sur vous doit tomber ma vengeance:
    Hâtez-vous de vous retirer.
    Le mépris d'un ingrat m'offense;
Qu'il souffre les tourments qu'il me fait endurer.

Dorine et Arcas se retirent.

AURORA
On someone other than you must my vengeance fall:
    Make haste to withdraw yourselves.
    The contempt of a heartless one offends me;
Let him suffer the torments that he has made me endure.

Dorine and Arcas exit.

Scène troisième

L'Aurore, Iphis

Scene 3

Aurora, Iphis

L'AURORE / **AURORA**

O vous, implacable ennemie
Des coeurs que l'Amour rend heureux,
Déesse des soupçons, barbare Jalousie,
Pour entendre ma voix de vos gouffres affreux,
Suspendez les fureurs dont vous êtes saisie.
    Par les charmes les plus puissants,
Inspirez à Procris une haine cruelle;
    Peignez-lui Cephale infidèle,
    Troublez son esprit et ses sens.
Ah! toutes les horreurs que votre rage inspire,
Tous les maux que produit votre funeste empire,
N'égaleront jamais les troubles que je sens.
	O you, implacable enemy
	Of hearts that Love has made happy,
	Goddess of suspicion, barbarous Jealousy,
	In order to hear my voice from your hideous abyss,
	Suspend the uproar in which you are involved.
	    Using the most powerful spells,
	Inspire in Procris a cruel hatred;
	    Depict Cephalus as unfaithful to her,
	    Disturb her spirit and her consciousness.
	Oh! All the horrors which your rage inspires,
	All the ills which your deadly empire produces
	Will never equal the pain that I feel.

On entend une symphonie lugubre. / *A lugubrious symphony is heard.*

Sortons, la Jalousie en ces lieux va se rendre.
    Cette affreuse divinité
    Ne pourrait souffrir la clarté
Que je suis malgré moi, contrainte de répandre.
    Hélas!
	Let us leave, Jealousy is going to come to this place.
	    This frightful divinity
	    Would not be able to suffer the brilliance
	Which, in spite of myself, I am constrained to spread abroad.
	    Alas!

IPHIS
    Qui vous fait soupirer?
A remplir vos désirs tout semble conspirer,
La haine que Procris fera voir à Cephale,
    Pourra vers elle empêcher son retour.

IPHIS
    Who makes you sigh?
Everything conspires to fulfill your desires,
The hatred that will strike Procris when she sees Cephalus,
    Will be able to hinder his return to her.

L'AURORE
    Iphis ma peine est sans égale,
    Je connais trop bien son amour,
Ma rage et tes conseils lui vont ravir le jour.

AURORA
    Iphis, my pain is without equal,
    I know too well his love,
My rage and your counsels to him are going to ruin him.

Non, je ne puis souffrir que ce héros périsse,
   Divinité, que mes fureurs
   Viennent d'armer pour son supplice . . .

IPHIS
Procris vient, bannissez vos injustes terreurs.
Qui vous rend en ce jour si contraire à vous-même?
Une indigne pitié doit-elle vous trahir?

L'AURORE
Tes conseils sur mon coeur ont un pouvoir suprême.
C'en est fait que l'enfer soit prêt à m'obéir . . .
De ma vengeance, Iphis, j'aurai peine à jouir.
Quand je songe à l'objet de mon ardeur extrême,
   J'oublie, hélas! que je le dois haïr,
   Et je sens trop bien que je l'aime.

Scène quatrième

PROCRIS
Funeste mort, donnez-moi du secours!
Ah! par pitié venez trancher mes jours!
   Mon infortune est certaine.
C'est peu de perdre, hélas! l'objet de mes amours,
Je me vois condamnée à m'unir pour toujours,
   A l'objet de toute ma haine.
Rien ne peut me tirer de cette affreuse peine.
   Funeste mort, donnez-moi du secours!
Ah! par pitié venez trancher mes jours!

On entend un bruit souterrain.

Quel bruit lugubre et sourd ici se fait entendre?
   Mille abîmes se sont ouverts!

Scène cinquième

Le théâtre change, et représente l'antre où La Jalousie fait son séjour.

Procris, La Jalousie, La Rage, Le Désespoir

PROCRIS
Je me vois transportée en d'horribles deserts!
   Ciel! quelle nuit vient me surprendre?
Pourquoi frémir? l'enfer touché de mes soupirs,
Veut-il par le trépas finir mes déplaisirs?

Elle apperçoit La Jalousie.

   Venez, implacable furie,
Venez, je m'abandonne à vos barbares mains.
   Terminez ma mourante vie:
Si de quelques frayeurs je vous parais saisie,
   Ce n'est pas votre barbarie,
   C'est votre pitié que je crains.

No, I cannot allow this hero to perish,
   Divinity, whom my fury
   Just strengthened for his torment . . .

IPHIS
Procris is coming, banish your unfounded terrors.
Who renders you so unlike yourself on this day?
Must an unworthy pity betray you?

AURORA
Your counsels have the highest power over my heart.
It is already accomplished that hell is ready to obey me . . .
Concerning my vengeance, Iphis, I will hardly revel in it.
When I dream of the object of my extreme ardor,
   I forget, alas, that I must hate him.
   And I know all too well that I love him.

Scene 4

PROCRIS
Grievous death, give me aid!
Oh! For pity's sake come cut short my days!
   My misfortune is certain.
It is little to lose, alas, the object of my love,
I see myself condemned to be united forever,
   To the object of all my hatred.
Nothing can extract me from this horrible punishment.
   Grievous death, give me aid!
Oh! For pity's sake come cut short my days.

A subterranean noise is heard.

What ominous, rumbling noise can be heard here?
   Thousands of chasms are opening!

Scene 5

The scene changes to the den where Jealousy makes his abode.

Procris, Jealousy, Rage, Despair

PROCRIS
I see myself transported to a horrible desert!
   Heaven! What darkness has just surprised me?
Why do I tremble? Does hell, touched by my sighs,
Wish by my death to end my grief?

She perceives Jealousy.

   Come, implacable fury,
Come, I abandon myself to your barbarous hands.
   End my faltering life;
If I appear to you filled with dread,
   It is not your savagery,
   It is your pity that I fear.

LA JALOUSIE Pour calmer vos ennuis le ciel ici m'appelle, 　L'enfer s'interesse pour vous; Voulez-vous conserver une flamme immortelle 　Pour un volage, un infidèle? 　　Ah! ne suivez que vos transports jaloux; Pour accabler l'ingrat d'une haine cruelle, 　Que, s'il se peut, votre courroux Egale les plaisirs de son ardeur nouvelle.	**JEALOUSY** The heavens have called me here to calm your anxiety, 　Hell is concerned for you; Would you preserve an immortal flame 　For a fickle one, an unfaithful one? 　　Oh! Follow only your jealous inclinations; To overcome the ingrate with a cruel hatred, 　Let your wrath, if possible, Equal the pleasures of his new passion.
PROCRIS Graces aux dieux, je suis au comble des malheurs. 　Le sort me fût toujours contraire; Mais je ne croyais pas, ô ciel! que ta colère Dû finir, par ce coup, ma vie et mes douleurs!	**PROCRIS** Thanks to the gods, I am at the height of misfortune. 　Fate might always be opposed to me, But I did not believe, oh heaven, that your wrath Had to finish, by this blow, my life and my sorrows!
Elle tombe évanouie.	*She falls unconscious.*
LA JALOUIE, LA RAGE et LE DESESPOIR 　Pour obéir à la déesse, Inspirons à Procris nos transports furieux. 　Profitons de cette faiblesse 　Qui va cacher notre rage à ses yeux: Venez, démons, venez, montrez-vous en ces lieux; 　Que chacun de nous s'empresse 　D'obéir à la déesse.	**JEALOUSY, RAGE, and DESPAIR** 　In order to obey the goddess, Let us inspire in Procris our furious ecstasy. 　Let us profit by this weakness Which will hide our fury from her eyes: Come, demons, come, show yourselves in this place; 　Let each of us be eager 　To obey the goddess.

Scène sixième

La Jalousie, La Rage, Le Désespoir, Troupe de Démons, Procris évanouie

Scene 6

Jealousy, Rage, Despair, Band of Demons, Procris unconscious

LE CHOEUR 　Accourons, traînons nos fers. Nous allons dans ces lieux pour remplir votre attente, Répandre la terreur, le trouble et l'épouvante; 　Accourons, traînons nos fers, 　Transportons ici les enfers.	**CHORUS** 　Let us hasten, let us drag our chains. In order to fulfill your expectations we are going To spread dread, trouble and terror in this place; 　Let us hasten, let us drag our chains, 　Let us bring here the creatures of hell.
Entrée de démons *La Jalousie s'approche de Procris*	*Opening dance of the demons* *Jealousy approaches Procris*
LA JALOUSIE 　Sortez d'un honteux esclavage. Méprisez l'Inconstant qui cause votre ennui. 　Que le dépit, la fureur et la rage 　Vous animent seuls aujourd'hui. Non, non, vous ne sauriez lui faire trop d'outrage, La haine que l'on sent pour un amant volage, Se mesure à l'amour que l'on avait pour lui.	**JEALOUSY** 　Leave a shameful bondage. Scorn the unfaithful one who causes your distress. 　Let spite, fury and rage 　Alone animate you today. No, no, you can't do him too much injury, The hatred that one feels for a fickle lover, Is in proportion to the love that one had for him.
LE CHOEUR 　Sortez d'un honteux esclavage. Méprisez l'inconstant qui cause votre ennui. 　Que le dépit, la fureur et la rage 　Vous animent seuls aujourd'hui. Non, non, vous ne sauriez lui faire trop d'outrage,	**CHORUS** 　Leave a shameful bondage. Scorn the unfaithful one who causes your distress. 　Let spite, fury and rage 　Alone animate you today. No, no, you can't give him too much injury,

La haine que l'on sent pour un amant volage,	The hatred that one feels for a fickle lover,
Se mesure à l'amour que l'on avait pour lui.	Is in proportion to the love that one had for him.

Les démons et La Jalousie inspirent leur fureur à Procris, et se retirent. / *The demons and Jealousy cast their spell on Procris and leave.*

Scène septième / Scene 7

Le théâtre change, et représente les mêmes jardins qui avaient paru auparavant. Procris sort de son évanouissement, agitée des fureurs que La Jalousie vient de lui inspirer.

The scene changes to the same gardens which had appeared previously. Procris awakens from her fainting spell, agitated by the fury that Jealousy has just inspired in her.

Procris, Cephale, Dorine / *Procris, Cephalus, Dorine*

PROCRIS
L'ingrat! mais, dieux! où suis-je?

You ingrate! But, gods! Where am I?

CEPHALE / CEPHALUS
Enfin le ciel propice. . . .

Finally favorable heaven. . . .

PROCRIS
Perfide, je te vois? va, fuis loin de mes yeux:
   Par tes mensonges odieux
   Tu ne peux plus couvrir ton injustice.
Cherche des lieux remplis de traîtres, d'imposteurs,
Où l'on puisse imiter tes trahisons secrètes.
Pour le malheur, hélas! des funestes ardeurs,
   Tu n'auras que trop de retraite.

Treacherous one, I see you? Go, fly far from my eyes:
   With your odious lies
   You can no longer cover up your unjust acts.
Look for a place full of traitors, of imposters,
Where people can imitate your secret treachery.
For the misery, alas, caused by those deadly passions,
   You will have only too much privacy.

CEPHALE / CEPHALUS
Que dites-vous, Cruelle? ah! vous voulez en vain,
Sous un voile trompeur, cacher votre inconstance.

What are you saying, cruel one? Oh! In vain you wish,
Under a false veil, to hide your fickleness?

PROCRIS
   Pour me venger de ton offense,
   A ton rival je vais donner la main;
J'acheterai bien cher une triste vengeance;
J'en mourrai, je le sens, mais mon coeur sans effroi, . . .

[Verra de son destin les horreurs inhumaines,]
Non, traître je ne puis, par de trop rudes peines,
Me punir de l'amour que j'ai senti pour toi.

   In order to avenge myself for your transgression,
   To your rival I will give my hand;
I will buy a wretched revenge at great cost;
I will die because of it, I feel it, but my heart without dismay, . . .

[Will see the brutal horrors of its destiny,]
No, traitor, I cannot, by too harsh a pain,
Punish myself for the love that I felt for you.

CEPHALE / CEPHALUS
Vous m'accusez, quand j'ai lieu de me plaindre. . . .

You accuse me, when I have good reason to complain. . . .

PROCRIS
   Tes détours seront superflus:
Crois-moi, ne cherche point à feindre;
Mon coeur est détrompé, je ne t'écoute plus.
   Va retrouver ta conquête nouvelle
Que ne puis-je, à tes yeux, plus charmante et plus belle,

   Sur elle remporter le prix!
De ton perfide coeur me rendre souveraine,

   Your tricks will be ineffective:
Believe me, don't try anymore to pretend;
My heart is undeceived, I hear you no longer.
   Go and join your new conquest.
Would that I could, more charming and beautiful in your eyes,

   Triumph over her!
And be the queen of your treacherous heart,

Pour payer à jamais de froideur et de haine
   L'ardeur dont tu serais épris.

Elle sort.

CEPHALE
Sans vouloir m'écouter, l'Ingrate se retire!
Ah! c'est au désespoir que je dois recourir!
Je ne puis plus souffrir un si cruel martyre.
   Courons la voir, l'apaiser, ou mourir.

Acte V

Le théâtre représente un bois.

Scène première

Procris, Dorine

PROCRIS
Ne me parle plus d'un parjure.
Prends-tu quelque plaisir d'aigrir mon désespoir?
Ah! plutôt pour m'aider à suivre mon devoir,
Dis-moi que j'en reçois la plus cruelle injure,
   Et quoique mon coeur en murmure,
Que ma gloire m'oblige à ne jamais le voir.
A ne jamais le voir? ô gloire trop cruelle!
Cephale, hélas! que ne m'es-tu fidèle?
Quelle que fût des dieux l'impitoyable loi,
Prête à mourir du coup qui nous sépare,
   J'aurais, malgré le ciel barbare,
La douceur d'expirer en te donnant ma foi?
Quel plaisir, en mourant, de te voir, de t'entendre?
   Tes yeux me donneraient des pleurs,
Et le soin de tes jours pourrait seul me défendre

De te rendre témoin de toutes mes douleurs.
Mais, Ingrat, tu me fuis, et ma tendresse est vaine;

   Ton lâche coeur se plaît à me trahir!
Cruel, ah! quand tu vois que ma mort est certaine,
   Dois-tu, pour redoubler ma peine,
Contraindre, en expirant mon coeur à te haïr?

DORINE
Cephale au désespoir m'a fait voir ses alarmes;
   J'ai vu ses yeux baignés de larmes,
Vous chercher pour bannir votre cruelle erreur.

PROCRIS
Non, non, il veut encore tromper mon faible coeur;
Dorine, mon trépas n'aura rien qui l'étonne.
   Revenez, ma juste fureur.
   Je ne saurais avoir trop en horreur
   Le perfide qui m'abandonne.
C'en est fait, je le hais; je ne veux plus songer

In order to pay back forever with coldness and hatred
   The passion with which you would be smitten.

She exits.

CEPHALUS
Without wishing to hear from me, the ingrate departs!
Oh! It is to despair that I should return!
I can no longer suffer such a cruel torture.
   Let us hasten to see her, to appease her, or die.

Act 5

The scene is a forest.

Scene 1

Procris, Dorine

PROCRIS
Speak to me no more of a perjurer.
Do you take some pleasure in aggravating my grief?
Oh! In order to help me to follow my duty,
Tell me that I receive from him the cruellest wrong,
   And although my heart complains,
Let my pride oblige me to never see him again.
To never see him again? Oh, too cruel a pride!
Cephalus, alas! Were you not faithful to me?
Whatever was the gods' merciless law,
Ready to die from the blow which separates us,
   I would have had, despite barbarous heaven,
The sweetness of dying giving you my faith?
What pleasure, in dying, to see you, to hear you?
   Your eyes would have shed tears for me,
And concern for your well-being would alone have
   prevented me
From making you a witness of all my sadness.
But, ungrateful one, you fly from me, and my tenderness
   is empty;
   Your shameful heart wishes to betray me!
Cruel one, oh! When you see that my death is certain,
   Must you, in order to increase my pain,
Constrain my dying heart to hate you?

DORINE
Cephalus in despair has shown me his distress;
   I saw his eyes bathed in tears,
Seeking you in order to correct your grievous error.

PROCRIS
No, no, he still wishes to deceive my weak heart;
Dorine, only my death will shake him.
   Return, my rightful fury.
   I would not know how to abhor too much
   The perfidious one who abandons me.
It is done, I hate him; I wish no longer to dream

Qu'à suivre un fier devoir qui seul peut me venger.	But to follow a proud duty that alone can avenge me.
Inutile courroux, impuissante vengeance,	Useless wrath, impotent vengeance,
En vain, pour me tromper, je fais ce que je puis.	In vain, in order to fool myself, I do that which I can.

DORINE / DORINE

De vos transports calmez la violence:
On vient.

Calm the violence of your delirium:
Someone is coming.

PROCRIS / PROCRIS

Hélas! doit-on me contraindre au silence,
Quand la plainte peut seule adoucir mes ennuis?

Alas! Must I be constrained to silence,
When lamentation alone is able to alleviate my vexation?

Scène seconde / Scene 2

Procris, Borée, Dorine
Troupe de Thraces et d'Athéniens

Procris, Boreas, Dorine
Band of people from Thrace and Athens

BOREE / BOREAS

Belle Princesse, enfin, approuvez-vous ma flamme?
Et lorsqu'un doux hymen vous unit en ce jour,
M'est-il permis de croire que votre âme
   Veut bien partager mon amour?
Vous vous troublez, vous êtes interdite?
Ingrate, mes soupirs n'ont-ils pu vous toucher?

Beautiful princess, do you finally approve of my passion?
And since a sweet wedding will bind you on this day,
May I be permitted to believe that your soul
   Is willing to share my love?
You are troubled, you are confused?
Ungrateful one, have not my sighs been able to touch you?

PROCRIS / PROCRIS

Ne soyez pas surpris du trouble qui m'agite;
Pardonnez à mon coeur le désordre qu'excite
   Un amour qu'il veut vous cacher.

Do not be surprised at the distress which disturbs me;
Excuse my heart the disorder that stirs up
   A love that it wishes to hide from you.

BOREE / BOREAS

Qu'entends-je? mes craintes sont vaines;
Vous consentez à couronner mes feux?
   Après de mortelles peines,
Que l'hymen a d'appas pour deux coeurs amoureux;
   Non, il n'a point de douces chaînes,
   Si l'Amour n'en forme les noeuds.

What do I hear? My fears are false;
You consent to reward my ardor?
   After extreme difficulties,
How marriage holds charms for two amorous hearts;
   No, there is no point in sweet bonds,
   If Love does not tie the knots.

PROCRIS et BOREE / PROCRIS AND BOREAS

   Après de mortelles peines,
Que l'hymen a d'appas pour deux coeurs amoureux;
   Non, il n'a point de douces chaînes,
   Si l'Amour n'en forme les noeuds.

   After extreme difficulties,
How marriage holds charms for two amorous hearts;
   No, there is no point in sweet bonds,
   If Love does not tie the knots.

BOREE / BOREAS

Rien ne me trouble plus, et ma joie est certaine;
O vous, chers confidents de mes tristes soupirs,
Et que je rends témoins de mon bonheur suprême,
Si vos coeurs prennent part à mes tendres soupirs,
   Honorez la beauté que j'aime.
   Empressez-vous de rendre à ses beaux yeux,
   L'hommage que l'on rend aux dieux.

Nothing can trouble me further, and my joy is certain.
Oh you, dear confidants of my sad sighs,
And whom I make witnesses of my supreme happiness,
If your hearts participate in my affectionate sighs,
   Honor the beauty whom I love.
   Eagerly present to her beautiful eyes,
   The homage one gives to the gods.

LE CHOEUR / CHORUS

Empressons-nous de rendre à ses beaux yeux,
   L'hommage que l'on rend aux dieux.

Let us eagerly present to her beautiful eyes,
   The homage one gives to the gods.

Première Entrée / *First Dance*

BOREE / BOREAS

Est-il de plus douce victoire,	Is there a sweeter victory,
Que celle des amants que l'Amour rend heureux?	Than that of lovers whom Love renders happy?
Quel triomphe! quelle gloire!	What triumph! What glory!
De voir une beauté qui méprisait nos feux,	To see a beauty who was scorning our passion,
Céder et se rendre à nos voeux.	Give in and yield to our desires.
Est-il de plus douce victoire,	Is there a sweeter victory,
Que celle des amants que l'Amour rend heureux?	Than that of lovers whom Love renders happy?

LE CHOEUR / CHORUS

Est-il de plus douce victoire,	Is there a sweeter victory,
Que celle des amants que l'Amour rend heureux.	Than that of lovers whom Love renders happy?
Quel triomphe! quelle gloire!	What triumph! What glory!
De voir une beauté qui méprisait nos feux,	To see a beauty who was scorning our passion,
Céder et se rendre à nos voeux.	Give in and yield to our desires.
Est-il de plus douce victoire,	Is there a sweeter victory,
Que celle des amants que l'Amour rend heureux?	Than that of lovers whom Love renders happy?

Les Thraces recommencent leurs danses. / *The people from Thrace begin their dances again.*

BOREE / BOREAS

Approuvez les ardeurs d'une âme impatiente,	Sanction the ardors of an impatient spirit,
Je vais presser le Roi d'accomplir mes désirs.	I am going to pressure the king to fulfill my desires.
Les moments qu'il diffère à remplir mon attente,	Each moment that he postpones accomplishing my expectation,
Il les dérobe à mes plaisirs.	Will detract from my delight.

Scène troisième / Scene 3

Procris, Dorine

PROCRIS

Ah! pendant ces moments, où je suis libre encore,	Oh! During these moments while I am still free,
Prévenons les malheurs qui me sont destinés.	Let us avert the unhappiness that is reserved for me.
C'est traîner trop long temps des jours infortunés,	Those wretched days drag out too long,
Et nourrir en mon coeur l'ennui qui le dévore!	And nourish in my heart the anxiety that consumes it.
Mourons. . . .	Let me die. . . .

Scène quatrième / Scene 4

L'Aurore, Procris, Dorine / *Aurora, Procris, Dorine*

L'AURORE / AURORA

Modérez vos transports,	Restrain your desperation,
Procris, à votre sort l'Aurore s'interesse.	Procris, Aurora has an interest in your destiny.
Pour couronner votre tendresse,	In order to reward your tenderness,
Je viens employer mes efforts.	I have just employed my efforts.
Cephale vous conserve une immortelle flamme,	Cephalus conserves for you an eternal flame,
Une jalouse déité	A jealous deity
A fait inspirer à votre âme	Has caused in your soul
Un injuste soupçon de sa fidélité.	An unjust suspicion concerning his faithfulness.

PROCRIS
Quoi! Cephale? Cephale à mes maux est sensible?
Il m'aime? Ah! mon destin m'en paraît plus affreux!

L'AURORE
A mes désirs il n'est rien d'impossible,
Ne craignez point un hymen rigoureux.
Allez, près d'un amant, par des ardeurs nouvelles,
Renouveller vos flammes mutuelles,
Et des dieux apaisés oublier le courroux.
Combien est-il de coeurs fidèles,
Qui par des peines plus cruelles,
Voudraient bien acheter un succès aussi doux?

Scène cinquième

L'AURORE
Que fais-je? quel projet! une pitié fatale
A servir ces amants me va-t'elle engager?
Ciel! sans frémir puis-je songer
Au bonheur, dont mes soins vont combler ma rivale?
Mais plutôt, de ma flamme un indigne retour
Pourrait-il m'empêcher de vaincre mon amour?
Cesse de m'attaquer, importune tendresse!
Si les dieux sont jaloux, ils ne sont pas cruels.
Plus notre rang nous place au dessus des mortels,
Moins nous devons partager leur faiblesse.

Scène sixième

L'Aurore, Iphis

L'AURORE
Hé bien? de mes soins généreux,
Cephale est-il content? as-tu su l'en instruire?

IPHIS
Cephale, des mortels est le plus malheureux.

L'AURORE
Juste ciel! que vas-tu me dire?

IPHIS
Le Roi, soumis aux volontés des dieux,
A fait rompre un hymen à vos désirs contraire.
Borée, irrité, furieux,
A trouvé son rival assez près de ces lieux,
Procris n'a pu suspendre leur colère,
Déja de sa fureur prompt à se repentir,
Le Thrace allait prendre la fuite,
Lorsqu'un trait qu'au hazard Cephale fait partir,
Frappe, d'un coup mortel, la Princesse interdite.

PROCRIS
What! Cephalus? Cephalus is aware of my sorrows?
He loves me? Oh! my fate seems even more horrible!

AURORA
Nothing is impossible to my desires,
Fear not at all a harsh marriage.
Go to your beloved with new ardor,
To renew your mutual passion,
And to forget the wrath of the appeased gods.
How many faithful hearts,
Who by the cruelest pains,
Would wish to dearly buy an equally sweet success?

Scene 5

AURORA
What am I doing? What a plan! A disastrous pity
Is going to involve me in assisting these lovers?
Heaven! Without trembling am I able to think
Of the happiness with which my solicitude will fill my rival?
But rather, an unworthy change in my passion
Was it able to hinder me from subduing my love?
Stop this attack on me, troublesome tenderness!
If the gods are jealous, they are not cruel.
The higher our rank places us above mortals,
The less we must share their weakness.

Scene 6

Aurora, Iphis

AURORA
So then? Because of my generous attentions,
Is Cephalus now happy? Have you informed him of everything?

IPHIS
Of all mortals, Cephalus is the most unhappy.

AURORA
Just heaven! What are you going to tell me?

IPHIS
The king, submissive to the will of the gods,
Dissolved a wedding which was contrary to your desires.
Boreas, agitated, furious,
Found his rival quite near to this place,
Procris was not able to suspend their anger,
Quick to repent of his fury,
The Thracian man was going to run away,
When by accident Cephalus let fly an arrow,
Striking with a mortal blow the astounded princess.

L'AURORE
Qu'entends-je? ô destin rigoureux!
  Pourquoi t'opposer à ma gloire?
  Tu viens m'enlever la victoire
Que j'allais pour jamais remporter sur mes feux.
Cent mouvements divers trouvent place en mon âme;
Malgré tous mes efforts, une secrète flamme
    Cherche encore à s'y rallumer.
	AURORA
	What do I hear? O harsh destiny!
	  Why are you opposed to my glory? You just raised me to the victory
	That I would have carried off forever with my splendor.
	A hundred diverse emotions find a place in my soul;
	Despite all my efforts, a secret passion
	    Still seeks to rekindle itself there.

IPHIS Cephale vient.	**IPHIS** Cephalus is coming.

L'AURORE
  Fuyons, je crains qu'il ne me voie,
Cachons un lâche amour, qui veut se ranimer.
Cachons . . . que sais-je, Iphis? une maligne joie
Que ma gloire offensée à peine peut calmer . . .
	AURORA
	  Let us flee, I fear he may not want to see me,
	Let us conceal a shameful love, which wants to revive itself.
	Let us hide . . . what do I discern, Iphis? A malicious joy
	That my offended pride is scarcely able to calm . . .

Scène septième

Cephale, Arcas, Troupe d'Athéniens

Scene 7

Cephalus, Arcas, Band of Athenians

CEPHALE
Ah! laissez-moi mourir! votre pitié cruelle
Veut-elle prolonger les rigueurs de mon sort?
Malheureux que je suis! cette main criminelle
A ma chère Procris vient de donner la mort.
    Pourquoi m'arracher d'auprès d'elle?
    Pourquoi, par un barbare effort,
Me retenir au jour quand son ombre m'appelle?
Ah! laissez-moi mourir! votre pitié cruelle
Veut-elle prolonger les rigueurs de mon sort?
	CEPHALUS
	Oh! Let me die! Does your cruel pity
	Wish to prolong the rigors of my fate?
	Unhappy one that I am! This criminal hand
	Just inflicted death on my beloved Procris.
	    Why do I tear myself away from her?
	    Why, by a barbarous effort,
	Do I cling to the day when her ghost calls to me?
	Oh! Let me die! Does your cruel pity
	Wish to prolong the rigors of my fate?

Scène dernière

*Procris mourante, soutenue par Dorine.
Cephale, Troupe d'Atheniens*

Final Scene

*Procris dying, supported by Dorine.
Cephalus, Band of Athenians*

CEPHALE Mais, je la vois! Procris . . .	**CEPHALUS** Why, I see her! Procris . . .
PROCRIS Cephale . . .	**PROCRIS** Cephalus . . .

ENSEMBLE
    ô jour funeste!
	TOGETHER
	    O disastrous day!

CEPHALE Vous me fuyez? ah! restez dans ces lieux; Voulez-vous m'enlever le seul bien qui me reste?	**CEPHALUS** You are leaving me? Ah! Remain in this place; Do you wish to take away the only blessing that remains to me?
PROCRIS Hé bien! Cephale, hé bien! recevez mes adieux. A suivre vos désirs mon propre amour m'entraîne;	**PROCRIS** Ah, yes! Cephalus, ah, yes! Receive my farewell. To attend to your desires my pride hurries me away;

J'aurais voulu, de peur d'augmenter votre peine,	I would have wished, for fear of increasing your pain,
Me priver du plaisir de mourir à vos yeux.	To deny myself the pleasure of dying before your eyes.

CEPHALE / CEPHALUS

Je vais vous suivre en la nuit éternelle.	I am going to follow you into the eternal night.

PROCRIS

Non, vivez, je le veux; je veux revivre en vous.	No! Live, I desire it; I wish to live again in you.
Vous m'aimez, vous m'êtes fidèle,	You love me, you are faithful to me,
Mon sort doit me paraître doux.	My fate now seems sweet to me.
Adieu; le destin veut que je vous abandonne:	Farewell; destiny desires that I leave you:
Cher Cephale, aimez-moi toujours,	Dear Cephalus, love me always,
Mais que le souvenir de nos tristes amours	But so that the memory of our sad loves
Ne trouble point le repos de vos jours,	Scarcely troubles the tranquility of your days,
Oubliez-moi plutôt, c'est moi qui vous l'ordonne.	Forget me soon, it is I who orders this of you.
Tout mon corps s'affaiblit, je frémis, je me meurs,	My entire body is becoming weak, I am trembling, I am dying,
Déja du noir séjour j'entrevois les horreurs;	Already from the dark abode I perceive the horrors;
A mes yeux obscurcis la lumière est ravie.	To my darkened eyes the light is entrancing.
Reçois ma main, Cephale, et sois sûr qu'en ce jour,	Receive my hand, Cephalus, and be assured that on this day,
Le dernier soupir de ma vie,	The last breath of my life,
Est encore un soupir d'amour.	Is yet a breath of love.

Elle tombe entre les bras de Dorine qui l'emmène. / *She falls into the arms of Dorine who takes her away.*

CEPHALE / CEPHALUS

Achève, ô ciel barbare! assouvis ta colère!	Finish it off, oh barbarous heaven! Gratify your wrath!
Ah! je sens qu'à la fin tu te rends à mes cris!	Oh! I perceive that in the end you yield to my cries!
Tu cesses de m'être sévère,	You cease being severe to me,
Je succombe à mes maux, rien ne m'est plus contraire,	I give in to my troubles, nothing is opposed to me any longer,
Et je vais aux enfers rejoindre ma Procris.	And I am going to the underworld to rejoin my Procris.

Plate 1. *Cephale et Procris* (Paris: Ballard, 1694), p. 27, "Lieux écartés," mm. 1–25. Courtesy Music Library, University of California, Berkeley.

Plate 2. *Cephale et Procris*, Premier dessus de violon partbook, Ouverture, mm. 1–47.
Courtesy Bibliothèque Nationale de France, Paris.

Plate 3. *Cephale et Procris,* (Paris: Ballard, 1694), p. 3, Ouverture, mm. 44–66. Courtesy Music Library, University of California, Berkeley.

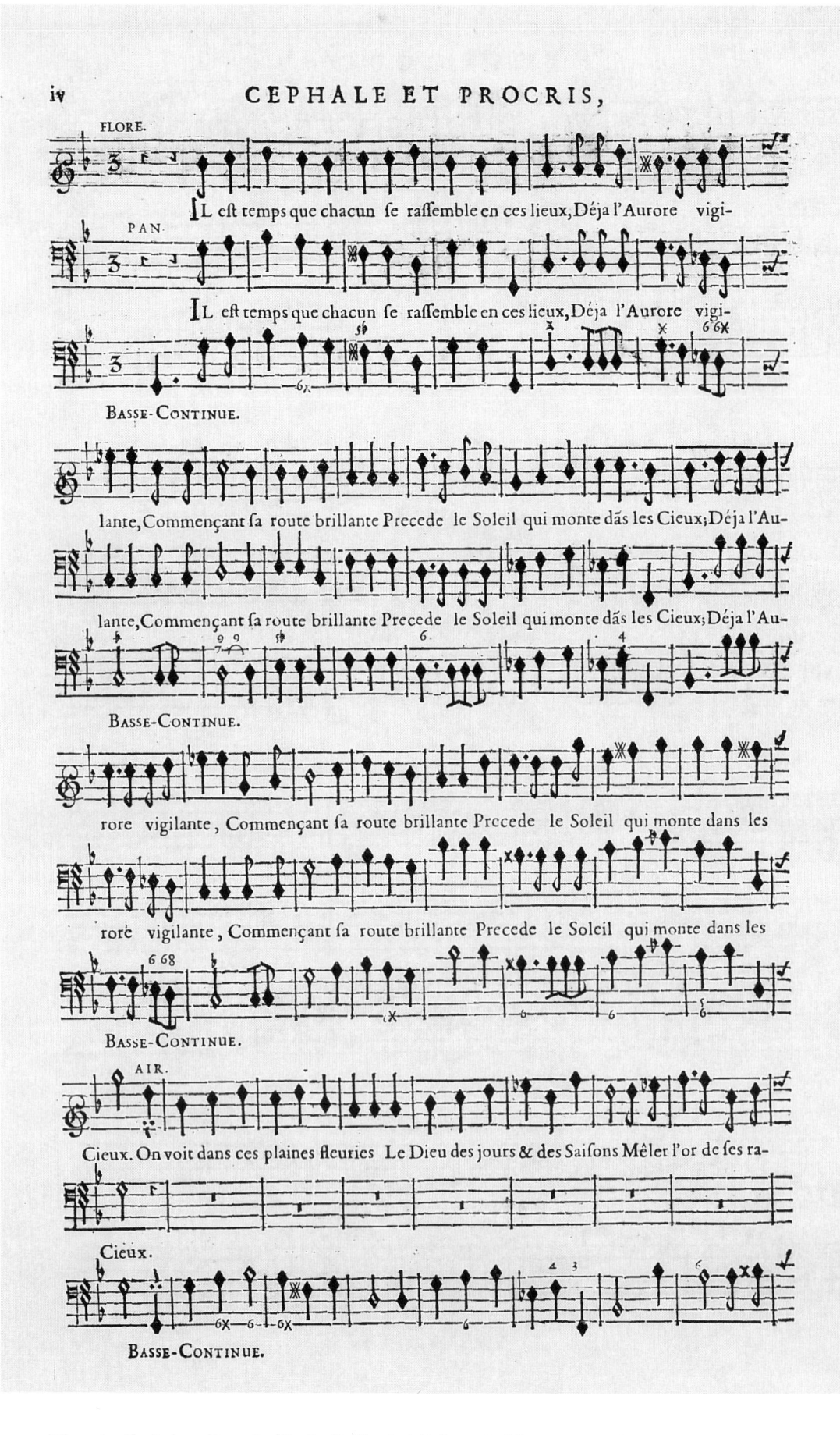

Plate 4. *Cephale et Procris*, (Paris: Ballard, 1694), p. 4, "Il est temps," mm. 1–30 (Prologue). Courtesy Music Library, University of California, Berkeley.

Cephale et Procris

Tragédie Lyrique

Music by Elisabeth-Claude Jacquet de La Guerre
Text by Joseph-François Duché de Vancy

CAST

(in order of appearance)

Prologue

Flore	Dessus
Pan	Basse
Choeur de la Suite de Pan et de Flore	DHcTB
Deux Nymphes	Dessus
Nerée	Haute-contre
Un dieu de la mer	Haute-contre

The Tragedy

Borée, *Prince de Thrace, rival de Cephale*	Basse
Procris, *fille d'Erictée, aimée de Cephale*	Dessus
Dorine, *confidente de Procris*	Dessus
Arcas, *ami de Cephale, amant de Dorine*	Basse
Chœur d'Athéniens	DHcTB
Le Roi (Erictée), *Roi d'Athènes*	Basse
Cephale, *amant de Procris*	Haute-contre
Deux Athéniennes	Dessus
La Prêtesse de Minerve	Dessus
Chœur de Thraces	DHcTB
Un Thrace	Haute-contre
Une Bergère	Dessus
Un Pâtre	Haute-contre
L'Aurore	Dessus
Iphis, *Nymphe, confidente de L'Aurore*	Dessus
Une suivante de La Volupté	Dessus
Chœur des suivantes de La Volupté	DDHc
La Jalousie	Taille
La Rage	Haute-contre
Le Désespoir	Basse
Chœur de Démons	Basse
Chœur de Démons (2e)	HcTB

NON-SINGING ROLES

Troupe d'Athéniens
Troupe de Thraces
Troupe de Pâtres et Bergères
La Volupté
Suite de La Volupté
Troupe de Plaisirs, de Graces, et quatres Amours
Dieux Zéphires

Prologue

Le théâtre représente un bois. La mer paraît dans le fonds.

Ouverture

*Italic voice names indicate parts added by the editor (see the critical report).

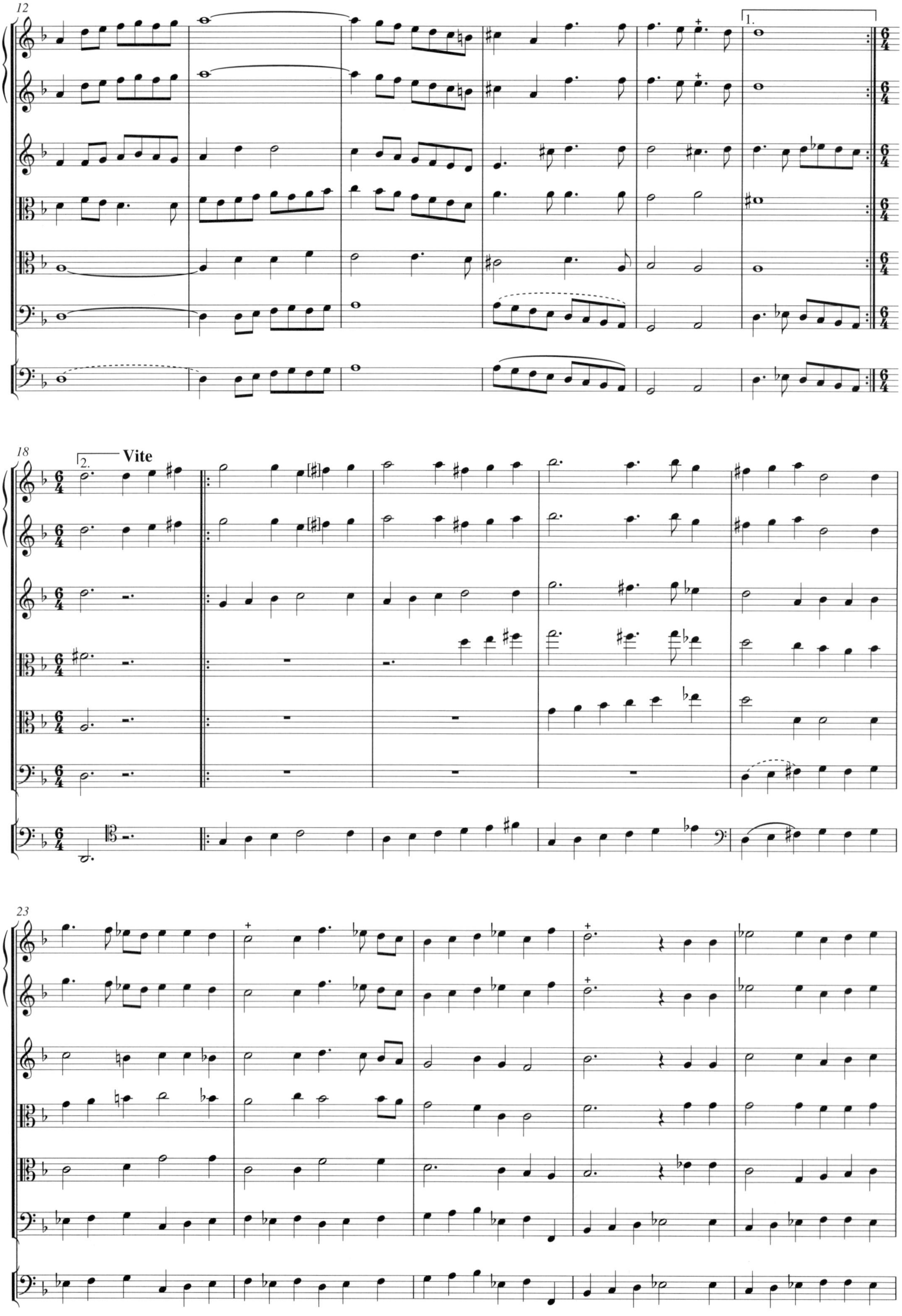
12
1.
18
2.
Vite
23

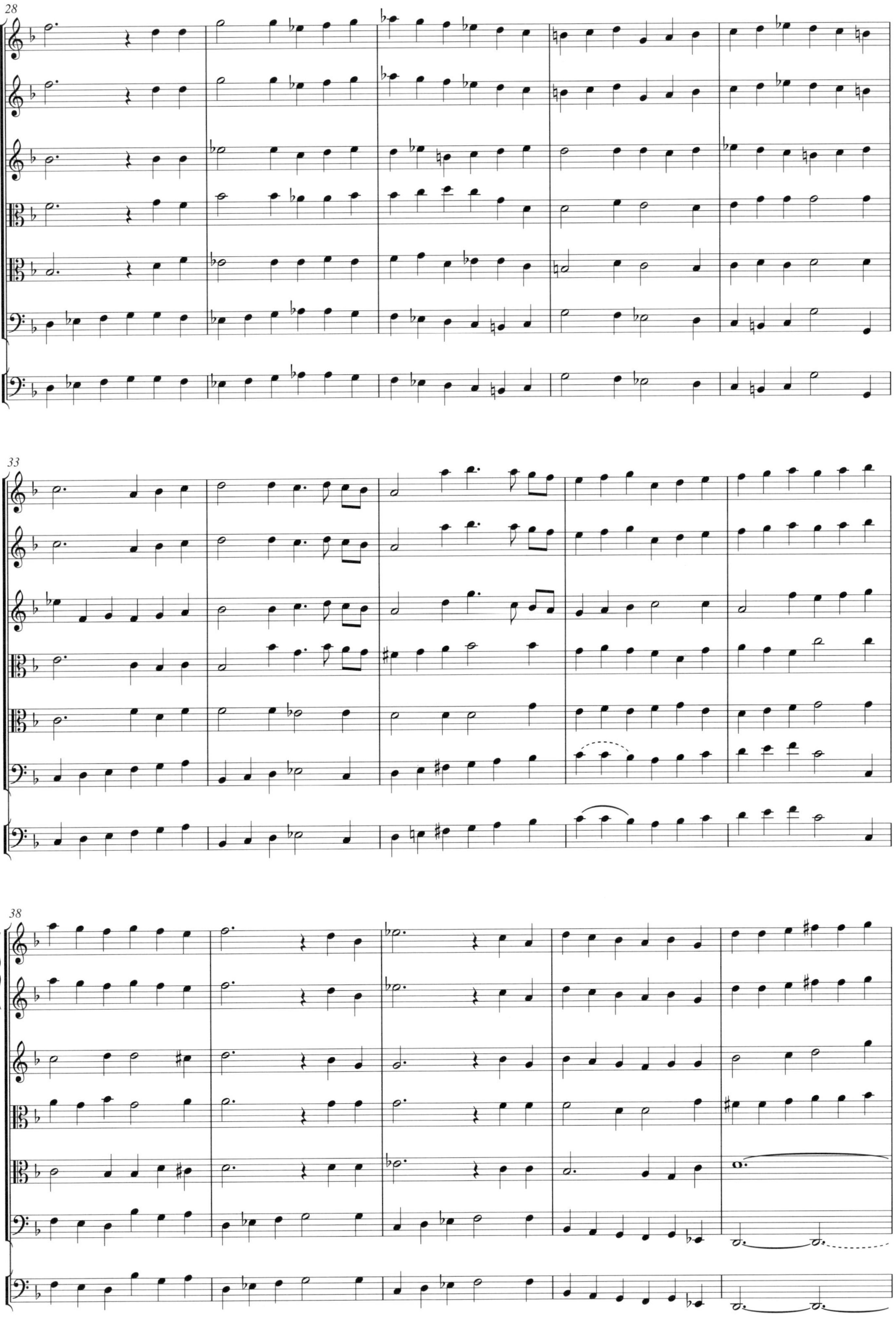
28
33
38

Lentement
43
Trio. Doux
[Violons seule]
Fort
[tous]
[7]
48
Trio. Doux
[Violons seule]
Fort
[tous]
52
Trio. Doux
[Violons seule]
Fort
[tous]
6♯

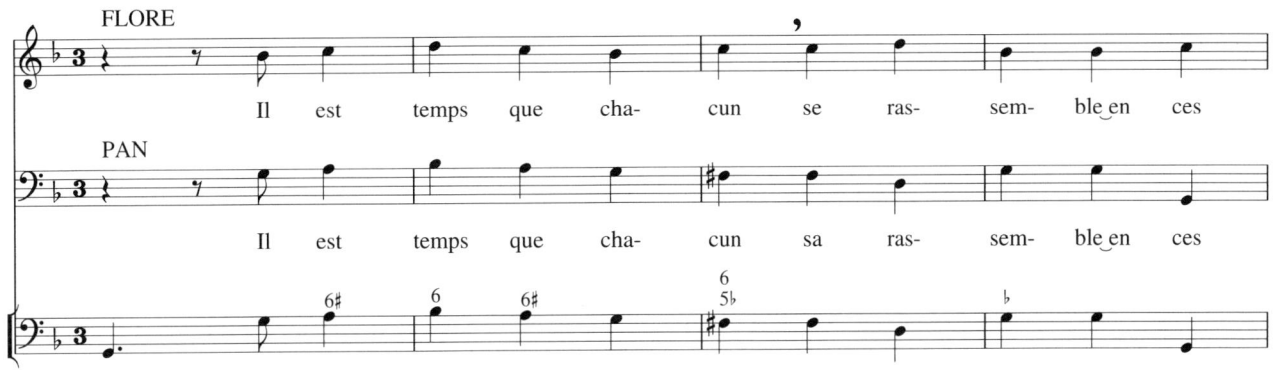

FLORE: Il est temps que chacun se rassemble en ces

PAN: Il est temps que chacun sa rassemble en ces

Basse continue

Air

FLORE

On voit dans ces plaines fleuries le dieu des jours et des saisons mêler l'or de ses rayons à l'émail de nos prairies. On es. Partout mille oiseaux divers célèbrent le retour de ce flambeau du monde, et par les plus tendres concerts, accordent leurs chansons au murmure de l'onde, que le zéphire emporte dans les airs.

[enchaîner]

FLORE
PAN
Rien ne doit re- tar- der nos fê- tes. Le dé- sir de chan-
Basse continue
-ter le plus puis-sants des rois, nous fit as- sem- bler dans ces bois; si l'on voit s'é- le-
-ver d'ef-froy- a- bles tem- pê- tes, vains en- ne- mis, trem- blez pour vos su-per- bes
tê- tes; la Gloire, as- ser- vi- e à ses loix, va cou-ron- ner ses der- niè- res con-
Rien ne peut é- chap- per à
-quê- tes par de nou- veaux ex- ploits. Rien ne peut é- chap- per à

sa sa- ges- se ex- trê- me, le vi- ce est pour ja- mais à ses pieds ab- ba-
sa sa- ges- se ex- trê- me, le vi- ce est pour ja- mais à ses pieds ab- ba- tu.

-tu.
Ce n'est point de son di- a- dè- me qu'il em- prun- te l'é- clat dont il est re- vê-

Tou- jours plus no- ble et plus grand par lui- mê- me, sa gloi- re, sa gran- deur su-
-tu.

-prê- me, sont au- des- sous de sa ver- tu. Chan- tons, chan- tons sa va- leur im- mor-
Chan- tons, chan- tons sa va- leur im- mor-

-te- le, chan- tons, chan- tons sa va- leur im- mor- tel- le. Pu- bli- ons ses faits glo- ri-
-tel- le, chan- tons, chan- tons sa va- leur im- mor- tel- le. Pu- bli- ons ses faits glo- ri-

-eux; pu- bli- ons ses faits glo- ri- eux; pu- bli- ons ses faits glo- ri-

-eux; pu- bli- ons ses faits glo- ri- eux; pu- bli- ons ses faits glo- ri-

-eux; que sa gloi- re soit é- ter- nel- le, qu'el- le du- re au- tant que les

-eux; que sa gloi- re soit é- ter- nel- le, qu'el- le du- re au- tant que les

dieux; que sa gloi- re soit é- ter- nel- le, que sa gloi- re soit é- ter-

dieux; que sa gloi- re soit é- ter- nel- le, que sa gloi- re soit é- ter-

-nel- le, qu'el- le du- re au- tant que les dieux.

-nel- le, qu'el- le du- re au- tant que les dieux.

[enchaîner]

Choeur de la suite de Pan et de Flore

-tons sa valeur immortelle. Publions ses faits glorieux; pu-bli-

-tons sa valeur immortelle. Publions ses faits glorieux; pu-bli-

-tons sa valeur immortelle. Publions ses faits glorieux; pu-bli-

-tons sa valeur immortelle. Publions ses faits glorieux; pu-bli-

-tons sa valeur immortelle. Publions ses faits glorieux; pu-bli-

-ons ses faits glo- ri- eux; pu- bli- ons ses faits glo- ri- eux;

-ons ses faits glo- ri- eux; pu- bli- ons ses faits glo- ri- eux;

-ons ses faits glo- ri- eux; pu- bli- ons ses faits glo- ri- eux;

-ons ses faits glo- ri- eux; pu- bli- ons ses faits glo- ri- eux.

-ons ses faits glo- ri- eux; pu- bli- ons ses faits glo- ri- eux.

Chan-tons, chan-

Chan-tons, chan-

Chan-tons, chan-

Chan-tons, chan-

-tons sa valeur immortelle, publions ses faits glorieux.

18
Chan-tons, chan-tons, chan-tons, chan-tons, chan-tons, chan-
Chan-tons, chan-tons, chan-tons, chan-tons, chan-tons, chan-
Chan-tons, chan-tons, chan-tons, chan-tons, chan-
Chan-tons, chan-tons, chan-tons, chan-tons, chan-tons, chan-
Chan-tons, chan-tons, chan-tons chan-tons, chan-

-tons sa valeur immortelle. Publions ses faits glorieux;

tous

[tous]

[tous]

pu- bli- ons ses faits glo- ri-

pu- bli- ons ses faits glo- ri-

pu- bli- ons ses faits glo- ri-

pu- bli- ons ses faits glo- ri-

29
Trio
[Violons seule]
[Violons seule]
tous
[tous]
-eux; que sa gloi- re soit é- ter- nel- le, qu'el-le du- re au- tant que les dieux. Que sa
que sa gloi- re soit é- ter- nel- le, qu'el-le du- re au- tant que les dieux. Que sa
-eux; que sa gloi- re soit é- ter- nel- le, qu'el-le du- re au- tant que les dieux. Que sa
-eux; Que sa
-eux; Que sa

gloi- re soit é- ter- nel- le, soit é- ter- nel- - le, qu'el-le

gloi- re soit é- ter- nel- le, soit é- ter- nel- - le, qu'el-le

gloi- re soit é- ter- nel- - le, que sa gloi- re soit é- ter-

gloi- re soit é- ter- nel- - le, qu'el-le du- re, qu'el-le

gloi- re soit é- ter- nel- le, que sa gloi- re soit é- ter- neldu- re au- tant que les dieux. Que sa gloi- re soit é- ter- nel- le, qu'el- le

du- re au- tant que les dieux. Que sa gloi- re soit é- ter- nel- le, qu'el- le

-nel- - le, que sa gloi- re soit é- ter- nel- le, qu'el- le

du- re au- tant que les dieux. Que sa gloi- re soit é- ter- nel- le, que sa

- le, que sa gloi- re soit é- ter- nel-

du- re au- tant que les dieux. Que sa gloi- re soit é- ter- nel- le, qu'el- le
du- re au- tant que les dieux. Que sa gloi- re soit é- ter- nel- le, qu'el- le
du- re au- tant que les dieux. Que sa gloi- re soit é- ter- nel- le, qu'el- le
gloi- re soit é- ter- nel- le, qu'el- le du- re, qu'el- le
- le, qu'el- le gloi- re soit é- ter- nel- le, qu'el- le

46
[Violons seule]
tous
[Violons seule]
[Violons seule]
[B. Vn.]
[tous]
[B. Vn.]
du- re au-tant que les dieux.
du- re au-tant que les dieux.
du- re au-tant que les dieux.
du- re au-tant que les dieux.
du- re au-tant que les dieux.

50
[tous]
[tous]
[tous]
Que sa gloi- re soit é- ter- nel- le, soit é- ter-
Que sa gloi- re soit é- ter- nel- le, soit é- ter-
Que sa gloi- re soit é- ter- nel- le, soit é- ter-
Que sa gloi- re soit é- ter-
Que sa gloi- re soit é- ter-

-nel- le, qu'elle du-re au- tant que les dieux! Qu'elle du- re au- tant que les dieux!

Entrée des Nymphes de la suite de Flore.
Rondeau

10
tous
Trio
[Violons seule]
[tous]
[Violons seule]
15
[tous]
[tous]
20
Trio
[Violons seule]
[Violons seule]

25
tous
[tous]
6
6♯
♯
♭
5♭
♭
♯
5♭
♭
♯
30
Trio
[Violons seule]
[Violons seule]
[tous]
[tous]
[♯]
♯
♭
6
6♯
♯
35

Passe-pied pour les violons

Fort vite

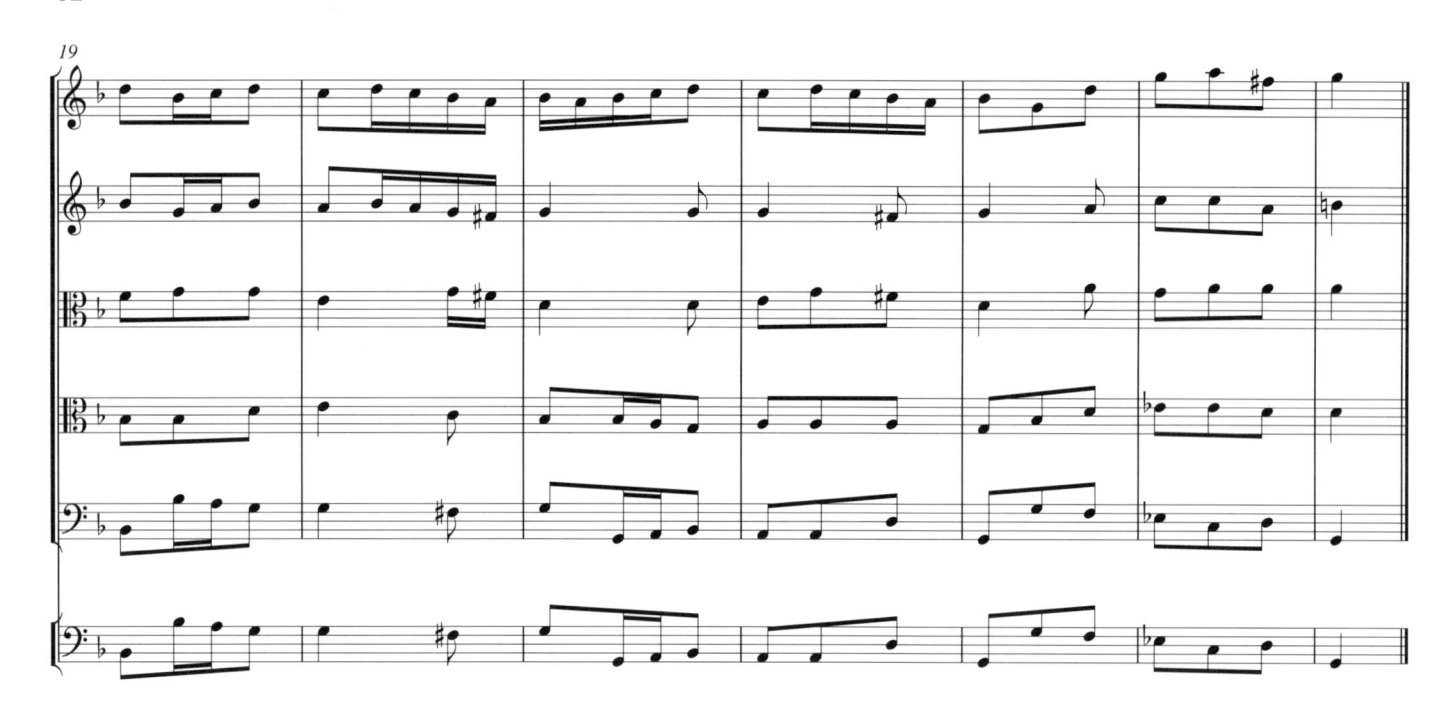

Passe-pied pour les hautbois

Deux Nymphes

DESSUS 1: Qu'un coeur est heu-reux dans un doux es-cla-va-ge! Qu'un coeur est heu-reux dans l'em-pi-re a-mou-reux! Qu'un reux! Dans la vi-ve ar-deur qu'in-spi-re le bel â-ge, quand mil-le plai-

DESSUS 2: Qu'un coeur est heu-reux dans un doux es-cla-va-ge! Qu'un coeur est heu-reux dans l'em-pi-re a-mou-reux! Qu'un reux!

Basse continue

34

*Les Nymphes recommencent leurs danses, après lesquelles Nerée paraît sur la mer
dans un char conduit par des tritons. Il est accompagné de huit dieux de la mer.*

Passe-pied pour les violons
[Reprise]

Passe-pied pour les hautbois
[Reprise]

Adagio

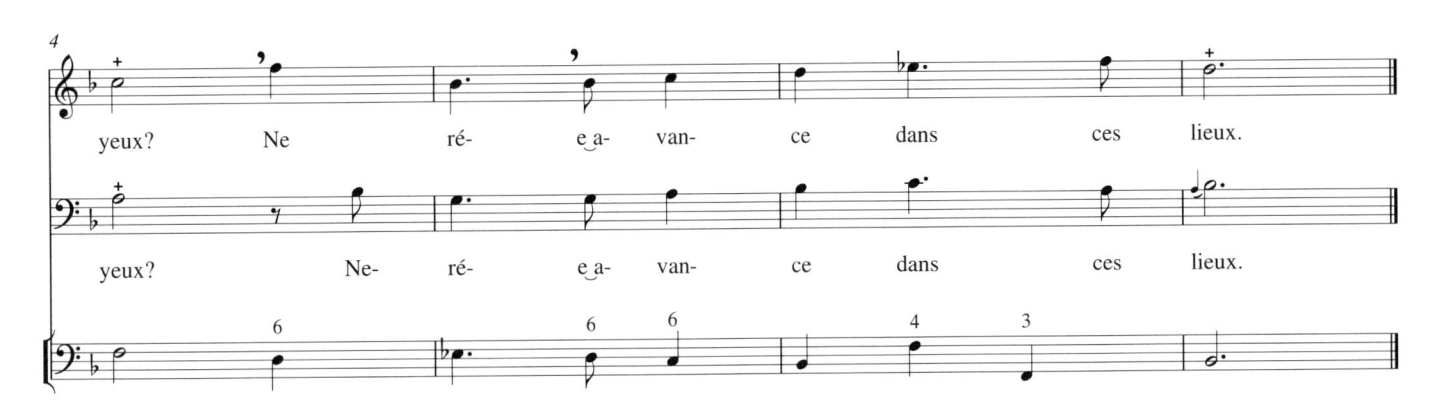

FLORE: Quel- le di- vi- ni- té se pré- sen- te à nos yeux? Ne ré- e- a- van- ce dans ces lieux.

PAN: Quel- le di- vi- ni- té se pré- sen- te à nos yeux? Ne- ré- e- a- van- ce dans ces lieux.

Basse continue

Marche pour Nerée et les Dieux Marins

Adagio

NERÉE

Je sors de l'empire de l'onde pour prendre part à vos concerts. L'Envie agite l'univers, et veut de sa fureur embraser tout le monde; mais sa jalouse rage en vain veut éclatter, quels projets odieux pourront exécuter des ennemis tremblants au seul nom de la France? Et qui craindraient de rien tenter, s'ils ne connaissaient la clémence du héros glorieux qu'ils osent irriter?

FLORE

O vous! qu'un sort heureux sous ses loix a fait naître, que le ciel à jamais protège votre maître! Que de ses ans rien n'arrête le cours! Ne demandez ni grandeur ni victoire. Pour vous combler de bonheur et de gloire, c'est assez que les dieux prennent soin de ses jours.

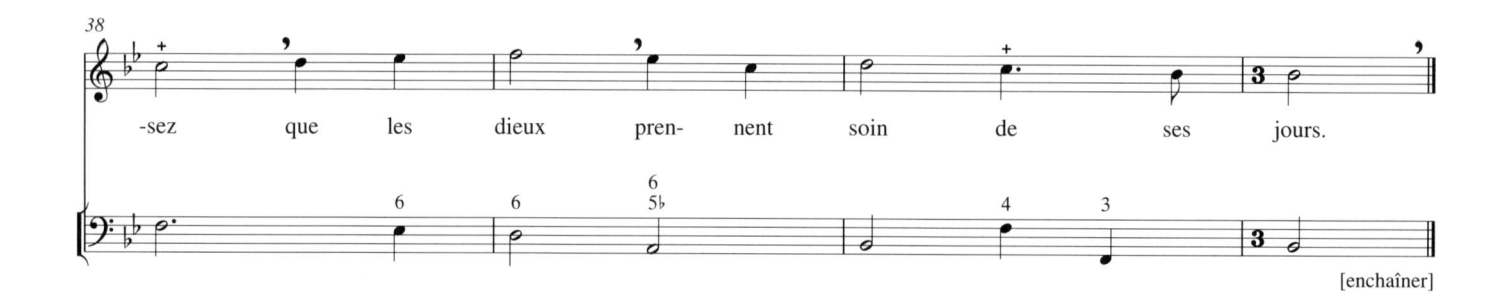

[enchaîner]

Choeur

Dessus 1: Cher- chons à sa- tis- fai- re les plus doux de nos voeux;

Dessus 2: Cher- chons à sa- tis- fai- re les plus doux de nos voeux;

Haute-contre: Cher- chons à sa- tis- fai- re les plus doux de nos voeux;

Taille: Cher- chons à sa- tis- fai- re les plus doux de nos voeux;

Basse: Cher- chons à sa- tis- fai- re les plus doux de nos voeux;

présentons- lui nos concerts et nos jeux, heu- reux, heu- reux! si nous pou-

Trio de hautbois

[Hautbois]

[Basson]

-vons lui plai- re. Pré- sen- tons- lui nos con- certs et nos jeux.

-vons lui plai- re. Pré- sen- tons- lui nos con- certs et nos jeux.

-vons lui plai- re. Pré- sen- tons- lui nos con- certs et nos jeux.

-vons lui plai- re. Pré- sen- tons- lui nos con- certs et nos jeux.

-vons lui plai- re. Pré- sen- tons- lui nos con- certs et nos jeux.

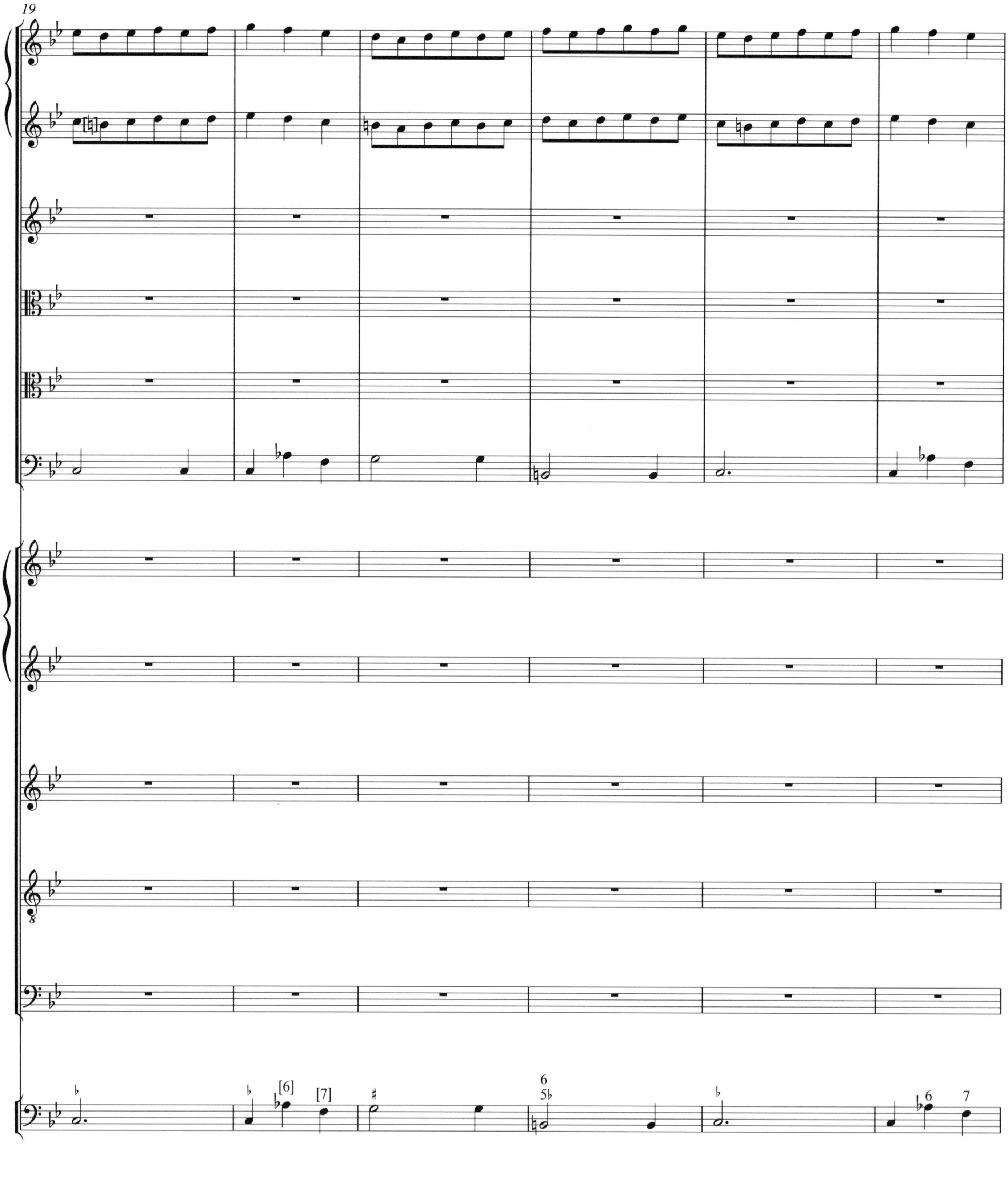
19
[6]
[7]
6
5♭
6
7

Pré- sen- tons- lui nos con- certs, et nos jeux, pré- sen- tons-

-lui nos con- certs, et nos jeux, heu- reux, heu- reux! si nous pou-

Trio de hautbois

[Hautbois]

[Basson]

-vons lui plai- re.

-vons lui plai- re.

-vons lui plai- re.

-vons lui plai- re.

-vons lui plai- re.

Pré- sen- tons- lui nos con- certs, et nos

49
[Trio de hautbois]
[Hautbois]
[Basson]
jeux.
jeux.
jeux.
jeux.
jeux.
6
5♭
[6]
6
5♭

50

Heu- reux, heu- reux! si nous pou- vons ___ lui

Heu- reux, heu- reux! si nous pou- vons ___ lui

Heu- reux, heu- reux! si nous pou- vons lui

Heu- reux, heu- reux! si nous pou- vons lui

Heu- reux, heu- reux! si nous pou- vons lui

plai- re, heu- reux, heu- reux! si nous pou- vons lui plai- re.

Loure

Entrée des dieux de la mer.

Un Dieu de la mer

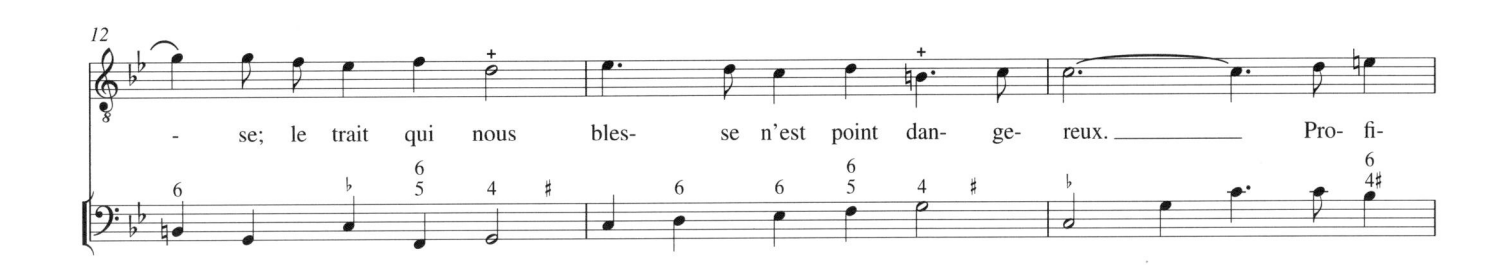

[HAUTE-CONTRE]

L'A- mour sou-met tout le mon- de, jus- ques dans l'on- de tout sent ses feux; L'A--mour sou-met tout le mon- de, jus- que dans l'on- de tout sent ses feux; pro- fi--tons de no- tre jeu- nes- se, sui- vons la ten- dres- se; le trait qui nous bles- se n'est point dan- ge- reux. Pro- fi-

Basse continue

-tons de no- tre jeu- nes- se, sui- vons la ten- dres- se; le trait qui nous bles- se doit nous ren- dre heu- reux. ____ Prof- fi- reux. ____

[enchaîner]

Les dieux de la suite de Nerée recommencent leurs danses.
Les nymphes de Flore s'y joignent, et forment avec eux la dernière Entrée.

Loure
[Reprise]

Lentement

Dessus de violon 1, 2
Hautbois 1, 2

Haute-contre de violon

Taille de violon

Quinte de violon

Basse de violon
Basson

Basse continue

Gigue

Vite

Dessus de violon 1, 2
Hautbois 1, 2

Haute-contre de violon

Taille de violon

Quinte de violon

Basse de violon
Basson

Basse continue

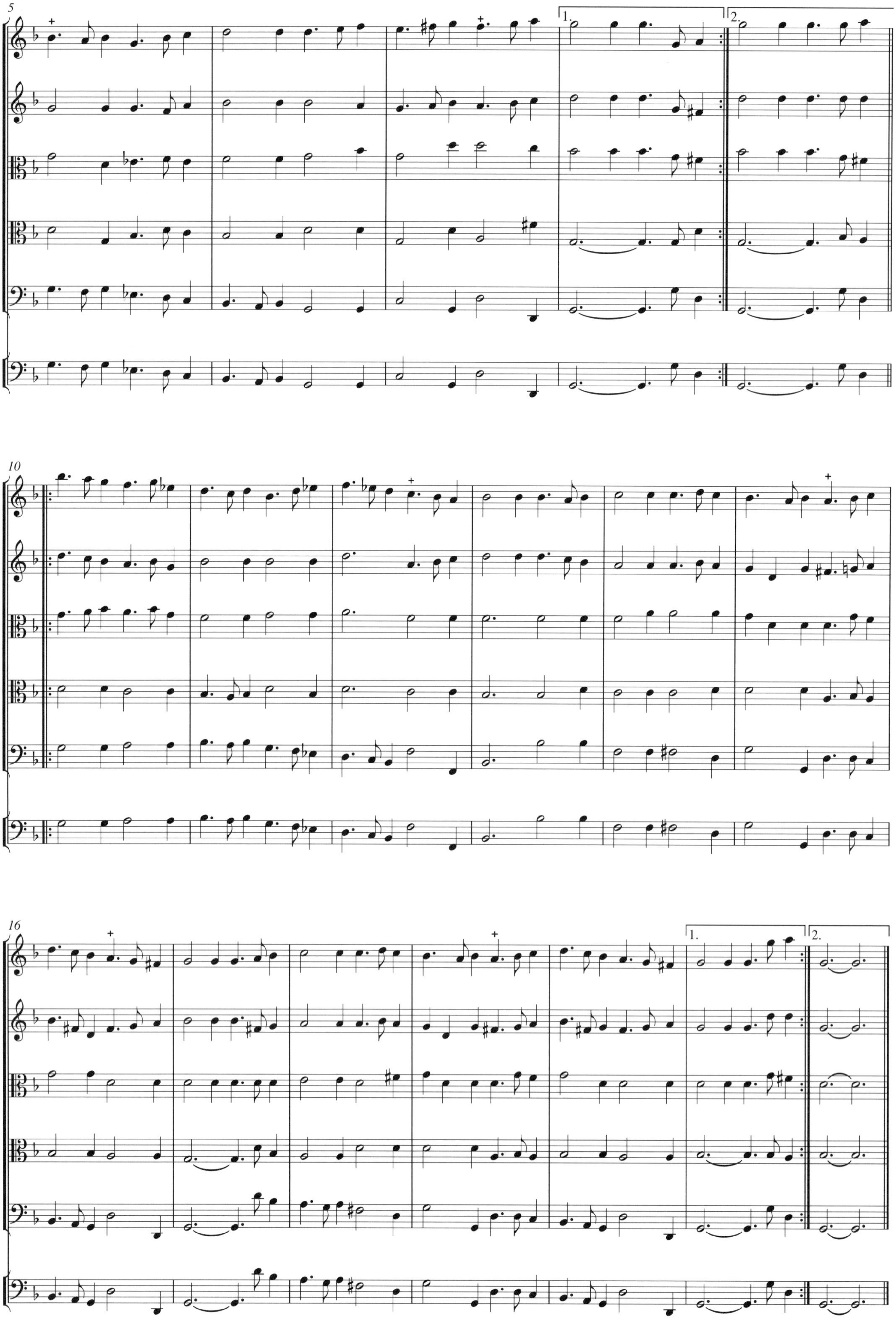

NEREE

Dans des lieux que le ciel ga-ran-tit de l'o-ra-ge, re-tra-çons de Pro-cris les tra-gi-ques a-mours. Heu-reux! si de ses maux la vi-ve et tris-te i-ma-ge peut nous ré-sou-dre à fuir un es-cla-va-ge tou-jours fu-nes-te au re-pos de nos jours!

[enchaîner]

Allegro

PAN

A l'a-bri du fra-cas des ar-mes, al-lons, al-lons à nos con-certs mê-ler des chants nou-veaux; à l'hon-neur de tant de hé-ros, qui vont au mi-lieu des a-

-lar- - mes nous as-su-rer un doux re-pos; à l'hon-neur de tant de hé-

-ros, qui vont au mi-lieu des a-lar- - mes nous as-su-rer un doux re- pos.

[enchaîner]

Choeur

Vite

Dessus de violon 1, 2 / Hautbois 1, 2
Haute-contre de violon
Taille de violon
Quinte de violon
Basse de violon / Basson

Vite

Dessus 1: Vo- lez, vo- lez, vo- lez
Dessus 2: Vo- lez, vo- lez, vo- lez
Haute-contre: Vo- lez, vo- lez, vo- lez vo- lez,
Taille: Vo- lez, vo- lez, vo-
Basse: Vo- lez, vo- lez,

Basse continue

4
_ ô guer- riers in- vin- ci- bles! Vo- lez, vo- lez, vo-
_ ô guer- riers in- vin- ci- bles! Vo- lez, vo- lez, vo-
_ ô guer- riers in- vin- ci- bles! Vo- lez, vo- lez, vo-
-lez, ô guer- riers in- vin- ci- bles! Vo- lez, vo- lez, vo-
_ ô guer- riers in- vin- ci- bles! Vo- lez,
9
-lez, ô guer- riers in- vin- ci- bles! E- ten- dez vos ex-
-lez, ô guer- riers in- vin- ci- bles! E- ten- dez vos ex-
-lez, vo- lez, vo- lez, ô guer- riers in- vin- ci- bles! E- ten- dez vos ex-
-lez, ô guer- riers in- vin- ci- bles! E- ten- dez vos ex-
ô guer- riers in- vin- ci- bles! E- ten- dez vos ex-

14
-ploits au bout de l'u- ni- vers. Vo- lez, vo- lez, vo- lez,
-ploits au bout de l'u- ni- vers. Vo- lez, vo- lez, vo- lez,
-ploits au bout de l'u- ni- vers. Vo- lez, vo- lez, vo- lez, ô guer-
-ploits au bout de l'u- ni- vers. Vo-lez,
-ploits au bout de l'u- ni- vers. Vo- lez, ô guer-
19
– ô guer- riers in- vin- ci- bles! E- ten- dez vos ex- ploits au bout
– ô guer- riers in- vin- ci- bles! E- ten- dez vos ex- ploits au bout
-riers in- vin- ci- bles! E- ten- dez, é- ten- dez vos ex- ploits au bout
– ô guer- riers in- vin- ci- bles! E- ten- dez vos ex- ploits au bout
-riers in- vin- ci- bles! E- ten- dez, é- ten- dez vos ex- ploits au bout

de l'u- ni- vers, é- ten- dez, é- ten- dez vos ex- ploits au bout de l'u- ni- vers, é- ten- dez, é- ten- dez vos ex- ploits au bout de l'u- ni- vers: nous al-

-lons en des lieux pai- si- bles cé- lé- brer par nos chants vos tri- om- phes di- vers, vos tri- om- phes di- vers, vos tri- om- phes, vos tri- om- phes, vos tri- om- phes di-

46
-vers, vos tri- om- phes di- vers. Vo- lez, vo- lez, vo-
-vers, vos tri- om- phes di- vers. Vo- lez, vo- lez, vo-
vers, vos tri- om- phes di- vers. Vo- lez, vo- lez, vo- lez, vo- lez, vo-
-vers, vos tri- om- phes di- vers. Vo- lez, vo- lez, vo- lez, vo-
-vers, vos tri- om- phes di- vers. Vo- lez,
51
-lez, ô guer- riers in- vin- ci- bles! E- ten- dez vos ex-
-lez, ô guer- riers in- vin- ci- bles! E- ten- dez vos ex-
-lez, vo- lez, ô guer-riers in- vin- ci- bles! E- ten- dez vos ex-
-lez, vo- lez, vo- lez, ô guer- riers in- vin- ci- bles! E- ten- dez vos ex-
ô guer- riers in- vin- ci- bles! E- ten- dez vos ex-

-ploits au bout de l'u- ni- vers.

Nous allons en des lieux paisibles célébrer, célébrer par nos chants vos triomphes, vos triomphes diphes di-

-vers, vos tri- om- phes di- vers.

Nous al-

86
Nous al- lons en des lieux pai- si- bles cé- lé- brer par nos
Nous al- lons en des lieux pai- si- bles cé- lé- brer par nos
-lons en des lieux pai- si- bles cé- lé- brer par nos chants vos tri- om-
Nous al- lons en des lieux pai- si- bles cé- lé- brer par nos chants vos tri-
Nous al- lons en des lieux pai- si- bles cé- lé- brer par nos chants vos tri-
91
chants vos tri- om- phes di- vers.
chants vos tri- om- phes di- vers.
- - phes di- vers.
-om- phes, vos tri- om- phes di- vers.
-om- - phes di- vers.

96
101
Vo- lez, vo- lez, vo- lez, ô guer-
Vo- lez, vo- lez, vo- lez, ô guer-
Vo- lez, vo- lez, vo- lez, vo- lez, ô guer-
Vo- lez, vo- lez, vo- lez, ô guer-
Vo- lez, vo- lez, ô guer-

106
-riers in- vin- ci- bles, vo- lez, vo- lez, vo- lez,
-riers in- vin- ci- bles, vo- lez, vo- lez, vo- lez,
-riers in- vin- ci- bles, vo- lez, vo- lez, vo- lez, vo- lez, vo-
-riers in- vin- ci- bles, vo- lez, vo- lez, vo- lez,
-riers in- vin- ci- bles, vo- lez,
111
ô guer- riers in- vin- ci- bles! E- ten- dez vos ex- ploits au bout
ô guer- riers in- vin- ci- bles! E- ten- dez vos ex- ploits au bout
-lez, ô guer- riers in- vin- ci- bles! E- ten- dez vos ex- ploits au bout
ô guer- riers in- vin- ci- bles! E- ten- dez vos ex- ploits au bout
ô guer- riers in- vin- ci- bles! E- ten- dez vos ex- ploits au bout

de l'u- ni- vers. Vo- lez, vo- lez, vo- lez, _____ ô guer-
de l'u- ni- vers. Vo- lez, vo- lez, vo- lez, _____ ô guer-
de l'u- ni- vers. Vo- lez, vo- lez, vo- lez, ô guer- riers in- vin-
de l'u- ni- vers. Vo- lez, _____ ô guer-
de l'u- ni- vers. Vo- lez, ô guer- riers in- vin-

-riers in- vin- ci- bles! E- ten- dez vos ex- ploits au bout de l'u- ni-
-riers in- vin- ci- bles! E- ten- dez vos ex- ploits au bout de l'u- ni-
-ci- bles! E- ten- dez, é- ten- dez vos ex- ploits au bout de l'u- ni-
-riers in- vin- ci- bles! E- ten- dez vos ex- ploits au bout de l'u- ni-
-ci- bles! E- ten- dez, é- ten- dez vos ex- ploits au bout de l'u- ni-

FIN DU PROLOGUE
On reprend l'Ouverture.

Acte I

Scène première

Borée, Procris

Le théâtre représente une place de la ville d'Athènes, ornée pour les jeux.
Le temple de Minerve paraît dans le fonds.

BOREE

Me fuirez-vous toujours? Arrêtez, Inhumaine, votre injuste courroux ne peut-il se calmer? Ah! pour mériter votre haine, quel crime ai-je commis que de vous trop aimer? Vos mépris, votre indifférence, sont-ils le prix de ma constance?

[enchaîner]

[Air]

Doux

BOREE

Un seul de vos regards pourrait charmer les dieux, par tout vous allu-

-mez une secrète flamme: Un me: Ne pourra-t'on jamais faire naître en votre âme l'amour que l'on prend dans vos yeux, ne pourra-t'on jamais faire naître en votre âme l'amour que l'on prend dans vos yeux?

PROCRIS
Malheureux qui ressent l'amoureuse puissance! Il ne goûte en aimant que des biens imparfaits; pour rendre deux coeurs satisfaits, il fau-

Basse continue

-drait que l'a- mour, la paix et l'in- no- cen- ce fus- sent tou- jours d'in-tel- li-

-gen- ce, et c'est ce qui ne fût ja- mais. Vous tâ- chez vai- ne-

BOREE

-ment de pa- raî- tre in-vin- ci- ble, je sais ce qui vous por- te à mé- pri- ser mes soins, cru-

-el- le, hé- las! vous me haï- ri- ez moins si vous é- tiez in- sen- si- ble, cru-

-el- le, hé- las! vous me haï- ri- ez moins si vous é- tiez in- sen- si- ble.

Ce- pha- le va bien- tôt pa- raî- tre dans ces lieux. Sa va- leur a domp- té les peu- ples de la

Thrace; de vos fiers ennemis il a puni l'audace, Philomèle est vengée, il est victorieux. Vous aimerez, dans ce haut rang de gloire, un jeune amant que vos yeux ont charmé; mais, s'il prétend sur moi remporter la victoire, vous pourrez quelque jour, sensible à sa mémoire, vous repentir de l'avoir trop aimé.

Scène seconde

Procris, Dorine

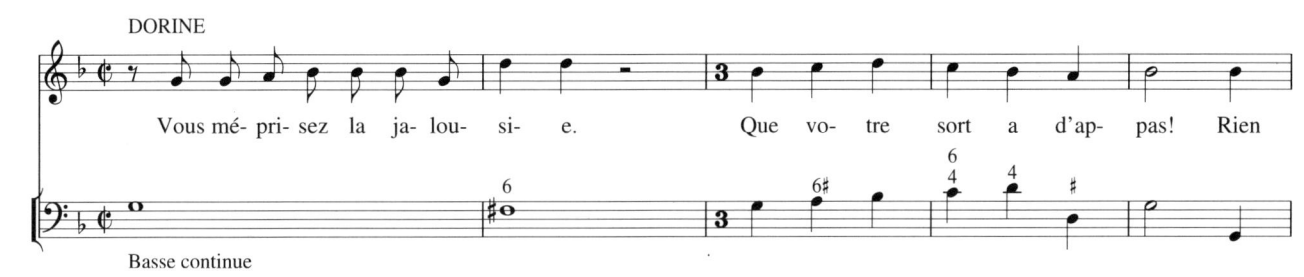

DORINE
Vous méprisez la jalousie. Que votre sort a d'appas! Rien

ne sau- rait trou- bler vo- tre pai- si- ble vi- e. Vous pas- sez vos beaux jours sans crain-

-te, sans en- vi- e. On vous ai- me, et vous n'ai- mez pas. Que vo- tre

PROCRIS   **DORINE**

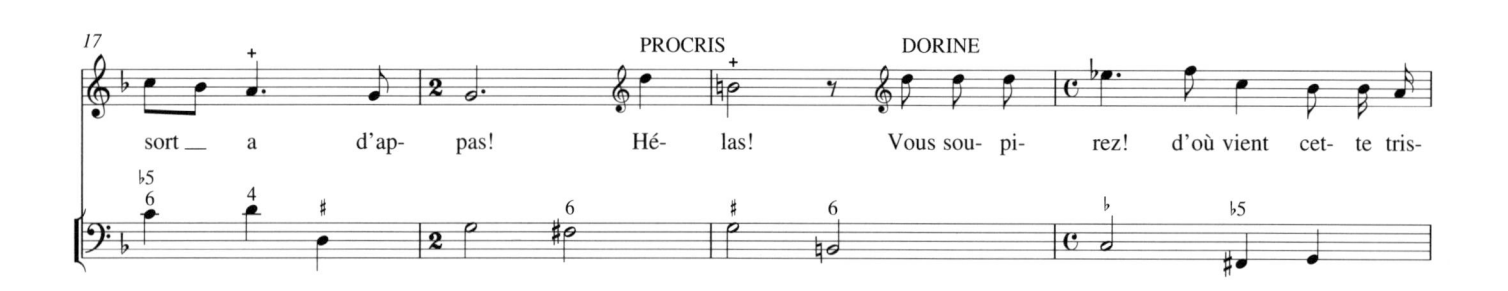

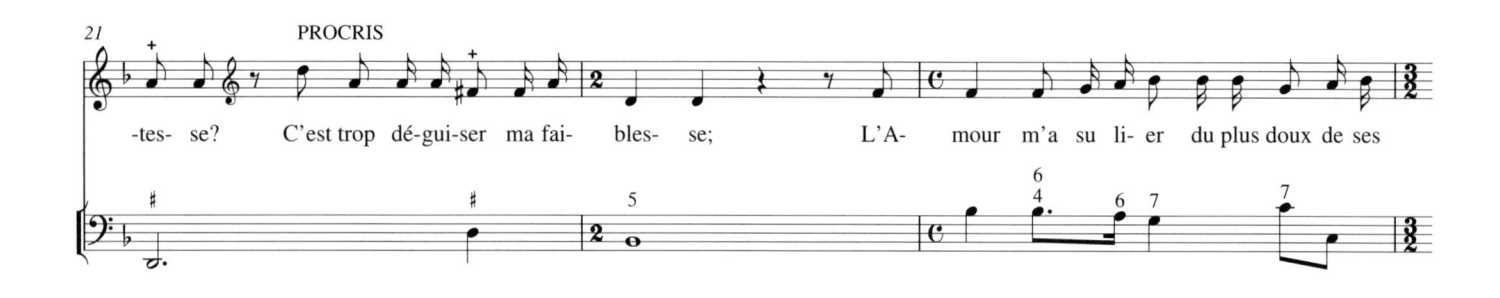

sort a d'ap- pas! Hé- las! Vous sou- pi- rez! d'où vient cet- te tris-

PROCRIS

-tes- se? C'est trop dé-gui-ser ma fai- bles- se; L'A- mour m'a su li- er du plus doux de ses

noeuds; par- don- ne, si j'ai pu te ca- cher ma ten- dres- se, suis- je la seu- le, hé-

-las! qui feint d'ê- tre maî- tres- se d'un coeur sou- mis aux loix de l'em- pi- re a- mou- reux?

[enchaîner]

Air

PROCRIS: J'ai- me, il faut l'a-vou- er, il ne m'est pas pos- si- ble de fuir un doux en- ga- ge- ment: mais le seul nom de mon a- mant m'ex- cu- se as- sez d'ê- tre sen- si- ble, mais ___ le seul nom de mon a- mant m'ex- cu- se as- sez d'ê- tre sen- si- ble.

[enchaîner]

DORINE: Cé- pha- le a-t'il su vous char- mer? Cha-cun sait que pour vous son ar- deur est ex- trê- me.

PROCRIS: Tu le con- nais; crois- tu que quand il ai- me, on puis- se ne le pas ai- mer?

DORINE: Aux plus ten- dres dou- ceurs vo-tre a-mour vous pré- pa- re; le

78

Roi doit, en ce jour, vous don-ner un é- poux; en fa- veur de Ce- pha- le on dit qu'il se dé-

[PROCRIS]
-cla- re. Je n'o- se at- ten- dre un sort qui me pa- raît trop doux.

[enchaîner]

Air

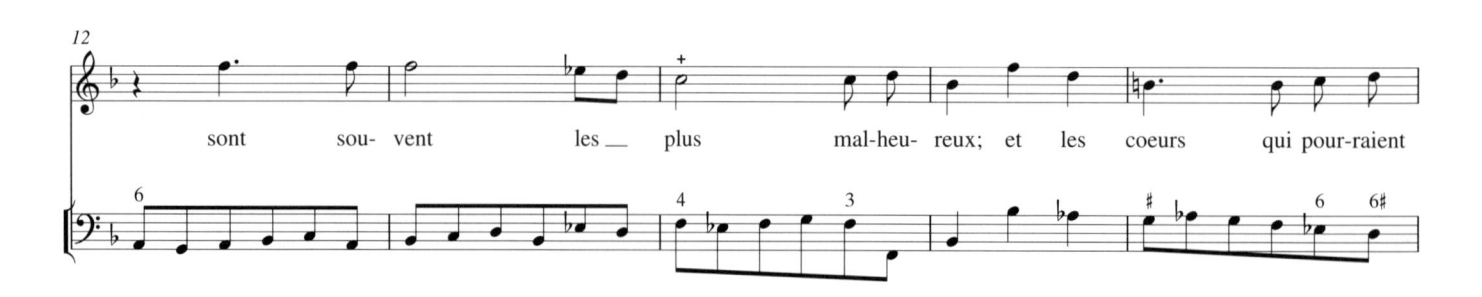

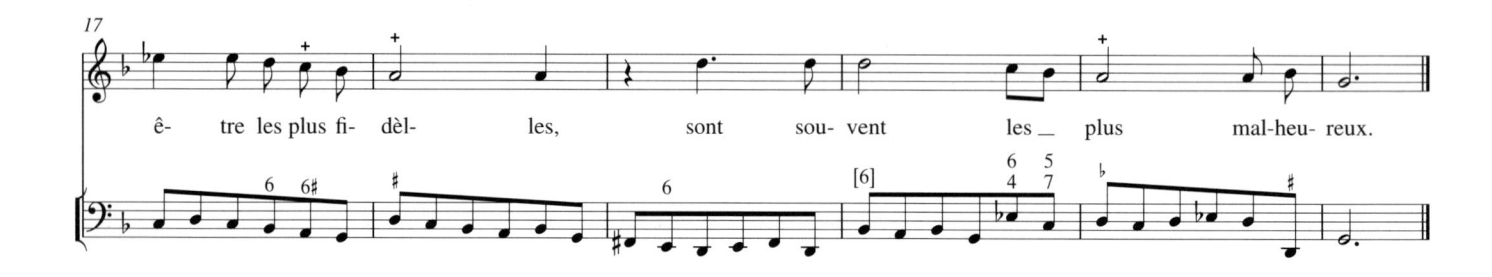

PROCRIS
On voit les ar- deurs les plus bel- les é- prou- ver un sort ri- gou-

Basse continue

-reux; On reux; et les coeurs qui pour-roient ê- tre les plus fi- dèl- les,

sont sou- vent les plus mal-heu- reux; et les coeurs qui pour-raient

ê- tre les plus fi- dèl- les, sont sou- vent les plus mal-heu- reux.

Scène troisième
Procris, Arcas

ARCAS: Le de-voir de Ce-pha-le au-près du Roi l'ap-pel-le. Doit-il ap-pre-hen-der en-core vo-tre ri-gueur? Il vous con-ser-ve dans son coeur u-ne flam-me im-mor-tel-le. A-près a-voir vain-cu nos en-ne-mis ja-loux, et por-té son cou-ra-ge au com-ble de la gloi-re, vous l'al-lez voir à vos ge-noux, moins con-tent des hon-neurs d'u-ne il-lus-tre vic-toi-re, que d'a-voir com-bat-tu pour vous. En cet heu-reux é-tat, que faut-il qu'il es-pé-re?

PROCRIS: Mes dé-sirs sont sou-mis aux or-dres de mon pè-re, c'est à lui de re-gler mes voeux. Ce-

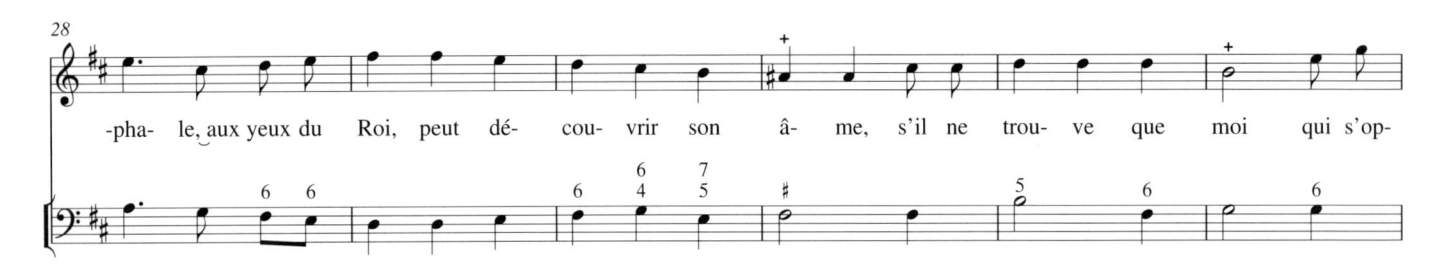

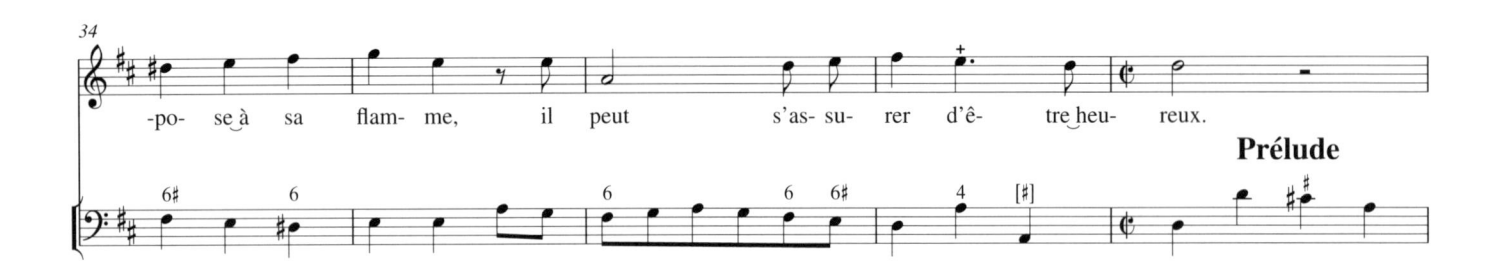

-pha- le, aux yeux du Roi, peut dé- cou- vrir son â- me, s'il ne trou- ve que moi qui s'op-

-po- se à sa flam- me, il peut s'as- su- rer d'ê- tre heu- reux.

Prélude

[enchaîner]

Scène quatrième
Arcas, Dorine

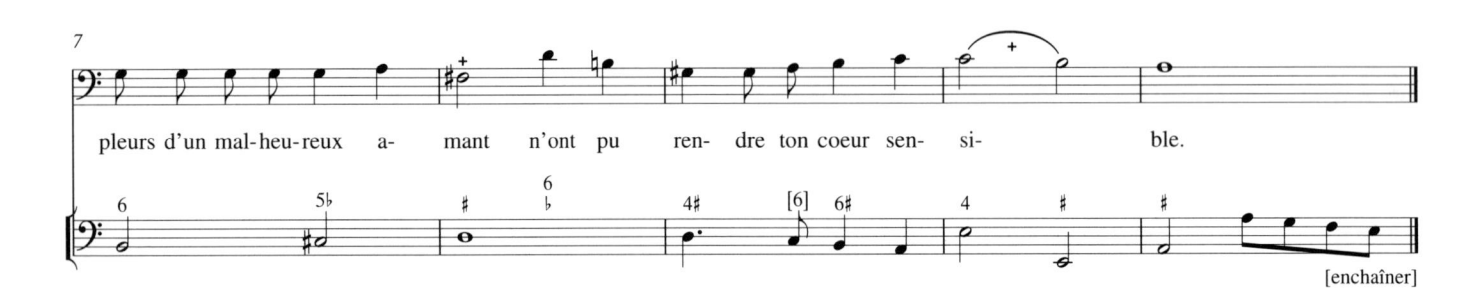

ARCAS
Se- ras- tu tou- jours in- fle- xi- ble? Je lan- guis pour toi vai- ne- ment. Les

Basse continue

pleurs d'un mal-heu-reux a- mant n'ont pu ren- dre ton coeur sen- si- ble.

[enchaîner]

[Air]

ARCAS: En vain le chan-ge-ment s'of-fre à me sou- la- ger, je ne sau- rais ê- tre vo- la- -ge; In- gra- te, ta beau-té m'en-ga- ge, et ta ri- gueur ne me peut dé- ga- ger, In- gra- te, ta beau- té m'en-ga- ge, et ta ri- gueur, et ta ri- gueur ne me peut dé- ga- ger.

[enchaîner]

DORINE: Tâ- che à vain- cre un a- mour, qui te rend mi- sé- ra- ble: je veux, pour t'é- par- gner des sou- pirs su- per- flus, prê- ter à ton dé- pit un se-

[Air]

DORINE

L'a- mour n'est point char- mant, s'il n'of- fre des plai- sirs, et tu portes par- tout le cha- grin, la tris- tes- se: L'a- se: pen- ses- tu, pour char- mer u- ne jeu- ne maî- tres- se, qu'il n'en coû- te que des sou- pirs, pen- ses- tu, pour char-

-cours fa- vo- ra- ble; Ar- cas, je ne te ver- rai plus. Cru- el- le, il te sied bien de bra- ver ma co- lè- re, tu sais que tes mé- pris ser- vent à m'en- flam- mer. Que ne sais- tu te fai- re ai- mer? A- prends-moi donc le se- cret de te plai- re?

[enchaîner]

-mer u-ne jeu-ne maî-tres-se, qu'il n'en coû-te que des sou-pirs?

[enchaîner]

ARCAS
Pro-mets-moi de m'ai-mer sans ces-se, de mes cru-els en-nuis tu fi-ni-ras le

Basse continue

DORINE
cours. Je t'ai-me, cher Ar-cas, j'ap-prou-ve ta ten-dres-se, mais peut-on s'as-sur-

ARCAS
-er qu'on ai-me-ra tou-jours? Quoi? tu crois donc chan-ger? Cru-el-le, quel ou-tra-ge!

[enchaîner]

[Air]

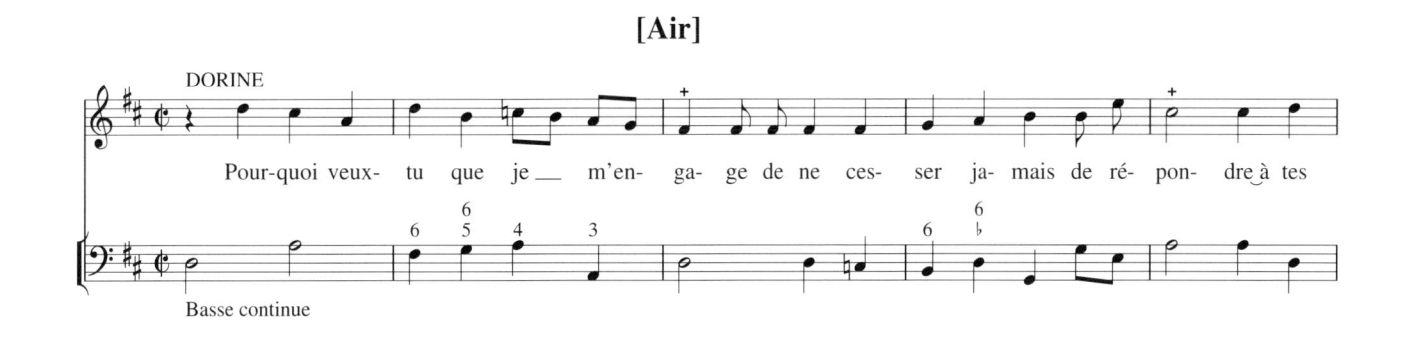

DORINE
Pour-quoi veux-tu que je m'en-ga-ge de ne ces-ser ja-mais de ré-pon-dre à tes

Basse continue

feux? feux? Crois-tu qu'un ser-ment a-mou-reux m'em-pê-che-rait d'ê-tre vo-

-lage, crois-tu qu'un ser-ment a-mou-reux m'em-pê-che-rait d'ê-tre vo-la-ge? Suis mes con-seils, Ar-cas, vi-vons tou-jours en paix, un long en-ga-ge-ment ra-re-ment a des char-mes.

ARCAS
Que pour les ten-dres coeurs la con-stan-ce a d'at-traits!

[enchaîner]

[Duo]

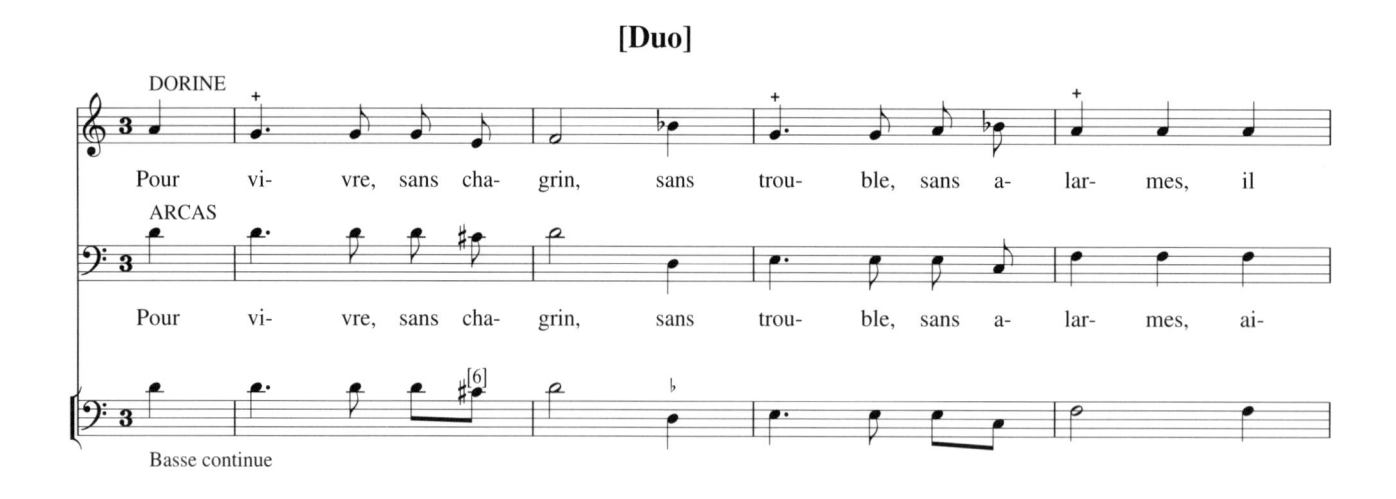

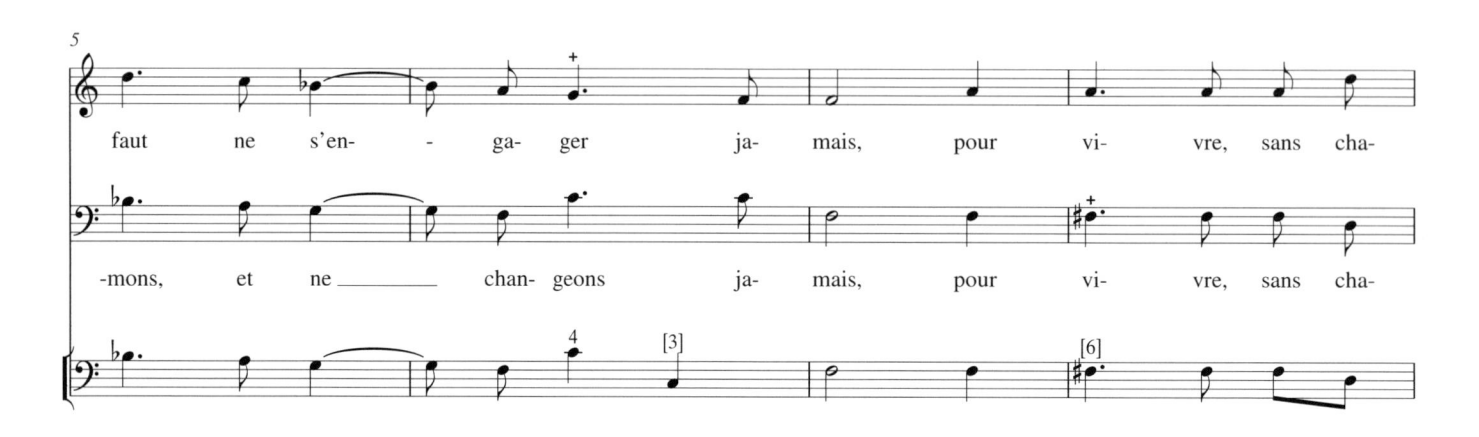

DORINE
Pour vi-vre, sans cha-grin, sans trou-ble, sans a-lar-mes, il

ARCAS
Pour vi-vre, sans cha-grin, sans trou-ble, sans a-lar-mes, ai-

Basse continue

faut ne s'en-ga-ger ja-mais, pour vi-vre, sans cha-

-mons, et ne chan-geons ja-mais, pour vi-vre, sans cha-

-grin, sans trou- - ble, sans a- lar- mes, il faut ne s'en- ga- ger ja-
-grin, sans trou- - ble, sans a- lar- mes, ai- mons et ne chan- geons ja-
-mais, il faut ne s'en- ga- ger ja- mais, ne s'en- ga- ger ja-
-mais, ai- mons et ne chan- geons ja- mais, et ne chan- geons ja- mais, ai-
-mais. il faut ne s'en- ga- ger ja- mais, ne s'en- ga- ger ja- mais, il
-mons et ne chan- geons ja- mais, et ne chan- geons ja- mais, ai- mons et ne chan- geons ja-
faut ne s'en- ga- ger ja- mais. Pour vi- vre, sans cha- grin, sans
-mais, et ne chan- geons ja- mais. Pour vi- vre, sans cha- grin, sans
trou- ble, sans a- lar- mes, il faut ne s'en- ga- ger ja- mais.
trou- ble, sans a- lar- mes, ai- mons et ne chan- geons ja- mais.

Scène cinquième

Dorine, Arcas, Troupe d'Athéniens, et d'Athéniennes

Marche

87

88

Chœur d'Athéniens

Cé- lé- brons d'un hé- ros la va- leur tri- om- phan- te, nos en- ne- mis sont sou-

-mis à ses loix. U- nis- sons nos coeurs et nos voix, chan- tons sa vic- toi- re é- cla-

-tante, chantons, chantons sa victoire éclatante, chantons ses glorieux ex-

-ploits, chan- tons sa vic- toi- re é- cla- tan- te, chan- tons sa vic- toi- re é- cla- tan- te, chan-

-tons, chan- tons ses glo- ri- eux ex- ploits.

36
[Violons seule]
[Violons seule]
[petit choeur]
U- nis- sons nos
[petit choeur]
U- nis- sons nos
petit choeur
U- nis- sons nos

coeurs et nos voix, u- nis- sons nos coeurs et nos voix, chan- tons la vic- toi- re é- cla-

-tante, chantons ses glorieux exploits. Unissons nos coeurs et nos voix, chan-

-tante, chantons ses glorieux exploits. Unissons nos coeurs et nos voix, chan-

-tante, chantons ses glorieux exploits. Unissons nos coeurs et nos voix, chan-

-tante, chantons ses glorieux exploits. Chan-

-tante, chantons ses glorieux exploits. Chan-

-tons sa vic- toi- re é- cla- tan- te, chan- tons ses glo- ri- eux ex- ploits. U- nis- sons nos

-tons sa vic- toi- re é- cla- tan- te, chan- tons ses glo- ri- eux ex- ploits. U- nis- sons nos

-tons sa vic- toi- re é- cla- tan- te, chan- tons ses glo- ri- eux ex- ploits. U- nis- sons nos

-tons sa vic- toi- re é- cla- tan- te, chan- tons ses glo- ri- eux ex- ploits.

-tons sa vic- toi- re é- cla- tan- te, chan- tons ses glo- ri- eux ex- ploits.

64
[tous]
[tous]
coeurs et nos voix,
[tous]
u- nis- sons nos coeurs et nos
coeurs et nos voix,
[tous]
u- nis- sons nos coeurs et nos
coeurs et nos voix,
[tous]
u- nis- sons nos coeurs et nos
U- nis- sons nos coeurs et nos
U- nis- sons nos coeurs et nos
[♯]

71
voix, chan- tons sa vic- toi- re é- cla- tan- te, u- nis-
voix, chan- tons sa vic- toi- re é- cla- tan- te, u- nis-
voix, chan- tons sa vic- toi- re é- cla- tan- te, u- nis-
voix, chan- tons sa vic- toi- re é- cla- tan- te, u- nis-
voix, chan- tons sa vic- toi- re é- cla- tan-

-ri- eux ex- ploits.

Célébrons d'un héros la va-

-leur tri- om- phan- te, nos en- ne- mis sont sou- mis à ses loix. U- nis- sons nos coeurs et nos voix, chan- tons sa vic- toi- re é- cla- tan- te, chan- tons, chan- tons sa vic- toi- re é- cla-

-tante, chantons ses glorieux exploits, chantons sa victoire éclatante, chan-

-tons sa vic- toi- re é- cla- tan- te, chan- tons, chan- tons ses glo- ri- eux ex- ploits.

Première Entrée
Air pour les Athéniens

108

Scène sixième

Tous les acteurs de la scene précédente.
Le Roi, Cephale

LE ROI

Re- dou- blez vos chants d'al- le- gres- se, for- mez les con- certs les plus doux. Mes ar- mes ont ren- du le re- pos à la Grè- ce, et Ce- pha- le est l'heu- reux é- poux que je des- ti- ne à la Prin- ces- se. Re- dou- blez vos chants d'al- le- gres- se, for- mez les con- certs les plus doux.

Seconde Entrée
Second air [d'Athéniens]

111

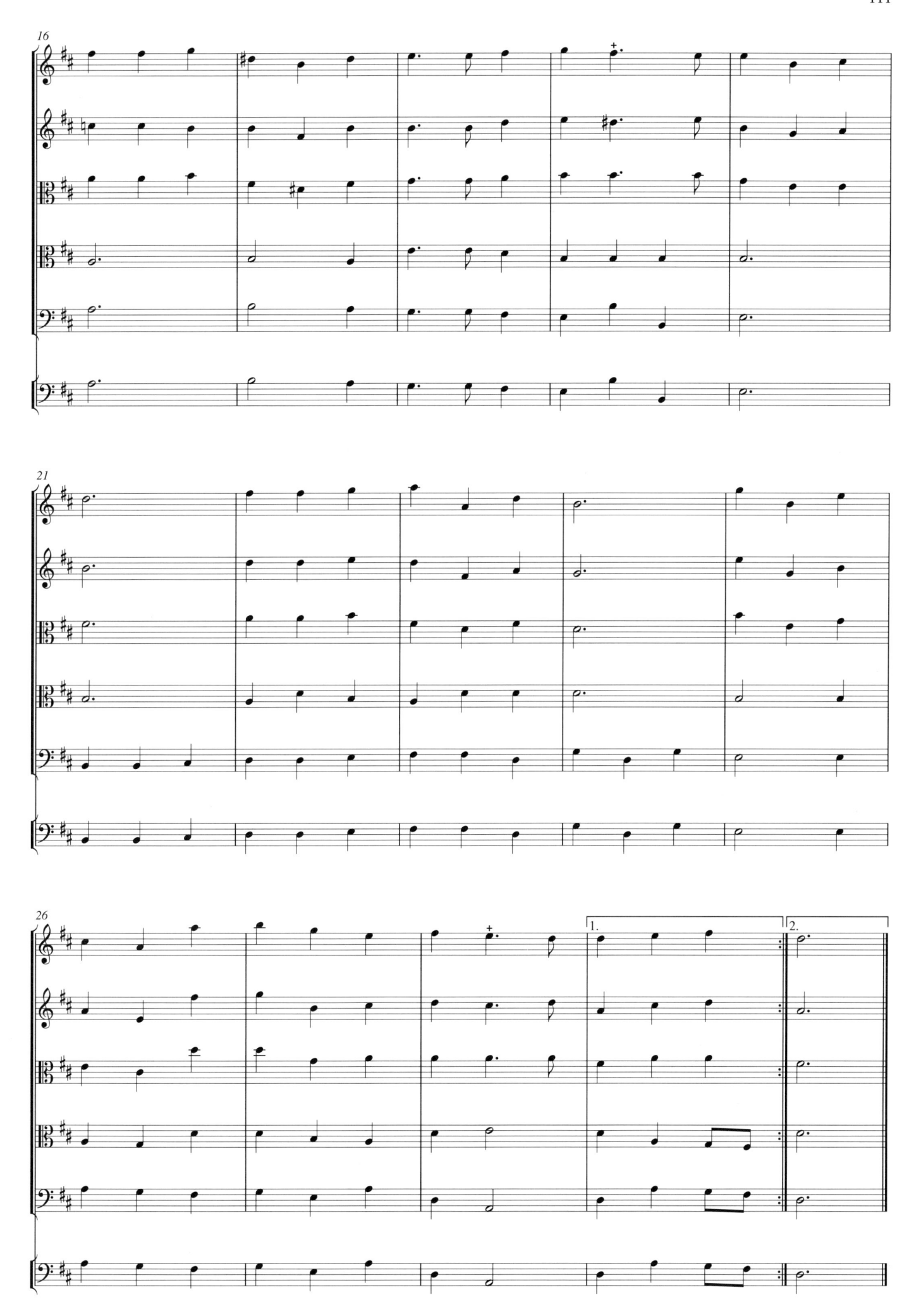

[Duo]
Deux Athéniennes

Ren- dons- nous, cè- dons à la ten- dres- se, du dieu des a- mours doit- on fuir les fa- veurs: veurs: les tran- sports d'u- ne heu- reu- se fai- bles- se pas- sent les dou- ceurs d'u- ne vai- ne sa- ges- se, les ar- deurs, les lan- gueurs, sont des plai- sirs faits pour les jeu- nes coeurs. Les tran- coeurs.

Le temple de Minerve s'ouvre, et la grande prêtresse en sort.

Scène septième

Tous les acteurs de la scène précédente.
Le Roi, La Prêtresse

LE ROI: Que vois-je? de Pallas j'apperçois la prêtresse.

LA PRETRESSE: Prince, que faites-vous? quel hymen odieux osez-vous arrêter sans consulter les dieux? Ecoutez ce qu'une déesse veut bien vous dire par ma voix. Le ciel désapprouve le choix que vous faites pour la Princesse. Si vous voulez qu'une profonde paix forme les noeuds sa-

-crés d'une auguste hymenée, accordez Procris à Borée, et condamnez Ce-phale à ne l'avoir jamais.

Elle se retire. **CEPHALE** Qu'entends-je? juste ciel! Sei-gneur, pourrez-vous croire que les dieux inhumains...

LE ROI Je conçois vos douleurs. Cet oracle est pour vous le plus grand des malheurs, mais l'amour au devoir doit céder la victoire. Révérons les arrêts que les dieux ont dictés; un héros doit trouver sa gloire, à soumettre à leurs

Ils entrent tous deux dans le temple.
FIN DU PREMIER ACTE
Entr'acte [Second Air d'Athéniens, pp. 110–111]

Acte II

Scène première

Procris seule

*Le théâtre représente un lieu solitaire au pied du Mont-Hymette.
On voit quelques hameaux dans l'éloignement.*

Prélude

Lieux è-car-tés, pai-si-ble so-li-tu-de, so-yez seuls les té-moins de ma vi-ve dou-leur. Des pei-nes des a-mants je souf-fre la plus ru-de; lieux é-car-tés, pai-si-ble so-li-tu-de, ca-chez le dé-ses-poir qui reg-ne dans mon coeur.

Hé- las! quand j'ig-no- rais la fa- ta- le puis- san- ce du dieu qui m'a ra- vi la paix, con--ten- te des plai- sirs qu'of- fre l'in- dif- fé- ren- ce, que mon sort é- tait plein d'at--traits! Pour- quoi, cru- el A- mour, par d'in- vin- ci- bles traits, as- tu dom- pté ma ré- si- stan- ce?

119

-mais. Lieux é- car- tés, pai- si- ble so- li- tu- de, so- yez seuls les té- moins de ma vi- ve dou- leur. Des pei- nes des a- mants je souf- fre la plus ru- de; lieux é- car- tés, pai- si- ble so- li- tu- de, ca- chez le dé- ses- poir, qui reg- ne dans mon coeur.

[enchaîner]

PROCRIS
Cephale vient; hélas! tout redouble ma peine. Ne puis-je, sans le voir, abandonner ce lieu? Mes pleurs vont me trahir! quel tourment! quelle gêne!

[Prélude]

[enchaîner]

Scène seconde

Procris, Cephale

CEPHALE
L'amour, belle Procris, près de vous me ramène, je viens vous dire un éternel adieu. Ma mort va contenter la haine des dieux inhumains et jaloux.

PROCRIS
Ce n'est point votre mort qu'exige leur cour-

122

CEPHALE
-roux. N'est-ce pas me livrer à la Parque inhumaine, que de me condam--ner à vivre loin de vous? Vous soupirez! vous me cachez vos larmes! Quoi? seriez-vous sensible à mes cruels ennuis? Dieux! que mes maux auraient de charmes!

PROCRIS
Vous voyez malgré moi le désordre où je suis.

[enchaîner]

Air

PROCRIS
Un coeur trop sévère fait un vain mystère des maux que son amour le contraint de souffrir: ses soins et ses peines pour

Basse continue

_ ca- cher ses chaî- nes ne ser- vent qu'à les dé- cou- vrir. Ses soins et ses pei- nes pour _ ca- cher ses chaî- nes ne ser- vent qu'à les dé- cou- vrir.

[enchaîner]

PROCRIS
Vous pa- ye- rez bien cher un a- veu trop sin- cè- re! Vous a- vez trou- vé seul le se- cret de me plai- re, je n'ai plus rien à vous ce- ler; mais, mal- gré tou- te ma fai- bles- se, aux vo- lon- tés des dieux mon coeur doit im- mo- -ler sa fa- ta- le ten- dres- se, ne me re- pro- chez point les maux que je vous

Basse continue

fais, lais- sez- moi rem- por- ter cet- te tris- te vic- toi- re... Si vous a- vez soin de ma

gloi- re, Prin- ce, ne me vo- yez ja- mais. **CEPHALE** Ah! puis- que vous m'ai- mez, per- met- tez que j'es-

PROCRIS -pè- re. Vous sa- vez qu'E- o- le est mon pè- re. Je puis l'ar- mer... En vain vous flat- tez mes dou-

-leurs; il faut bri- ser les noeuds d'u- ne chaî- ne si bel- le; Les dieux m'ont con- dam- né- e à d'é- ter- nel- les

pleurs; non, ce n'est plus que la Par- que cru- el- le, qui peut ter- mi- ner mes mal- heurs.

[enchaîner]

[Duo]

-las! un sort si ri- gou- reux, doit- il de tant d'a-mour ê- tre la ré- com- pen-

si ri- gou- reux, doit- il de tant d'a-mour ê- tre la ré- com- pen-

-se? Hé- las, hé- las! un sort si ri- gou- reux, doit- il de tant d'a-mour

-se? Hé- las, hé- las! un sort si ri- gou- reux, doit- il de tant d'a-mour

ê- tre la ré- com- pen- se? A- dieu, Prince, je fuis, nos

ê- tre la ré- com- pen- se?

pleurs sont su- per- flus. O sort bar- ba- re! Faut- il que le

Cru- el des- tin! Faut- il que le

sort nous sé- pa- re? A- dieu.

sort nous sé- pa- re? Bel- le Pro- cris, ne vous ver- rai- je plus?

Scène troisième

Cephale seul

Dieux cru- els, dieux im- pi- to- ya- bles! Suis-je as-sez mal-heu- reux au gré de vos dé--sirs? Vous m'en-le-vez tous mes plai- sirs, mon coeur dé-ses-pé- ré vous trou-ve in- e- xo- ra- bles. Dieux cru-

-els, dieux im- pi- to- ya- bles, suis-je as-sez mal-heu- reux au gré de vos dé- sirs?

On entend un bruit de symphonie.
Prélude de hautbois

CEPHALE

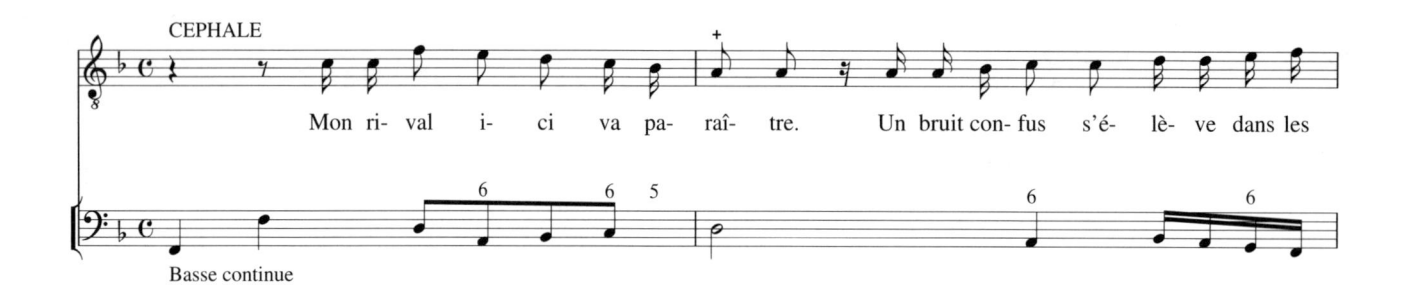

Mon rival ici va paraître. Un bruit confus s'élève dans les airs, sachons, sans nous faire connaître, le sujet de ses concerts.

Cephale se retire à l'écart.
[Trio de hautbois]

Scène quatrième

Borée, Troupe de Thraces de la suite de Borée, Cephale retiré à l'écart

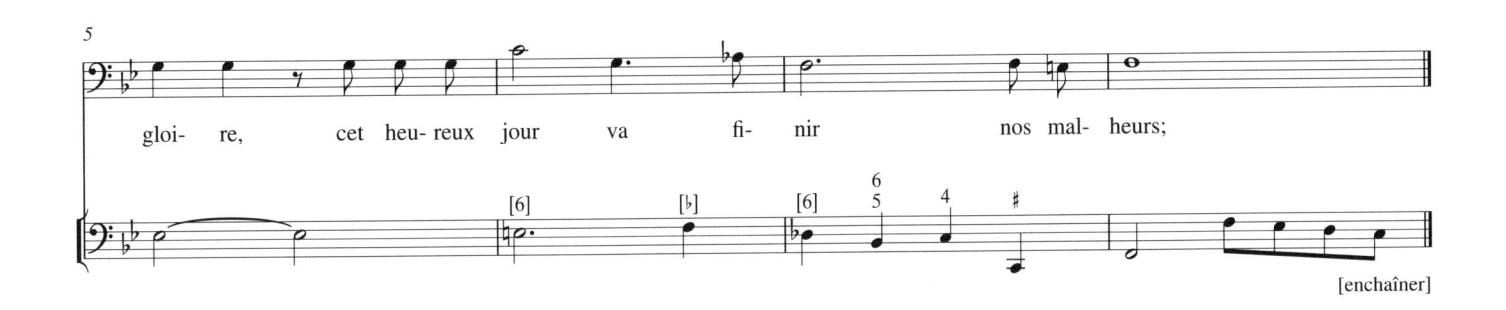

BOREE
Les dieux m'ont, à la fin accordé la victoire. Mon amour est comblé de gloire, cet heureux jour va finir nos malheurs;

Basse continue

[enchaîner]

[Air]

Doux

BOREE

Quel plai- sir pour les coeurs fi- dè- les! Quand un heu-reux suc- cès cou- ron- ne leurs ar- deurs, et qu'a- près des pei- nes cru- el- les, il est doux de chan- ter l'a- mour, et ses dou- ceurs, et qu'a- près des pei- nes cru- el- les, il est doux de chan- ter, il est doux de chan- ter l'a- mour, et ses dou- ceurs.

[enchaîner]

Choeur des Thraces

-ne leurs ar- deurs, et qu'a- près des pei- nes cru- el- les, il est doux de chan- ter l'a- mour, et ses dou-

-ceurs, et qu'a-près des pei- nes cru- el- les, il est doux de chan- ter, il est doux de chan- ter l'a- mour,

-ceurs, et qu'a-près des pei- nes cru- el- les, il est doux de chan- ter, il est doux de chan- ter l'a- mour,

-ceurs, et qu'a-près des pei- nes cru- el- les, il est doux de chan- ter, il est doux de chan- ter l'a- mour,

-ceurs, et qu'a-près des pei- nes cru- el- les, il est doux de chan- ter, il est doux de chan- ter l'a- mour, et ses dou-ceurs.

et ses dou-ceurs.

et ses dou-ceurs.

et ses dou-ceurs.

et ses dou-ceurs.

Et qu'a- près des pei- nes cru- el- les, il est doux de chan- ter l'a- mour, et ses dou- ceurs.

138

139

-dè- les! Quel plai- sir pour les coeurs fi- dè- les! Quand un heu-reux suc- cès cou- ron- ne leurs ar-

61
[Violons seule] [tous] [Violons seule] [tous]
[Violons seule] [tous] [Violons seule] [tous]
[petit choeur] [tous] [petit choeur] [tous]
-deurs. Quel plai- sir, quel plai- sir, quel plai- sir pour les coeurs fi- dè- les, quel plai- sir pour les
[petit choeur] [tous] [petit choeur] [tous]
-deurs. Quel plai- sir, quel plai- sir, quel plai- sir pour les coeurs fi- dè- les, quel plai- sir pour les
[petit choeur] [tous] [petit choeur] [tous]
-deurs. Quel plai- sir, quel plai- sir, quel plai- sir pour les coeurs fi- dè- les, quel plai- sir pour les
-deurs. Quel plai- sir, quel plai- sir pour les
-deurs. Quel plai- sir, quel plai- sir pour les
[6 4♯]
[5♭]
[♯]

coeurs fi- dè- les! Quand un heu-reux suc- cès cou-ron- ne leurs ar- deurs.

Et qu'a- près des
Et qu'a- près des
Et qu'a- près des
Et qu'a- près des
Et qu'a- près des

peines cruelles, il est doux de chanter, il est doux de chanter l'amour, et ses douceurs.

[Air]

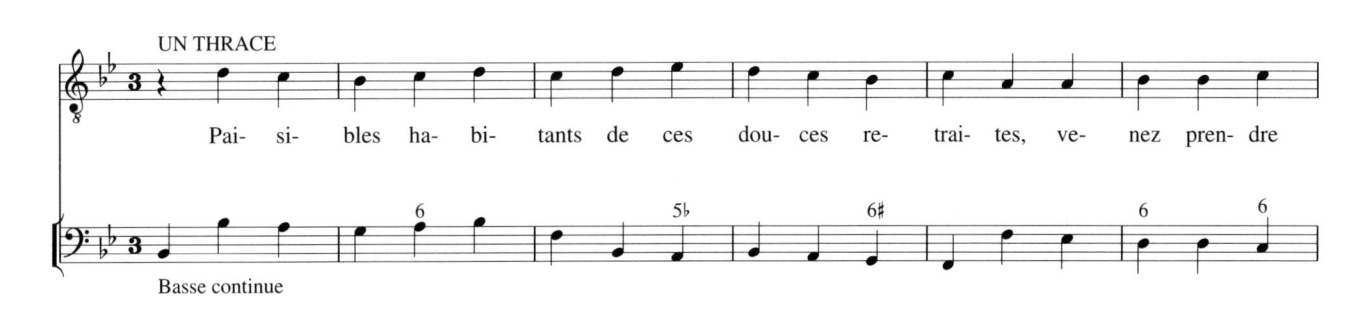

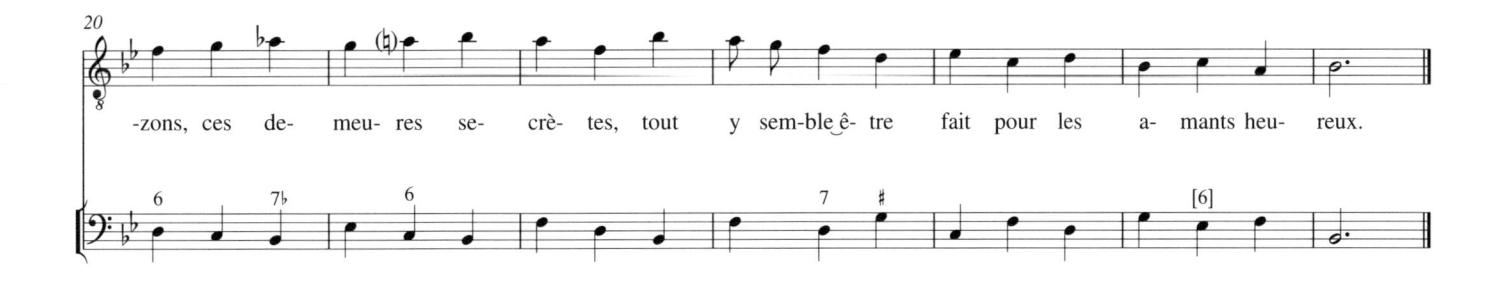

UN THRACE

Pai-sibles habitants de ces douces retraites, venez prendre part à nos jeux: jeux: cet ombre, ces gazons, ces demeures secrètes, tout y semble être fait pour les amants heureux, cet ombre, ces gazons, ces demeures secrètes, tout y semble être fait pour les amants heureux.

Scène cinquième

Tous les acteurs de la scène précédente. Troupe de pâtres et de bergères.
Première Entrée

Marche

147

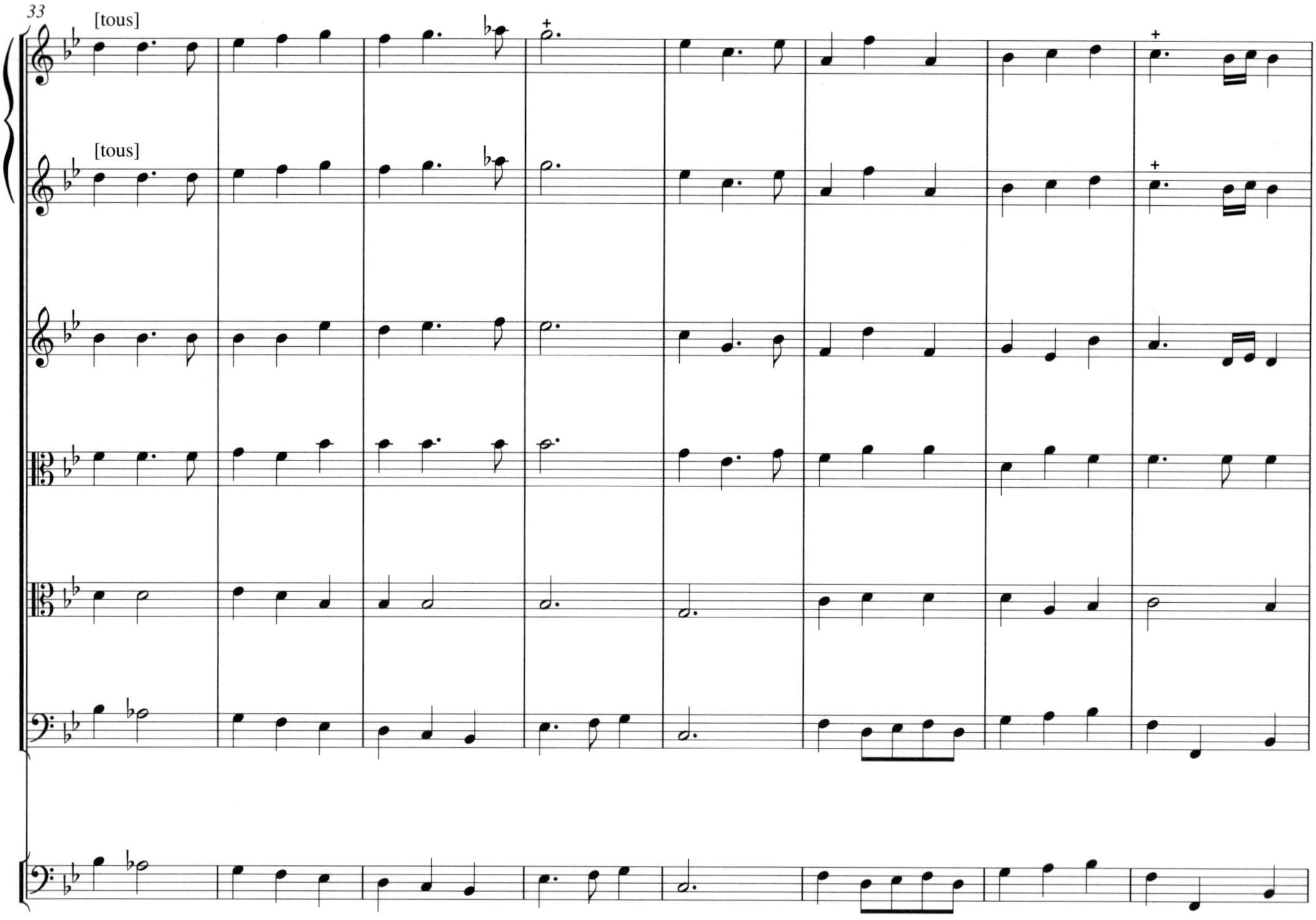
33
[tous]
[tous]

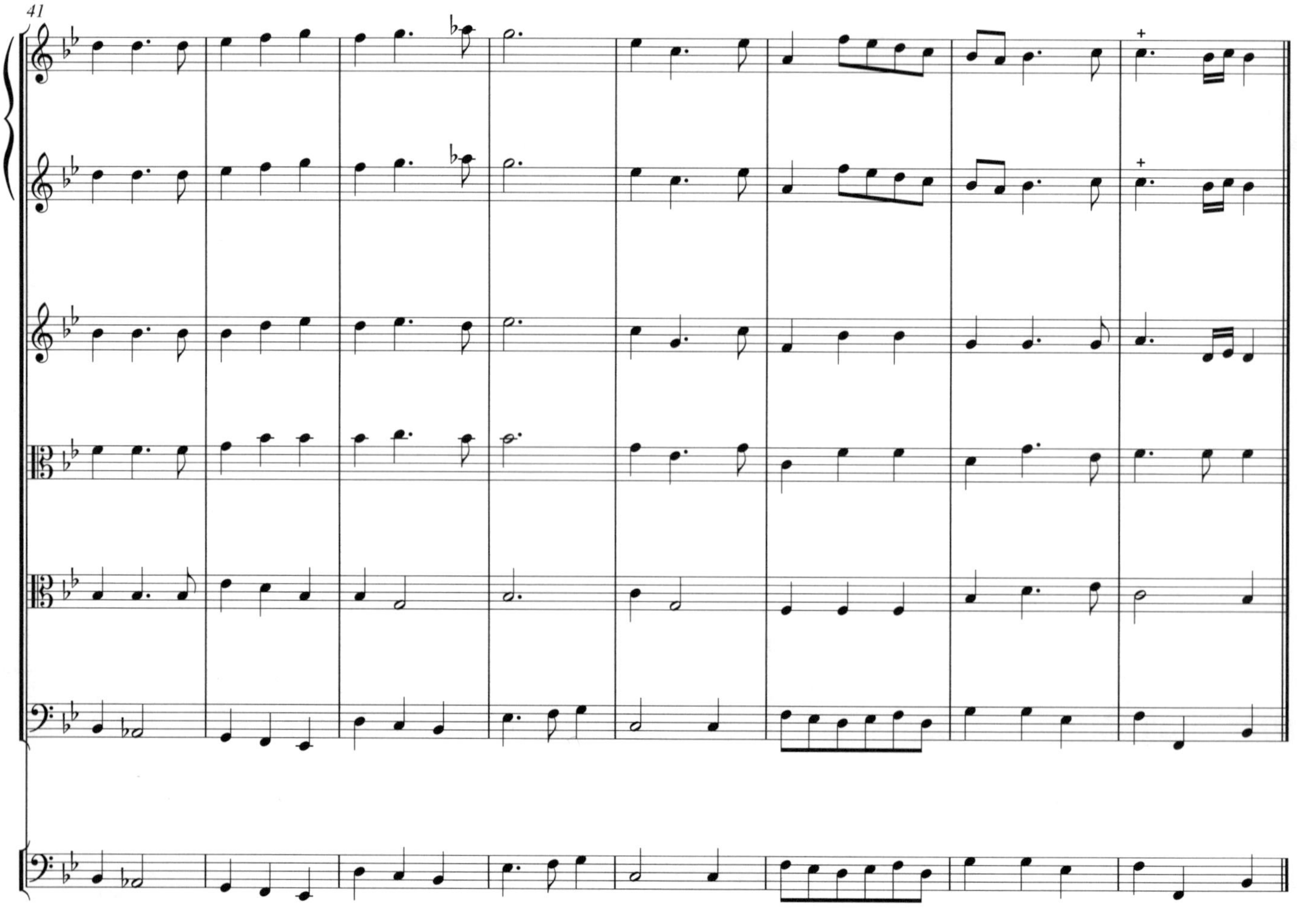
41

Les pâtres

[Duo]

Un pâtre et une bergère

UNE BERGERE: Les ros-si-gnols, dès que le jour com-men-ce, chan-tent l'a-mour qui les a-ni-me tous, tous, si les oi-seaux cè-dent à sa puis-san-ce, quel mal fai-sons-nous d'ai-mer à sen-tir ses coups? Si leur ins-tinct est rem-pli d'in-no-cen-ce, quel mal fai-sons-nous de sui-vre un pen-chant si doux? Si doux?

UN PATRE: Les ros-si-gnols, dès que le jour com-men-ce, chan-tent l'a-mour qui les a-ni-me tous, tous, si les oi-seaux cè-dent à sa puis-san-ce, quel mal fai-sons-nous d'ai-mer à sen-tir ses coups? Si leur ins-tinct est rem-pli d'in-no-cen-ce, quel mal fai-sons-nous de sui-vre un pen-chant si doux? Si doux?

Basse continue

Les pâtres et les bergères recommencent leur danses;
après quoi le même pâtre et la même bergère qui ont chanté le dernier Air, chantent le second couplet.

Bourée

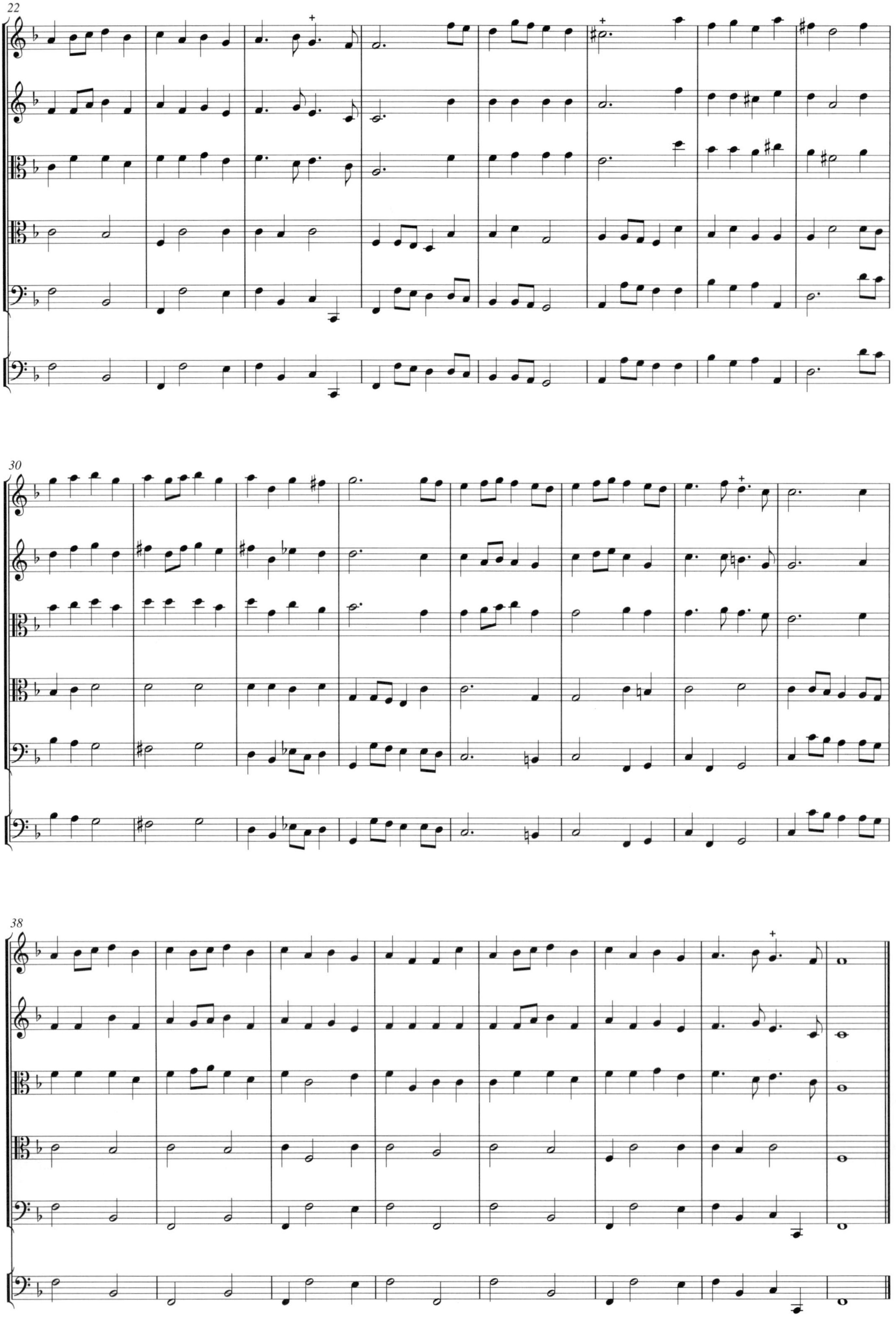
22
30
38

*Les danses des bergers continuent; quand elles sont finies,
Cephale sort du lieu où il s'était retiré, et s'adresse à Borée.*

Scène sixième

Cephale, Borée

CEPHALE
Vous n'êtes pas encore sûr de votre conquête.
Craignez du sort volage un dangereux retour. Dussé-je voir la foudre à tomber toute prête, ma mort seule pourra m'arracher mon amour.

BOREE
Je souffre d'un jaloux l'impuissante colère, ton amour te rend téméraire, tu suis une aveugle fureur; mais mon coeur généreux veut bien te faire grace: pour te punir de ton audace, c'est assez que tu

Scène septième

L'Aurore, Cephale, Iphis

L'Aurore descend dans une machine brillante.

CEPHALE *Cephale sans voir L'Aurore*

sois té-moin de mon bon-heur. Le traî-tre à me bra-ver por-te son in-so--len-ce? Cou-rons à la ven-gean-ce, n'é-cou--tons que l'ar-deur dont je suis a-ni-mé!

[enchaîner]

L'AURORE
Ce-pha-le, où cou-rez-vous? quel-le fu-reur vous gui-de?

CEPHALE
Je vais me ven-ger d'un per-fi-de, ou mou-rir pour l'ob-jet dont mon coeur est char--mé.

L'AURORE
Sus-pen-dez les tran-sports d'un gé-né-reux cou-ra-ge de la beau-

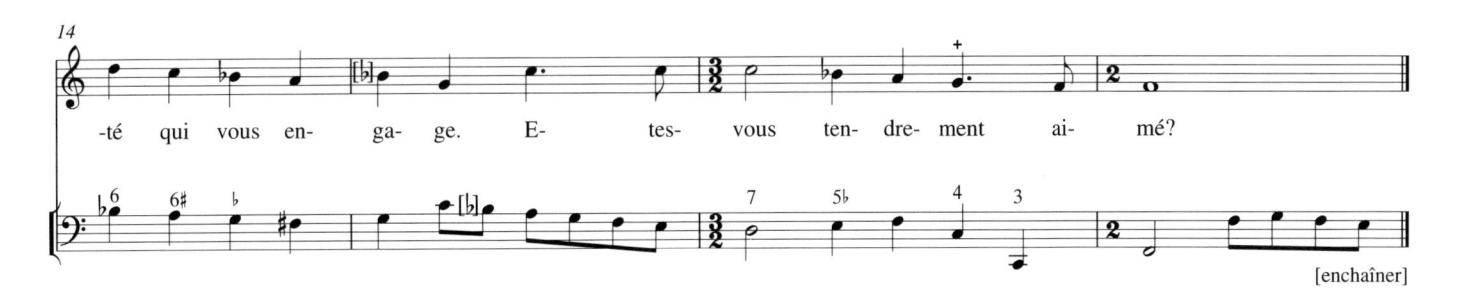

Air

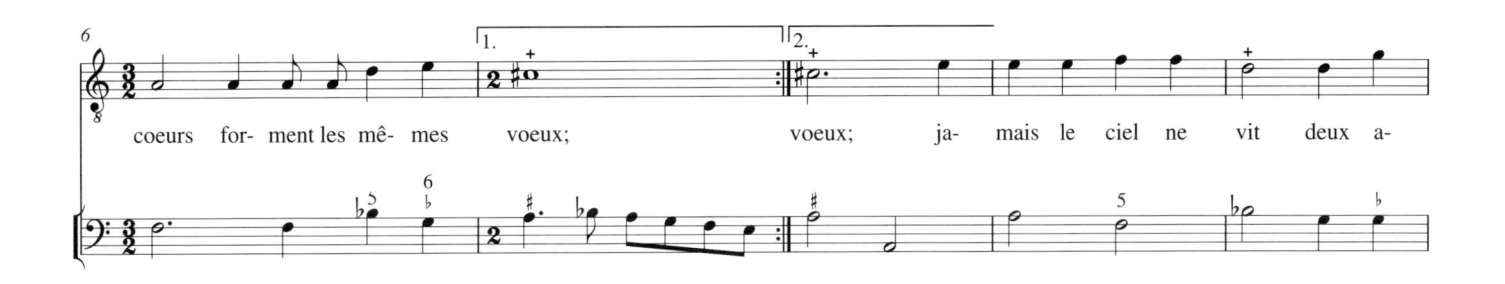

CEPHALE

Nous res- sen- tons des ar- deurs mu- tu- el- les, nos ten- dres coeurs for- ment les mê- mes voeux; voeux; ja- mais le ciel ne vit deux a- -mants plus fi- dè- les, et n'en fit de plus mal- heu- reux, ja- mais le ciel ne vit deux a- mants plus fi- dè- les, et n'en fit de plus mal- heu- reux.

[enchaîner]

L'AURORE

Procris peut vous tromper; peut-être que l'ingrate n'aime qu'un vain honneur dont le charme la flatte, elle cède à Borée, il triomphe à vos yeux; commencez à mieux la connaître; rarement l'Amour est le maître d'un coeur ambitieux. J'ouvre au père du jour la céleste barrière. Je précède en tous lieux le dieu de la lumière; la terre, à mon aspect, fait éclore ses fleurs; je suis cette Aurore charmante, dont la clarté toujours naissante, peint l'univers des plus vives couleurs, et qui même, au milieu de mes tendres douleurs, toujours ai-

-ma- ble, et tou-jours bien-fai- san- te, en- ri- chit si sou- vent la ter- re de mes pleurs.

[enchaîner]

Air

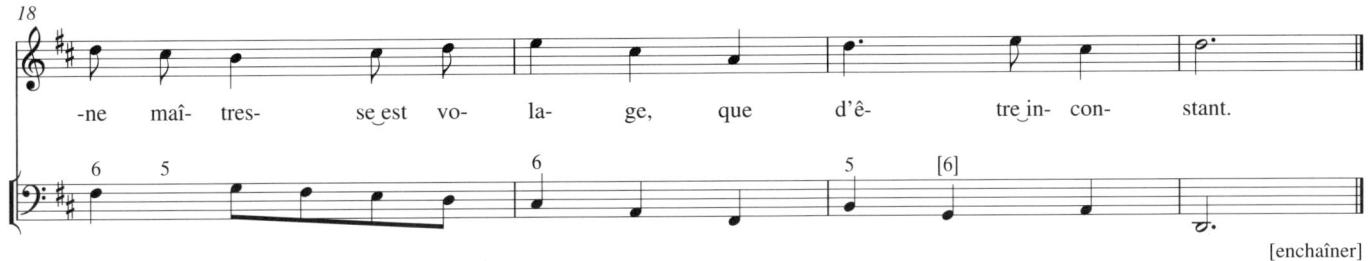

L'AURORE
Sui- vez un con- seil sa- lu- tai- re, vous souf- frez pour Pro-

Basse continue

-cris, el- le a trop su vous plai- re: gue- ris- sez vous en la quit-

-tant; c'est ê- tre sa- ge, quand u- ne maî- tres- se est vo-

-la- ge, que d'ê-tre in- con- stant, c'est ê- tre sa- ge, quand u-

-ne maî- tres- se est vo- la- ge, que d'ê- tre in- con- stant.

[enchaîner]

CEPHALE
Quoi! l'objet charmant que j'adore aurait feint de répondre à mes tendres amours? Ciel! quel nouveau chagrin m'agite, et me dévore! Ah! je ne sais si Procris m'aime encore; mais, hélas! je sens bien que je l'aime toujours.

L'AURORE
Je vais tout employer, pour contenter votre âme; ne craignez rien d'un rival odieux; pour mieux cacher le feu qui vous enflamme, ne paraissez point en ces lieux; allez, reposez-

-vous sur ces guides fidèles. Avant que de suivre vos pas, je veux, pour terminer tant de peines cruelles, vous assurer un destin plein d'appas. Volez, charmants zéphires, accompagnez Cephale, aux honneurs les plus grands ses jours sont destinés. Est-il un mortel qui l'égale? Volez, je vais le suivre, en des lieux fortunés.

160

Les zéphires enlevent Cephale.

Scène huitième
L'Aurore, Iphis
Ritournelle

[enchaîner]

IPHIS
Pour rendre un amant volage, vous mettez tout en usage; pourquoi prendre tant de soins? Je crois qu'il en coûte moins pour rendre un amant volage.

[enchaîner]

L'AURORE
Je connais ce jeune héros. Je sais quelle est sa constance, et sa flamme; Tu te souviens du jour qu'il troubla mon repos, il venait en ces lieux confier aux échos les tendres secrets de son âme: mon coeur se sentit enflammé, rien n'a pu jusqu'ici dissiper ma faiblesse; de Pallas j'ai vu la prêtresse, j'ai fait rompre un hymen, qu'elle allait confirmer; hé! que ne fait-on point, lorsque l'Amour nous blesse, pour tâcher de se faire aimer?

IPHIS
Laissez-vous occu-

-per d'u- ne dou- ce es-pé- ran- ce, Ce- pha- le, par vos soins, peut chan-ger en ce jour.

[enchaîner]

Air

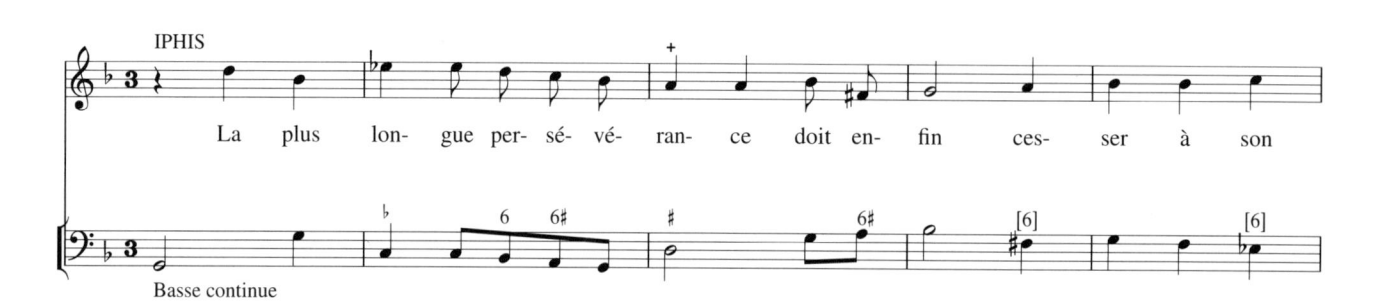

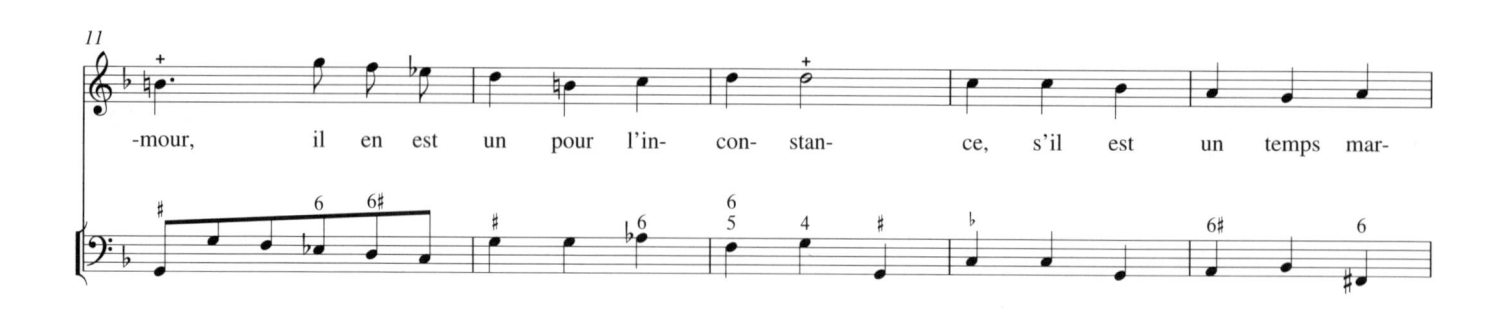

IPHIS

La plus lon- gue per- sé- vé- ran- ce doit en- fin ces- ser à son

Basse continue

tour; tour; s'il est un temps mar- qué pour se ren- dre à l'A-

-mour, il en est un pour l'in- con- stan- ce, s'il est un temps mar-

-qué pour se ren- dre à l'A- mour, il en est un pour l'in- con- stan- ce.

[enchaîner]

L'AURORE

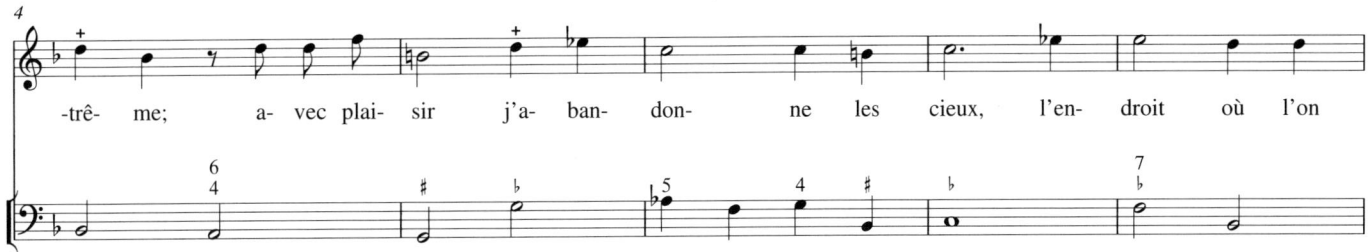

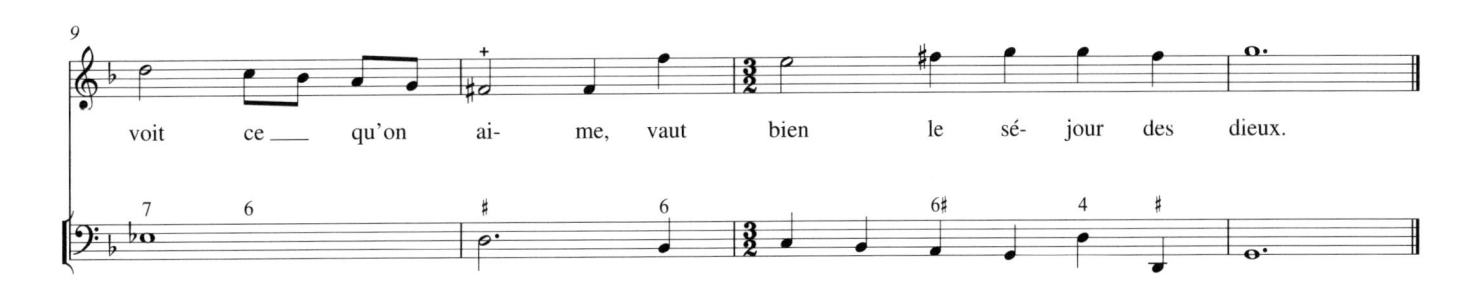

C'est trop demeurer dans ces lieux, allons trouver l'objet de mon amour extrême; avec plaisir j'abandonne les cieux, l'endroit où l'on voit ce qu'on aime, vaut bien le séjour des dieux.

FIN DU SECOND ACTE
On joue la Bourée (pp. 151–152) pour l'Entr'acte.

Acte III

Scène première

Le théâtre représente les lieux où la Volupté fait son séjour; cette déesse paraît dans le fonds du théâtre couchée sur un lit de fleurs.

Cephale seul

165

A- mour, que sous tes loix cru-el- les on suf- fre des maux ri-gou- reux! Par un es-poir trom- peur tu sais flat- ter nos voeux, pour nous li- vrer à des pei- nes mor- tel- les. A- mour, que sous tes loix cru- el- les on

souf- fre des maux ri- gou- reux! Quand tu con-trains deux coeurs à res- sen- tir tes feux, dois-
-tu lais- ser rom- pre des noeuds qui de-vroient leur for- mer des chaî- nes é- ter- nel- les? A-
-mour, que sous tes loix cru- el- les les coeurs con- stants sont mal-heu- reux! Et qu'il en est peu de fi-

-dè- les! A- mour, que sous tes loix cru- el- les on souf- fre des maux ri- gou- reux!

Scène seconde
Cephale, Iphis

IPHIS
Rien ne peut- il a- pai- ser vos a- lar- mes? Quoi? Ce- pha- le, en ces lieux char-mants, vous sou- pi- rez, vous ré- pan- dez de lar- mes?

CEPHALE
Ah! pour les mal- heu- reux a- mants, est- il quel- que sé- jour qui puis- se a- voir des char- mes?

IPHIS
Vous de- vez es- pé- rer la fin de vos mal- heurs.

[enchaîner]

Air

IPHIS

Tôt ou tard l'Amour répare les maux qu'il fait aux tendres coeurs. Et c'est souvent par d'extrêmes rigueurs qu'il nous prépare à ses plus charmantes faveurs. Tôt ou tard l'Amour répare les maux qu'il fait aux tendres coeurs.

[enchaîner]

Parlant à la Volupté.

IPHIS

Déesse dont toujours on aima la puissance, vous, qui par d'agréables loix, rendez, quand il vous plaît, les héros et les rois, esclaves des plaisirs que votre main dispense; tranquille Volupté, venez, avec les jeux, d'un trop fi- dè- le_a- mant a- pai- ser le mar- ty- re. Vous pou-vez com-

-bler tous nos voeux, tout rit, tout plaît sous vo- tre_em- pi- re; et si

quel- qu'un se plaint du pou- voir a- mou- reux, c'est moins de pei- ne qu'il sou-

-pi- re, que du plai- sir qui le rend trop heu- reux.

[enchaîner]

Scène troisième

Cephale, Iphis, La Volupté, Suite de la Volupté,
Troupe de Plaisirs, de Grâces, et quatres Amours
La Volupté et sa suite forment une entrée de ballet.

Symphonie

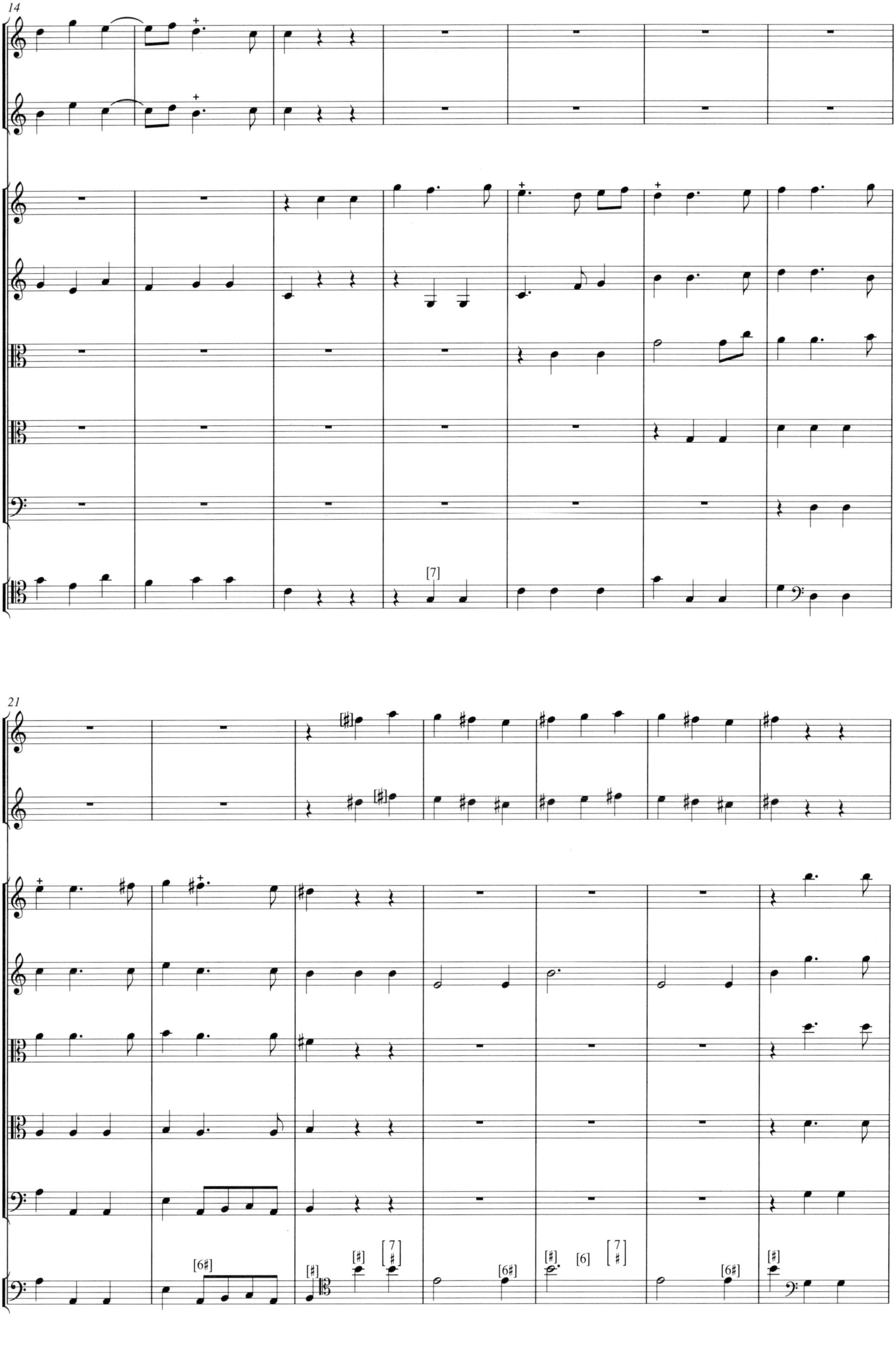

14
[7]
21
[6♯]
[♯]
[♯]
[7 ♯]
[6♯]
[♯]
[6]
[7 ♯]
[6♯]
[♯]

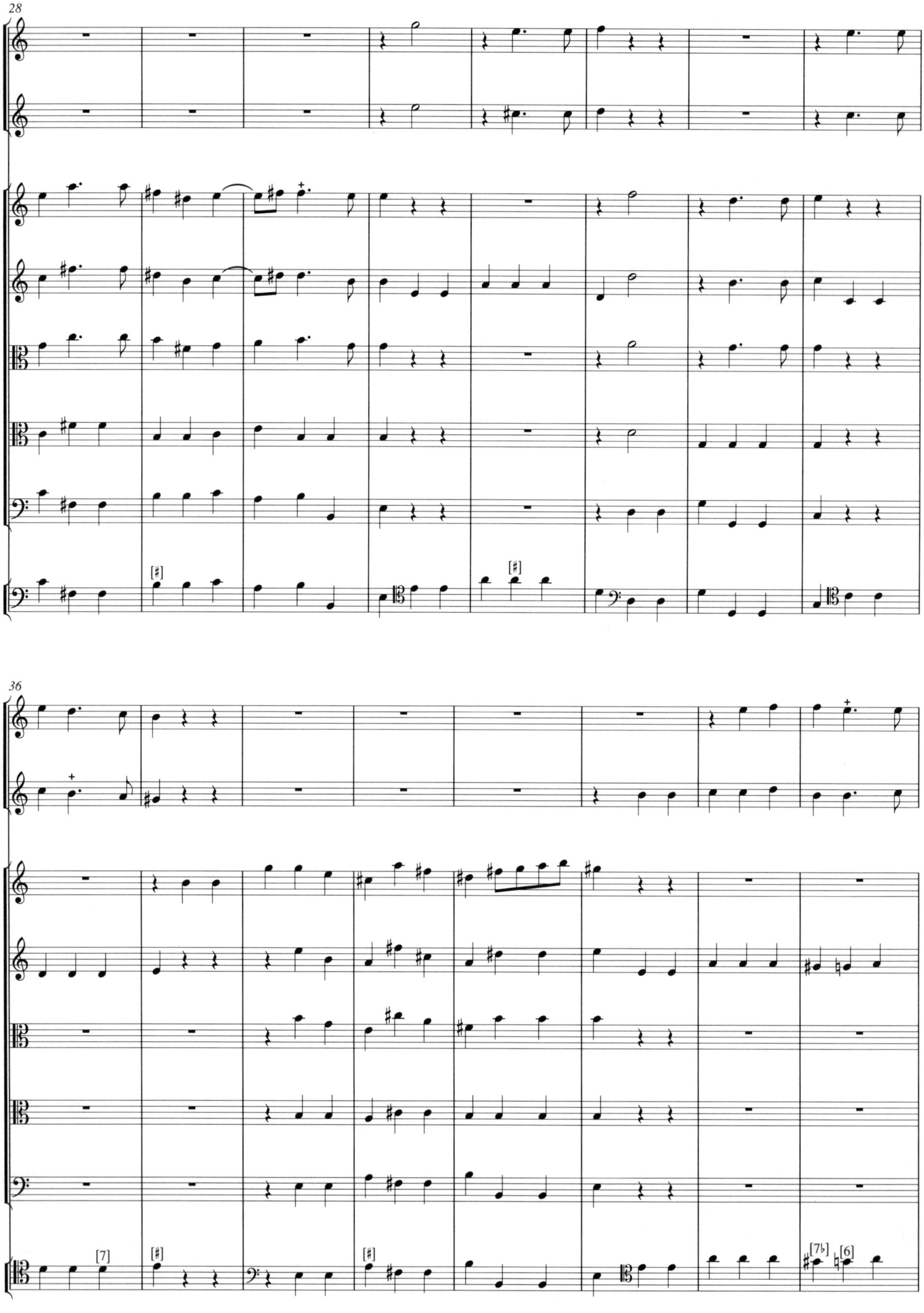
28
[♯]
[♯]
36
[7]
[♯]
[♯]
[7♭]
[6]

173

[Air]

UNE SUIVANTE DE LA VOLUPTÉ

Tendres amants, bravez vos peines. Le dieu qui vous donne des chaînes, doit à la fin vous secourir; la moindre grace que l'Amour fasse, sait nous payer des maux qu'il fait souffrir, la moindre grace que l'Amour fasse, sait nous payer des maux qu'il fait souffrir.

[enchaîner]

Chœur des suivants de la Volupté

Dessus 1: Tendres amants, bravez vos peines. Le dieu qui vous

Dessus 2: Tendres amants, bravez vos peines. Le dieu qui vous

Haute-contre: Tendres amants, bravez vos peines. Le dieu, le

175

[Air]

LA VOLUPTE

Loin de ces lieux, triste sagesse, doit-on défendre à la jeunesse de se former des noeuds charmants? Quelle folie, quand de sa vie un jeune coeur perd les plus doux moments, quelle folie quand de sa vie un jeune coeur perd les plus doux moments!

La Volupté et sa suite recommencent leurs danses.

Passacaille

14
[Violons seule]
[Violons seule]
21
[tous]
[tous]
28
[Violons seule]
[Violons seule]
[tous]
[tous]

179

56
[tous]
[tous]
64
[Violons seule]
[Violons seule]
[tous]
[tous]
72
[Violons seule]
[tous]
[Violons seule]
[Violons seule]
[tous]
[Violons seule]

181

[Air]

Gai

UNE SUIVANTE DE LA VOLUPTÉ

La douce folie que celle d'aimer! L'Amour doit former les beaux jours de la vie; la douce folie, que celle d'aimer! Plus ce dieu nous lie, plus il sait charmer, tout doit s'enflammer, le printemps y convie; la douce folie que celle d'aimer! La douce folie que celle d'aimer!

[enchaîner]

[enchaîner]

Choeur

Dessus 1: La dou- ce fo- li- e que cel- le d'ai- mer! L'A- mour doit for- mer les beaux jours de la vi- e; la dou- ce fo- li- e, que cel- le d'ai- mer! Plus ce dieu nous li- e, plus il sait char- mer, tout doit s'en- flam- mer, le prin- temps y con-

Dessus 2: La dou- ce fo- li- e que cel- le d'ai- mer! L'A- mour doit for- mer les beaux jours de la vi- e; la dou- ce fo- li- e, que cel- le d'ai- mer! Plus ce dieu nous li- e, plus il sait char- mer, tout doit s'en- flam- mer, le prin- temps y con-

Haute-contre: La dou- ce fo- li- e que cel- le d'ai- mer! L'A- mour doit for- mer les beaux jours de la vi- e; la dou- ce fo- li- e, que cel- le d'ai- mer! Plus ce dieu nous li- e, plus il sait char- mer, tout doit s'en- flam- mer, le prin- temps y con-

Basse continue

20
-vi- e; la dou- ce fo- li- e que cel- le d'ai- mer! La dou- ce fo- li- e que
-vi- e; la dou- ce fo- li- e que cel- le d'ai- mer! La dou- ce fo- li- e que
-vi- e; la dou- ce fo- li- e que cel- le d'ai- mer! La dou- ce fo- li- e que
27
cel- le d'ai- mer! Tout doit s'en- flam- mer, le prin- temps y con- vi- e; la dou- ce fo-
cel- le d'ai- mer! Tout doit s'en- flam- mer, le prin- temps y con- vi- e; la dou- ce fo-
cel- le d'ai- mer! Tout doit s'en- flam- mer, le prin- temps y con- vi- e; la dou- ce fo-
34
-li- e que cel- le d'ai- mer, la dou- ce fo- li- e que cel- le d'ai- mer!
-li- e que cel- le d'ai- mer, la dou- ce fo- li- e que cel- le d'ai- mer!
-li- e que cel- le d'ai- mer, la dou- ce fo- li- e que cel- le d'ai- mer!

Scène quatrième

L'Aurore, Iphis, Cephale, la Volupté, les Plaisirs, et les Grâces

L'AURORE
Pour dissiper votre tristesse, vous voyez les soins que j'ai pris: tâchez de surmonter une indigne faiblesse; la volage beauté, dont vous êtes épris, est plus digne de vos mépris, qu'elle ne fus d'avoir votre tendresse.

CEPHALE
De mon funeste sort, ciel! quelle est la rigueur?

L'AURORE
Vous soupirez encore pour elle?

CEPHALE
J'ai honte d'être trop fidèle, mais, hélas! le dépit qui déchire mon coeur, redouble ma peine cruelle, et n'affaiblit point mon ardeur.

L'AURORE

Cessez d'être sensible aux beautés des mortelles; cherchez un sort dont les dieux soient jaloux de tant de déités qui brillent parmi nous, les plus fières, les plus rebelles, ces seront de l'être pour vous. J'en dis peut-être trop; vous allez me connaître, Cephale, il ne faut plus vous rien dissimuler, en vain j'ai voulu vous celer que de mon faible coeur l'Amour s'est rendu maître; mes soins pour le cacher ont été superflus, contre lui la fierté n'est qu'un faible remède, hélas! quand ce dieu nous pos-

-sè- de, les dieux les plus puis- sants ne se pos- sè- dent plus. Vous voy- ez mon ar-

-deur, par- lez sans vous con- train- dre. De vos bien- faits mon coeur se sent com- blé, mais...

L'AURORE **CEPHALE**

dieux! Que di- tes vous? Que mon sort est à plain- dre! In- di- gne des hon-

L'AURORE

-neurs dont je suis ac- ca- blé... N'a- che- ve pas, In- grat, je pré- vois quel out-

-ra- ge tes in- ju- stes mé- pris se- raient à mes ar- deurs! Va lan- guir pour u- ne vo-

-la- ge? Va te li- vrer à d'é- ter- nels mal- heurs? Je ne se- rai pas seu- le à ré- pan- dre des pleurs... il fuit... il m'a-ban-don-ne à ma hon-te, et ma ra-ge...

Ce-pha-le, tu te perds, ces-se de m'ir-ri-ter: tu te re-pen-ti-rais d'a-voir su me dé-plai-re.

CEPHALE
Je n'ai rien fait pour mé-ri-ter ni vos soins, ni vo-tre co-lè-re.

[enchaîner]

Air

CEPHALE
Vous me fai-tes voir en ce jour un bar-ba-re cou-roux, u-ne ra-ge in-hu-mai-ne; je ne croy-ais pas que l'a-mour dût tant res-sem-bler à la hai-ne, je ne croy-ais pas que l'a-mour dût tant res-sem-bler à la hai-ne.

Basse continue

[enchaîner]

Air

L'AURORE
Vous me bravez, Cruel, vous con-nais-sez mon coeur, je vous ai fait voir sa fai-bles-se; vous ne sa-vez que trop, que tou-te ma fu-reur ne peut é-ga-ler ma ten-dres-se, vous ne sa-vez que trop, que tou-te ma fu-reur ne peut é-ga-ler ma ten-dres-se.

[enchaîner]

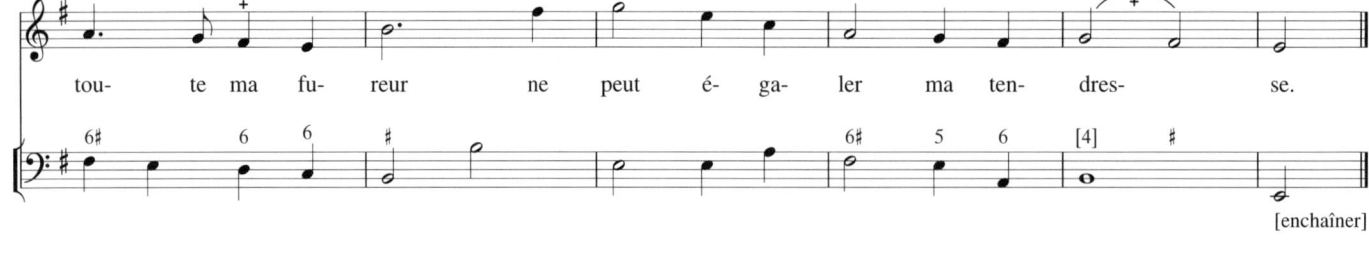

CEPHALE
De votre bon-té in-ter-rom-pez le cours. Vo-tre a-mour out-ra-gé de-man-de u-ne vic-ti-me, fai-tes fi-nir mes tris-tes jours, pu-nis-sez-moi, sui-vez un cou-roux lé-gi-

L'AURORE

-ti- me. Je ne vous pu- ni- rai qu'en vous ai- mant tou- jours. Ai- mez qui vous mé-

-pri- se, et fuy- ez qui vous ai- me: vous se- rez le té- moin de mes ten- dres ar-

-deurs; a vos yeux cha- que jour j'of- fri- rais mes dou- leurs, et jus- ques dans vo- tre coeur

mê- me, mes maux, et mon a- mour trou- ve- rons des ven- geurs. Par-

-tez, c'est trop gê- ner vo- tre âme im- pa- ti- en- te; al- lez of- frir à des trom- peurs ap-

-pas l'hom- ma- ge gé- né- reux d'u- ne flam- me con- stan- te. Zé- phires, ac- com- pa-

-gnez, et con- dui- sez ses pas.

[Prélude]

[enchaîner]

Scène cinquième

L'Aurore, Iphis

L'AURORE
Tu vois ma honte et mon supplice.

IPHIS
Vengez-vous de l'Ingrat qui cause vos ennuis.

L'AURORE
Quel triomphe pour lui! en l'état où je suis, s'il savait que forcée à lui rendre justice, ma raison me contraint d'approuver ses mépris!

IPHIS
Que dites-vous?

L'AURORE
Apprends quelle est mon infortune: jamais je ne l'ai tant aimé, mon coeur malgré lui-même, est surpris et charmé d'une vertu si peu commune... Ah! c'est de quoi mon coeur doit encore le punir; il me quitte... il me hait... et

sait encore me plaire! Vengeons-nous; je le puis... qui peut me retenir?... A mon juste courroux ma tendresse est contraire, et je crains bien que ma colère n'augmente mon amour, au lieu de le bannir.

FIN DU TROISIEME ACTE

Acte IV

Scène première

Dorine, Arcas

Le théâtre représente les jardins du palais d'Erictée.

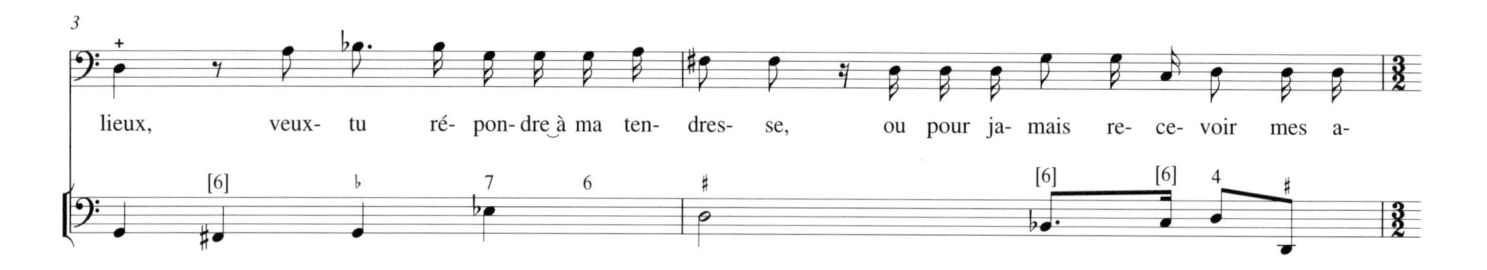

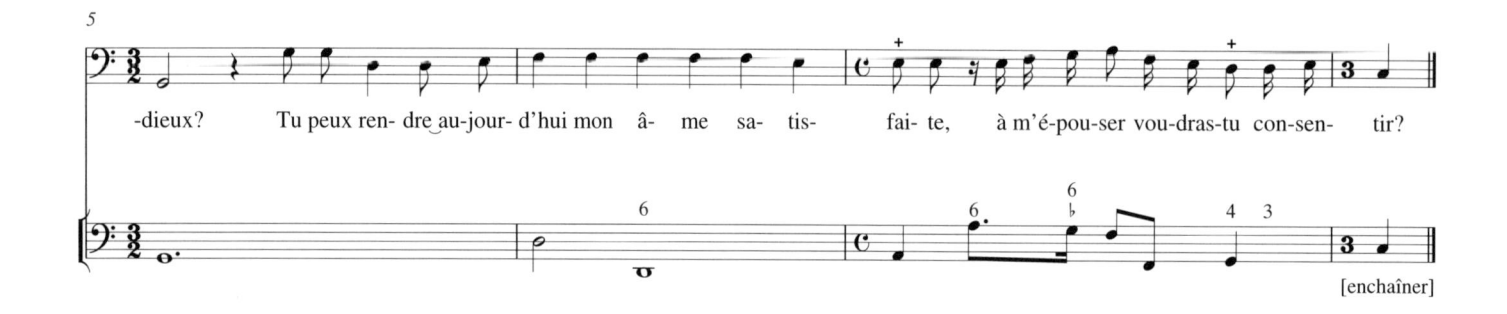

ARCAS
Bo- rée é- pou- se la Prin- ces- se. Je dois a- vec Ce- pha- le a- ban- don- ner ces lieux, veux- tu ré- pon- dre à ma ten- dres- se, ou pour ja- mais re- ce- voir mes a- dieux? Tu peux ren- dre au- jour- d'hui mon â- me sa- tis- fai- te, à m'é- pou- ser vou- dras- tu con- sen- tir?

[enchaîner]

[Air]

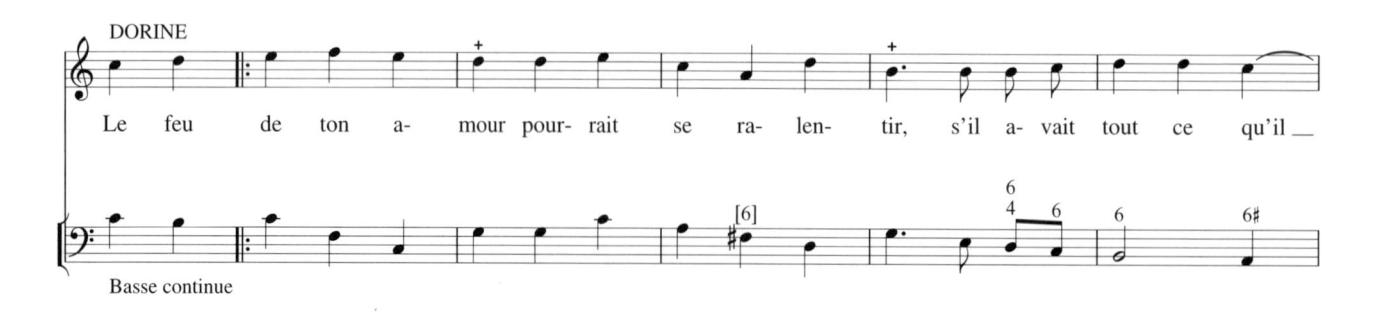

DORINE
Le feu de ton a- mour pour- rait se ra- len- tir, s'il a- vait tout ce qu'il sou- hai- te; Le feu te; quel- ques plai- sirs qu'on se pro- met- te, il n'est de- puis l'hy-

-men qu'un pas au re- pen- tir; quel- ques plai- sirs qu'on se pro- met- te, il n'est de- puis l'hy--men qu'un pas au re- pen- tir.

ARCAS
A d'é- ter- nels re- fus dois- je tou- jours m'at- ten- dre?

[enchaîner]

[Air]

DORINE
N'es- pè- rez pas que je me ren- de un jour, mon coeur de s'en- ga--ger sau- ra bien se dé- fen- dre: trop sou- vent l'hy- men le plus tendre é- teint le flam- beau de l'a- mour; trop sou--vent l'hy- men le plus ten- dre é- teint le flam- beau de l'a- mour.

Basse continue

[enchaîner]

[Air]

Les mépris d'une cruelle rendent le calme à mon coeur. Malheureux qui s'obstine à souffrir la rigueur d'une beauté rebelle. Dans l'empire amoureux le coeur le moins constant est bien souvent le plus content; dans l'empire amoureux le coeur le moins constant est bien souvent le plus content.

ARCAS

[enchaîner]

[Duo]

DORINE
Vi- vons tou- jours sans tris- tes- se, n'ai- mons qu'à ri- re et chan- ter. Quand l'a- mour nous bles- se, s'il of- fre un doux mo- ment, tâ- chons d'en pro- fi- ter; mais re- gar- dons un ex- cès de ten- dres- se com- me u- ne fai- bles- se qu'on doit é- vi- ter; mais re- gar- dons un ex- cès de ten- dres- se com- me u- ne fai- bles- se qu'on doit é- vi- ter.

ARCAS
Vi- vons tou- jours sans tris- tes- se, n'ai- mons qu'à ri- re et chan- ter. Quand l'a- mour nous bles- se, s'il of- fre un doux mo- ment, tâ- chons d'en pro- fi- ter; mais re- gar- dons un ex- cès de ten- dres- se com- me u- ne fai- bles- se qu'on doit é- vi- ter; mais re- gar- dons un ex- cès de ten- dres- se com- me u- ne fai- bles- se qu'on doit é- vi- ter.

Basse continue

Scène seconde

L'Aurore, Iphis, Dorine, Arcas

L'AURORE
Sur d'au-tres que sur vous doit tom-ber ma ven-gean- ce: hâ- tez- vous de vous re- ti- rer. Le mé-pris d'un in-grat m'of- fen- se; qu'il souf- fre les tour- ments qu'il me fait en- du- rer.

Dorine et Arcas se retirent.

Prélude

199

Doux
[Violons seule]

[B.Vn.]

O vous, im- pla- ca- ble en- ne-

-mi- e des coeurs que l'A-mour rend heu- reux, dé- es- se des soup- çons, bar- ba- re Ja- lou-

-si- e, pour en- ten- dre ma voix de vos gouf- fres af- freux, sus- pen- dez les fu-

Fort
[tous]

-reurs dont vous ê- tes sai- si- e.

201

-spi- re, tous les maux que pro- duit vo- tre fu- nes-te em- pi- re, n'é- ga- le- ront ja-

On entend une symphonie lugubre.

-mais les trou-bles que je sens.

L'AURORE
Sortons, la Jalousie en ces lieux va se rendre. Cette affreuse divinité ne pourrait souffrir la clarté que je suis malgré moi, contrainte de répandre.

IPHIS
Hélas! Qui vous fait soupirer? A remplir vos désirs tout semble conspirer, la haine que Procris fera voir à Céphale, pourra vers elle empêcher son retour.

L'AURORE
Iphis, ma peine est sans égale, je connais trop bien son amour, ma rage et tes con-

204

-seils lui vont ravir le jour. Non, je ne puis souffrir que ce héros pé-

IPHIS

-risse, divinité, que mes fureurs viennent d'armer pour son supplice... Procris

vient, bannissez vos injustes terreurs. Qui vous rend en ce jour si contraire à vous

L'AURORE

même? Une indigne pitié doit-elle vous trahir? Tes conseils sur mon

coeur ont un pouvoir suprême. C'en est fait, que l'enfer soit prêt à m'obé-

-ir... De ma vengeance, Iphis, j'aurai peine à jouir. Quand je songe à l'ob-

-jet de mon ar- deur ex- trê- me, j'ou- bli- e, hé- las! que je dois le ha- ïr, et je sens trop bien que je l'ai- me.

[Prélude]

Scène troisième

Procris seule

Prélude

Funeste mort, donnez-moi du secours! Ah! par pitié venez trancher mes jours! Mon infortune est certaine. C'est peu de perdre, hélas! l'objet de mes amours, je me vois condamnée à m'unir pour toujours, à l'objet de toute ma haine. Rien ne peut me ti- rer de cet- te af- freu- se pei- ne. Fu- nes- te mort, don- nez- moi du se- cours! Ah! par pi- tié ve- nez tran- chez mes jours!

On entend un bruit souterrain.

Quel bruit lu- gu- bre et sourd i- ci se fait en-

-ten- dre?   Mil- le a- bî- mes se sont ou-

-verts!

[enchaîner]

Scène quatrième

Le théâtre change, et représente l'antre où La Jalousie fait son séjour.

Procris, La Jalousie, La Rage, Le Désespoir

PROCRIS
Je me vois transportée en d'horribles deserts! Ciel! quelle nuit vient me surprendre? Pourquoi frémir? l'enfer touché de mes soupirs, veut-il par le trépas finir mes déplaisirs?

Elle apperçoit La Jalousie.

Scène cinquième
Procris, La Jalousie, La Rage, Le Désespoir

PROCRIS
Ve- nez, ve- nez, im- pla- ca- ble fu- ri- e, ve- nez, je m'a-ban--don- ne à vos bar- ba- res mains. Ter- mi- nez ma mou- ran- te vi- e; si de quel- ques fra- yeurs je vous pa- rais sai- si- e, ce n'est pas vo- tre bar- ba- ri- e, c'est vo- tre pi- tié que je crains.

[enchaîner]

LA JALOUSIE
Pour cal- mer vos en- nuis le ciel i- ci m'ap- pel- le, l'en- fer s'in- ter- es- se pour vous; vou- lez- vous con- ser- ver u- ne flam- me im- mor-

-tel- le pour un vo- la- ge, un in- fi- dè- le? Ah! ne sui- vez que vos trans- ports ja- loux; pour ac- ca- bler l'in- grat d'u- ne hai- ne cru- el- le, que, s'il se peut, vo- tre cou- roux é- ga- le les plai- sirs de son ar- deur nou- vel- le.

[enchaîner]

PROCRIS
Gra- ces aux dieux, je suis au com- ble des mal- heurs. Le sort me fût tou- jours con- trai- re; mais je ne cro- yais pas, ô ciel! que ta co- lè- re dû fi- nir, par ce coup, ma vi- e et mes dou- leurs!

Basse continue

[enchaîner]

Elle tombe évanouie.

LA RAGE: Pour obéir à la déesse, inspirons à Procris nos transports furieux. Profitons de cette faiblesse qui va cacher notre rage à ses yeux: venez, venez, démons, venez, venez montrez-vous en ces lieux; que chacun de nous s'empresse, que chacun de nous s'empresse d'obéir à la déesse.

LA JALOUSIE: Pour obéir à la déesse, inspirons à Procris nos transports furieux. Profitons de cette faiblesse qui va cacher notre rage à ses yeux: venez, venez, démons, venez, venez montrez-vous en ces lieux; que chacun de nous s'empresse, que chacun de nous s'empresse d'obéir à la déesse.

LE DESESPOIR: Pour obéir à la déesse, inspirons à Procris nos transports furieux. Profitons de cette faiblesse qui va cacher notre rage à ses yeux: venez, démons, venez montrez-vous en ces lieux; que chacun de nous s'empresse, que chacun de nous s'empresse d'obéir à la déesse.

Basse continue

Scène sixième

La Jalousie, La Rage, Le Désespoir, Troupe de Démons, Procris évanouie.

Chœur de Démons

DEMONS
Ac- cou- rons, ac- cou- rons, traî- nons nos fers, traî- nons nos fers. Nous al- lons dans ces lieux pour rem- plir vo- tre at- ten- te, ré-

8
-pan- - - dre la ter- reur, le
[6]
[6]
12
trou- ble et l'é- pou- van- te, nous al- lons dans ces lieux pour rem- plir vo- tre at-
[5♭]
16
-ten- te, ré- pan- - - dre, ré-
[6]

-pandre la terreur, le trouble et l'épouvante; accourons, accourons, accourons, accourons, traînons nos fers, traînons nos fers, Transportons ici les enfers.

Entrée de Démons

Air de Démons

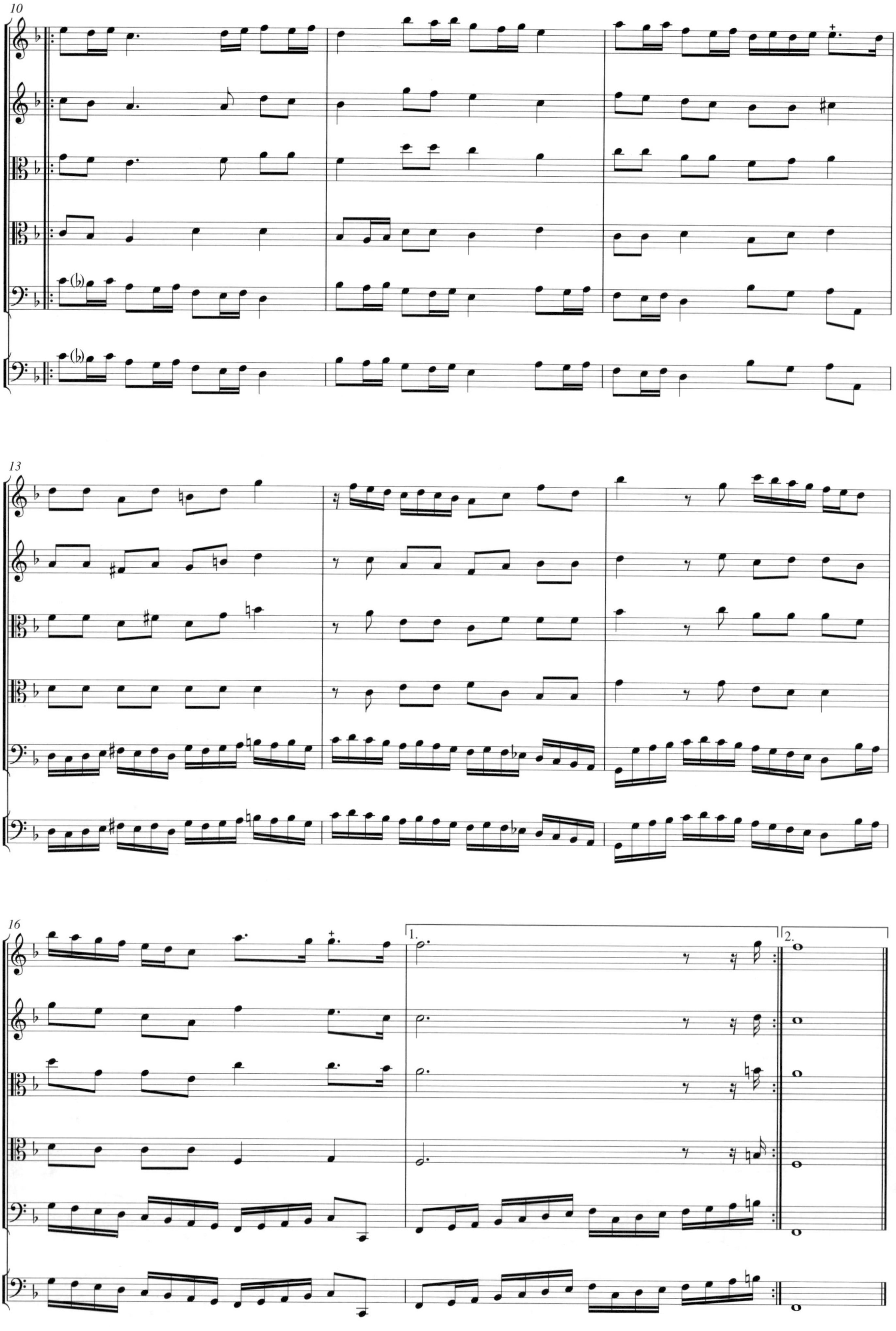
10
13
16
1.
2.

La Jalousie s'approche de Procris.

LA JALOUSIE

Sor- tez, sor- tez d'un hon-teux es- cla- va- ge. Mé-pri- sez l'In-con-stant qui cau- se vo- tre en- nui. Que le dé- pit, la fu- reur et la ra- ge vous a- ni- ment seuls au- jour- d'hui. Non, non, vous ne sau- -riez lui fai- re trop d'ou- tra- ge, la hai- ne que l'on sent pour un a- mant vo- la- ge, se me- sur- re à la a- mour que l'on a- vait pour lui, non, non, non, vous ne sau- riez lui fai- re trop d'ou- tra- ge, la hai- ne que l'on sent pour un a- mant vo- la- ge, se me- su- re à l'a- mour que l'on a- vait pour

[enchaîner]

Choeur de Démons

LA JALOUSIE: lui.

Haute-contre: Sortez, sortez d'un honteux esclavage. Méprisez l'Inconstant qui cause votre ennui. Que le dépit, la fureur et la

Taille: Sortez, sortez d'un honteux esclavage. Méprisez l'Inconstant qui cause votre ennui. Que le dépit, la fureur et la

Basse: Sortez, sortez d'un honteux esclavage. Méprisez l'Inconstant qui cause votre ennui. Que le dépit, la fureur et la

ra- ge, vous a- ni- ment seuls au-jour-d'hui. Non, non, non,
ra- ge, vous a- ni- ment seuls au-jour-d'hui. Non, non, non,
ra- ge, vous a- ni- ment seuls au-jour-d'hui. Non, non, non,

non, vous ne sau- riez lui fai- re trop d'ou- tra- ge, vous ne sau- riez lui fai- re trop d'ou-
non, vous ne sau- riez lui fai- re trop d'ou- tra- ge, vous ne sau- riez lui fai- re trop d'ou-
non, vous ne sau- riez lui fai- re trop d'ou- tra- ge, vous ne sau- riez lui fai- re trop d'ou-

-tra- ge, la hai- ne que l'on sent pour un a- mant vo- la- ge, se me-

-su- re à l'a-mour que l'on a- vait pour lui.

Non, non, vous ne sau-riez, non, non, vous ne sau-riez lui fai-re trop d'ou-tra-ge, la hai-ne que l'on sent pour un a- mant vo- la- ge, se me- su- re à l'a-mour que l'on a- vait pour lui.

Non, non, non, non vous ne sau-riez lui fai-re trop d'ou-tra-ge, non, non, non, non,

non vous ne sau-riez, vous ne sau- riez lui fai- re trop d'ou- tra- ge,

non vous ne sau-riez, vous ne sau- riez lui fai- re trop d'ou- tra- ge,

non vous ne sau- riez lui fai- re trop d'ou- tra- ge,

la hai- ne que l'on sent pour un a-mant vo- la- ge, se me- su- re à l'a-mour que l'on a- vait pour lui.

la hai- ne que l'on sent pour un a-mant vo- la- ge, se me- su- re à l'a-mour que l'on a- vait pour lui.

la hai- ne que l'on sent pour un a-mant vo- la- ge, se me- su- re à l'a-mour que l'on a- vait pour lui.

Second Air [de Démons]

*Les Démons et La Jalousie inspirent leur
fureur à Procris, et se reitrent.*

Scène septième

Procris, Cephale, Dorine

Le théâtre change, et représente les mêmes jardins qui avaient paru auparavant.
Procris sort de son évanouissement, agitée des fureurs que La Jalousie vient de lui inspirer.

PROCRIS: L'In- grat... mais, dieux! où suis- je? CEPHALE: En- fin le ciel pro- pi- ce... PROCRIS: Per- -fi- de, je te vois? va, fuis loin de mes yeux: par tes men- son- ges o- di- eux tu ne peux plus cou- -vrir ton in- jus- ti- ce. Cher- che des lieux rem- plis de traî- tres, d'im- pos- -teurs, où l'on puis- se i- mi- ter tes tra- hi- sons se- crè- tes. Pour le mal- heur, hé- -las! des fu- nes- tes ar- deurs, tu n'au- ras que trop de re- trai- te. CEPHALE: Que di- tes- vous, cru- -el- le? ah! vous vou- lez en vain, sous un voi- le trom- peur, ca- cher vo- tre in- con-

PROCRIS
-stance. Pour me venger de ton offense, à ton rival je vais donner la main; j'achèterai bien cher une triste vengeance; j'en mourrai, je le sens, mais mon coeur sans effroi, verra de son destin les horreurs inhumaines, non, traître, je ne puis, par de trop rudes peines, me punir de l'amour que j'ai senti pour toi.

CEPHALE
Vous m'accusez, quand j'ai lieu de me plaindre...

PROCRIS
Tes détours seront superflus: crois-moi, ne cherche point à feindre; mon coeur est détrom-

-pé, je ne t'é-cou- te plus. Va re-trou-ver ta con-quê-te nou- vel- le que ne puis-je, à tes yeux, plus char-man- te et plus bel- le, sur el-le rem-por-ter le prix! De ton per- fi- de coeur me ren-dre sou-ve- -rai- ne, pour pay- er à ja- mais de froi-deur et de hai- ne l'ar-deur dont tu se- rais é- -pris.

Elle sort.

CEPHALE

Sans vou- loir m'é- cou- ter, l'In- gra- te se re- ti- re! Ah! c'est au dé- ses- poir que je dois re- cou- rir! Je ne puis plus souf- -frir un si cru- el mar- ty- re. Cou-rons la voir, l'a- pai- ser, ou mou- rir.

FIN DU QUATRIEME ACTE

Acte V

Scène première

Procris, Dorine

Le théâtre représente un bois.

Ritournelle

PROCRIS

Ne me parle plus d'un parjure. Prends-tu quelque plaisir d'aigrir mon désespoir? Ah! plutôt pour m'aider à suivre mon devoir, dis-moi que j'en reçois la plus cruelle injure, et quoique mon coeur en murmure, que ma gloire m'oblige à ne jamais le voir. A ne jamais le voir? ô gloire trop cruelle! Céphale, hélas! que ne m'es-tu fidèle? Quelle que fût des dieux l'impitoyable loi, prête à mourir du coup qui nous sépare, j'aurais, malgré le ciel bar-

-ba- re, la dou- ceur d'ex- pi- rer en te don-nant ma foi? Quel plai-sir, en mou-

-rant, de te voir, de t'en- ten- dre? Tes yeux me don- ne- raient des

pleurs, et le soin de tes jours pour- rait seul me dé- fen- dre de te ren- dre té-

-moin de tou- tes mes dou- leurs. Mais, in- grat, tu me fuis, et ma ten- dres- se est

vai- ne, ton lâ- che coeur se plaît à me tra- hir! Cru- el, ah! quand tu

vois que ma mort est cer- tai- ne, dois- tu, pour re- dou- bler ma pei- ne, con- train- dre, en ex- pi-

-rant mon coeur à te ha-ïr? Ce-pha-le au dé-se-spoir m'a fait voir ses a-

DORINE

-lar-mes; j'ai vu ses yeux bai-gnés de lar-mes, vous cher-cher pour ban-nir vo-tre cru-el-le er-

PROCRIS

-reur. Non, non, il veut en-core trom-per mon fai-ble coeur; Do-ri-ne, mon tré-

-pas n'au-ra rien qui l'é-ton-ne. Re-ve-nez, re-ve-nez ma jus-te fu-

-reur. Je ne sau-rais a-voir trop en hor-reur le per-fi-de qui m'a-ban-don-ne.

C'en est fait, je le hais; je ne veux plus son-ger qu'à sui-vre un fier de-

-voir qui seul peut me venger. Inutile couroux, impuissante vengeance, en vain, pour me tromper, je fais ce que je puis.

DORINE
De vos transports calmez la violence: on vient.

PROCRIS
Hélas! doit-on me contraindre au silence, quand la plainte peut seule adoucir mes ennuis?

[enchaîner]

Scène seconde

Borée, Procris, Dorine, Troupe de Thraces et d'Athéniens

Prélude

238

Dessus de violon 1
Dessus de violon 2
BOREE
A- près de mor- tel- les pei- nes, que l'hy- men a d'ap- pas pour deux
Basse continue
Basse continue
coeurs a- mou- reux; reux; non, non, non, il n'a point de dou- ces chaî-
- nes, si l'A- mour n'en for- me les noeuds, non, non, non, il n'a
point de dou- ces chaî- - nes, si l'A- mour n'en for- me les noeuds.
[enchaîner]

[Duo]

PROCRIS: Après de mortelles peines, que l'hymen a d'appas, que l'hymen a d'appas pour deux cœurs amoureux ; non, non, non, il n'a point de douces chaînes, si l'Amour n'en forme les nœuds, non, non, il n'a point de douces chaînes, si l'Amour n'en forme les nœuds, non, non, non,

BOREE: Après de mortelles peines, que l'hymen a d'appas pour deux cœurs amoureux ; non, non, non, non, il n'a point de douces chaînes, si l'Amour n'en forme les nœuds, non, non, non, non, il n'a point de douces chaînes, si l'Amour n'en forme les nœuds,

Basse continue

il n'a point de dou- ces chaî- nes, il n'a point de dou- ces chaî- nes, si l'A-
non, non, non, non, il n'a point de dou- ces chaî- nes, si l'A-

-mour n'en for- me les noeuds, non, il n'a point de dou- ces chaî- nes, non il n'a
-mour n'en for- me les noeuds, non, il n'a point de dou- ces

point de dou- ces chaî- nes, si l'A- mour n'en for- me les noeuds.
chaî- nes, si l'A- mour n'en for- me les noeuds.

[enchaîner]

BORÉE
Rien ne me trouble plus, et ma joie est certaine; o

Basse continue

vous, chers confidents de mes tristes soupirs, et que je rends té-

[Air]

-moins de mon bon-heur su-prê- me, si vos coeurs pren-nent part à mes ten- dres sou- pirs, ho- no- rez la beau- té que j'ai- me.

[enchaîner]

Dessus de violon 1
Dessus de violon 2
BOREE
Basse continue

Em- pres- sez- vous, em- pres- sez- vous de ren- dre à ses beaux yeux, l'hom- ma- ge que l'on rend aux dieux, em- pres- sez- vous, em- pres- sez- vous de ren- dre à ses beaux yeux, l'hom- ma- ge que l'on rend aux

[enchaîner]

Choeur

BOREE: dieux.

Dessus 1, Dessus 2, Haute-contre: Em- pres- sons- nous, em- pres- sons- nous de ren- dre à ses beaux yeux, l'hom- ma- ge

Taille, Basse: Em- pres- sons- nous de ren- dre à ses beaux yeux, l'hom- ma- ge

Basse continue

6
[Violons seule]
[tous]
[Violons seule]
[tous]
[petit choeur]
[tous]
[petit choeur]
[tous]
que l'on rend aux dieux. Em- pres- sons- nous, em- pres- sons- nous, em- pres- sons- nous, em- pres- sons-
que l'on rend aux dieux. Em- pres- sons- nous, em- pres- sons- nous, em- pres- sons- nous, em- pres- sons-
que l'on rend aux dieux. Em- pres- sons- nous, em- pres- sons- nous, em- pres- sons- nous, em- pres- sons-
que l'on rend aux dieux. Em- pres- sons- nous, em- pres- sons-
que l'on rend aux dieux. Em- pres- sons- nous, em- pres- sons-
[4 2]
[3]
[6]
[7]
11
-nous de ren- dre à ses beaux yeux, l'hom- ma- ge que l'on rend aux dieux.
-nous de ren- dre à ses beaux yeux, l'hom- ma- ge que l'on rend aux dieux.
-nous de ren- dre à ses beaux yeux, l'hom- ma- ge que l'on rend aux dieux.
-nous de ren- dre à ses beaux yeux, l'hom- ma- ge que l'on rend aux dieux.
-nous de ren- dre à ses beaux yeux, l'hom- ma- ge que l'on rend aux dieux.

Premiere Entrée

Air

[Air]

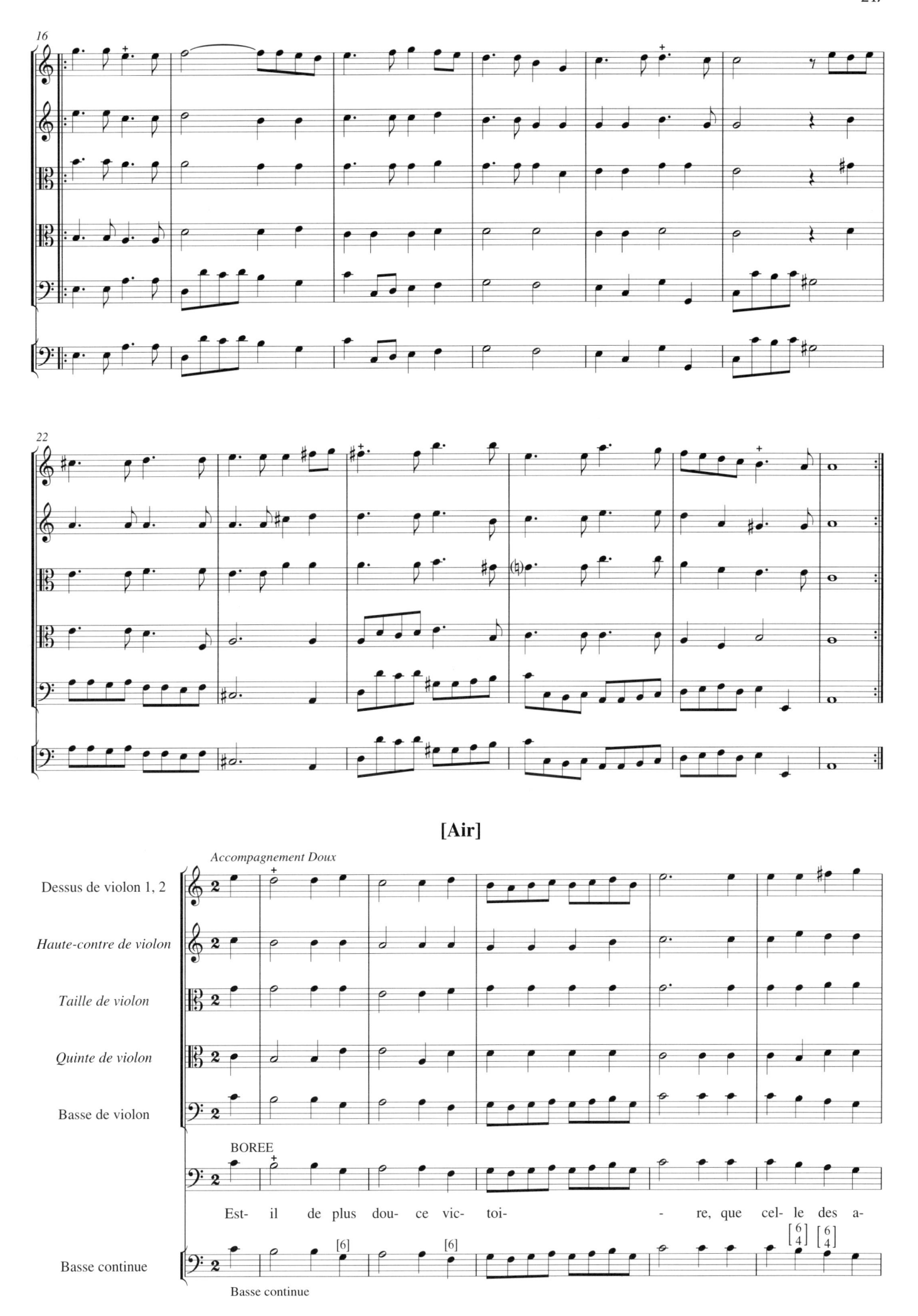

Accompagnement Doux

BOREE

Est- il de plus dou- ce vic- toi- - re, que cel- le des a-

-mants que l'A-mour rend heu- reux, est- il de plus dou- ce vic- toi- - re, que cel- le des a- mants que l'A- mour rend heu- reux? Quel tri- om- - phe, quel tri- om- - phe! quel- le gloi- re! de voir u- ne beau- té qui mé- pri- sait nos

249

44
- re, que cel- le des a- mants que l'A- mour rend heu- reux, est- il de plus
50
dou- ce vic- toi- - re, que cel- le des a- mants que l'A- mour rend heu- reux.

Choeur

Est-il de plus douce victoire, que celle des amants que l'Amour rend heureux? Est-il de plus douce vic-

-toi- re, de plus dou- ce vic- toi- re, que cel- le des a- mants que l'A-

-toi- re, de plus dou- ce vic- toi- re, que cel- le des a- mants que l'A-

-toi- re, de plus dou- ce vic- toi- re que cel- le des a- mants que l'A-

-toi- re, de plus dou- ce vic- toi- re, que cel- le des a- mants que l'A-

-mour rend heu- reux?

-mour rend heu- reux?

-mour rend heu- reux?

-mour rend heu- reux?

253

mé- pri- sait nos feux, cé- der et se ren- dre à nos voeux.

mé- pri- sait nos feux, cé- der et se ren- dre à nos voeux.

mé- pri- sait nos feux, cé- der et se ren- dre à nos voeux.

mé- pri- sait nos feux, cé- der et se ren- dre à nos voeux.

Quel tri-

Quel tri-

48
-om- - phe, quel tri- om- - - phe! quel-le gloi- re! de
-om- - phe, quel tri- om- - - phe! quel-le gloi- re! de
Quel tri- om- - phe, quel tri- om- - phe! quel-le gloi- re! de
Quel tri- om- - phe, quel tri- om- - phe! quel-le gloi- re! de
54
voir u- ne beau- té qui mé- pri- sait nos feux, cé- der et se ren- dre à nos voeux.
voir u- ne beau- té qui mé- pri- sait nos feux, cé- der et se ren- dre à nos voeux.
voir u- ne beau- té qui mé- pri- sait nos feux, cé- der et se ren- dre à nos voeux.
voir u- ne beau- té qui mé- pri- sait nos feux, cé- der et se ren- dre à nos voeux.

Est- il de plus dou- ce vic- toi- re, que cel- le des a-

-mants que l'A- mour rend heu- reux, est- il de plus dou- ce vic- toi- re, de plus
-mants que l'A- mour rend heu- reux, est- il de plus dou- ce vic- toi- re, de plus
-mants que l'A- mour rend heu- reux, est- il de plus dou- ce vic- toi-
-mants que l'A- mour rend heu- reux, est- il de plus dou- ce vic- toi-

dou- ce vic- toi- re, que cel- le des a- mants que l'A- mour rend heu- reux?
dou- ce vic- toi- re, que cel- le des a- mants que l'A- mour rend heu- reux?
-re, de plus dou- ce vic- toi- re, que cel- le des a- mants que l'A- mour rend heu- reux?
-re, de plus dou- ce vic- toi- re, que cel- le des a- mants que l'A- mour rend heu- reux?

Les Thraces recommencent leurs danses.

Premier Air

Second Air

Dessus de violon 1, 2
Hautbois 1, 2

Haute-contre de violon

Taille de violon

Quinte de violon

Basse de violon
Basson

Basse continue

BOREE
Ap-prou-vez les ar-deurs d'u-ne âme im-pa-ti- en- te, je vais pres-ser le Roi d'ac-com-plir mes dé- sirs. Les mo-ments qu'il dif-fè- re à rem-plir mon at- ten- te, il les dé-ro-be à mes plai- sirs.

Basse continue

Scène troisième
Procris, Dorine

PROCRIS

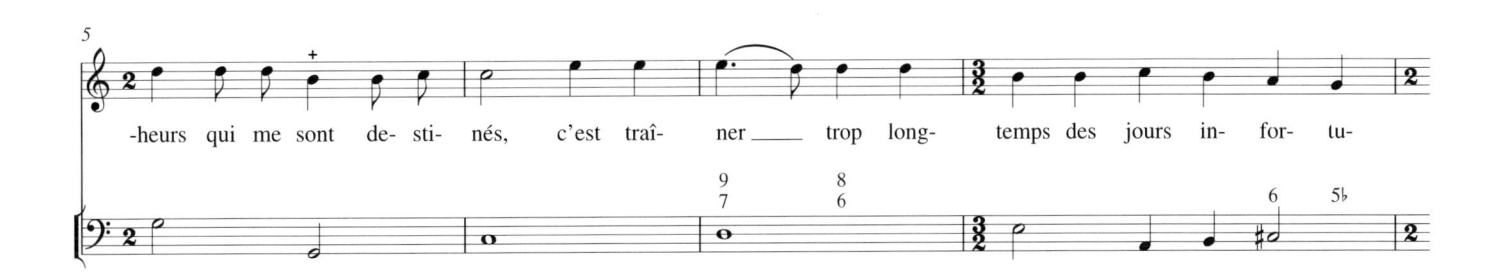

Ah! pendant ces moments, où je suis libre encore, prévenons les malheurs qui me sont destinés, c'est traîner trop longtemps des jours infortunés, et nourrir dans mon coeur l'ennui qui le dévore! Mourons...

Scène quatrième
L'Aurore, Procris, Dorine

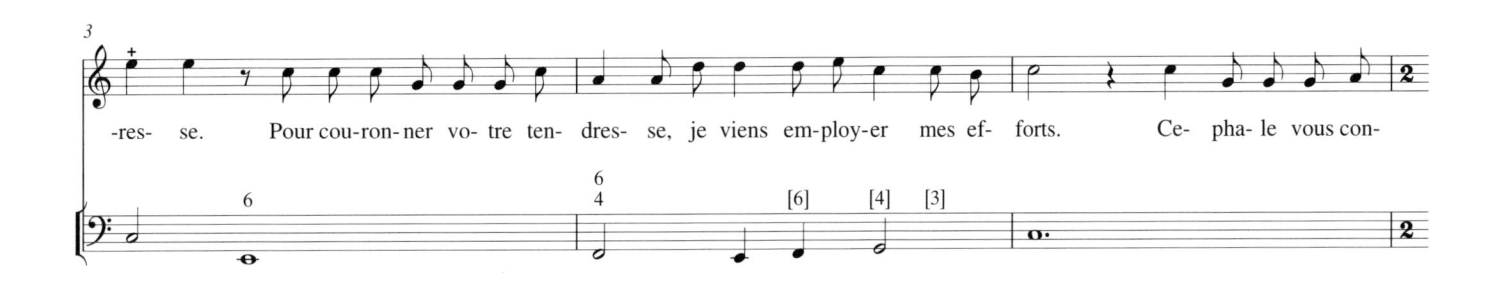

L'AURORE

Modérez vos transports, Procris, à votre sort l'Aurore s'intéresse. Pour couronner votre tendresse, je viens employer mes efforts. Cephale vous con-

-ser-ve u-ne im-mor-tel- le flam- me, u- ne ja- lou- se dé- i- té a fait in- spi- rer à vo-tre â- me un in- jus- te soup- çon de sa fi- dé- li- té.

PROCRIS
Quoi! Ce- pha- le? Ce- pha- le à mes maux est sen- si- ble? Il m'ai- me? Ah! mon de- stin m'en pa- raît plus af- freux!

L'AURORE
A mes dé- sirs il n'est rien d'im- pos- si- ble, ne crai- gnez point un hy- men ri- gou- reux. Al- lez, près d'un a- mant, par des ar- deurs nou-

-vel- les, re- nou- vel- ler vos flam- mes mu- tu- el- les, et des dieux a- pai- -sés ou- bli- er le cou- roux. Com- bien est- il de coeurs fi- -dè- les, qui par des pei- nes plus cru- el- les, vou- draient bien a- che- ter un suc- cès aus- si doux?

Prélude

[enchaîner]

Scène cinquième
L'Aurore

L'AURORE

Que fais-je? quel projet! une pitié fatale a servir ces amants me va-t'elle engager? Ciel! sans frémir puis-je songer au bonheur, dont mes soins vont combler ma rivale? Mais plutôt, de ma flamme un indigne retour, pourrait-il m'empêcher de vaincre mon amour? Cesse de m'attaquer, importune tendresse! Si les dieux sont jaloux, ils ne sont pas cruels, Plus notre rang nous place au dessus des mortels, moins nous devons partager leur faiblesse.

[enchaîner]

Scène sixième
L'Aurore, Iphis

L'AURORE
Hé bien ? de mes soins généreux, Céphale est-il content ? as-tu su l'en instruire ?

IPHIS
Céphale, des mortels est le plus malheureux.

L'AURORE
Juste ciel ! que vas-tu me dire ?

IPHIS
Le Roi, soumis aux volontés des dieux, a fait rompre un hymen à vos désirs contraire. Borée, irrité, furieux, a trouvé son rival assez près de ces lieux, Procris n'a pu suspendre leur colère, déjà de sa fureur prompt à se repentir, le Thrace allait prendre la

fui- te, lor- squ'un trait qu'au ha- zard, Ce- pha- le fait par- tir, frap- pe, d'un coup mor-

L'AURORE

-tel, la Prin- ces- se_in- ter- di- te. Qu'en- tends- je? ô des- tin ri- gou-

-reux! Pour- quoi t'op- po- ser à ma gloi- re? Tu viens m'en- le- ver la vic-

-toi- re que j'al- lais pour ja- mais rem- por- ter sur mes feux. Cent mou- ve- ments di-

-vers trou- vent pla- ce_en mon â- me; mal- gré tous mes ef- forts, u- ne se- crè- te

IPHIS **L'AURORE**

flam- me cher- che_en co- re_à s'y r'al- lu- mer. Ce- pha- le vient. Fu-

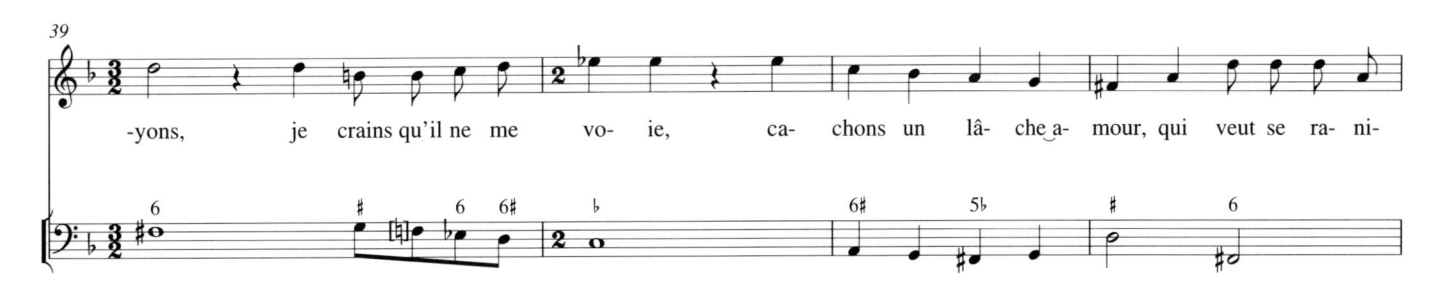

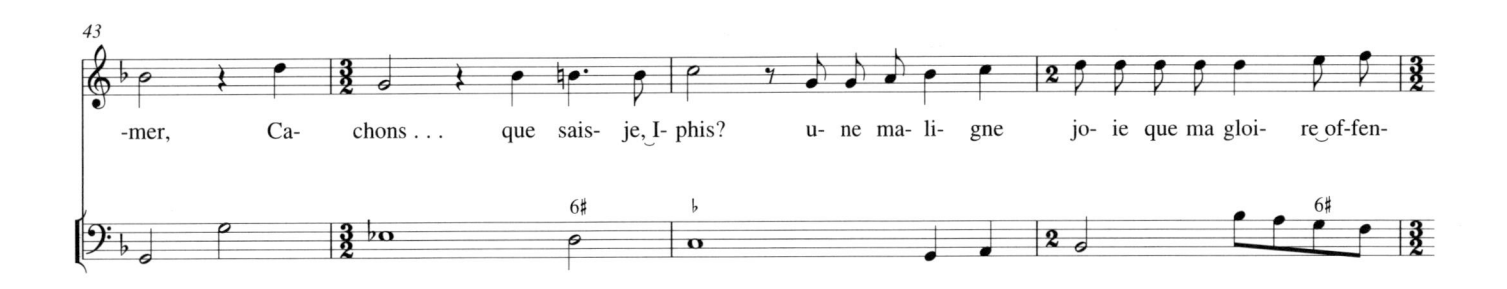

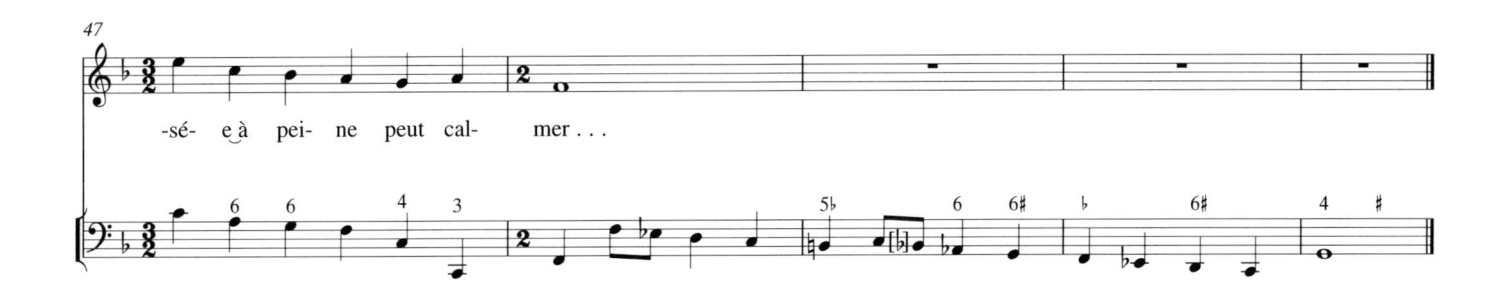

-yons, je crains qu'il ne me voie, ca- chons un lâ- che a- mour, qui veut se ra- ni- mer, Ca- chons... que sais- je, I- phis? u- ne ma- li- gne jo- ie que ma gloi- re of- fen- sé- e à pei- ne peut cal- mer...

Scène septième

Cephale, Arcas, Troupe d'Athéniens

CEPHALE

Ah! lais- sez- moi mou- rir! vo- tre pi- tié cru- el- le veut- el- le pro- lon- ger les ri- gueurs de mon sort? Mal- heu- reux que je suis! cet- te main cri- mi-

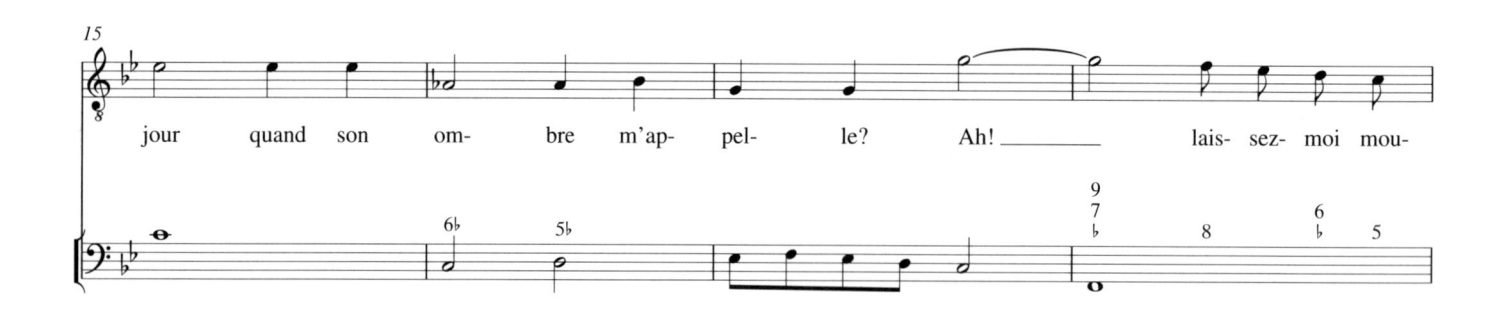

-nel- le à ma chè- re Pro- cris vient de don- ner la mort. Pour-quoi m'ar-ra- cher d'au-près d'el- le? Pour- quoi, par un bar- ba- re ef- fort, me re- te- nir au jour quand son om- bre m'ap- pel- le? Ah! _____ lais- sez- moi mou- rir! vo- tre pi- tié cru- el- le veut- el- le pro- lon- ger les ri- gueurs de mon sort?

Scène dernière

Procris mourante, soutenue par Dorine, Cephale.

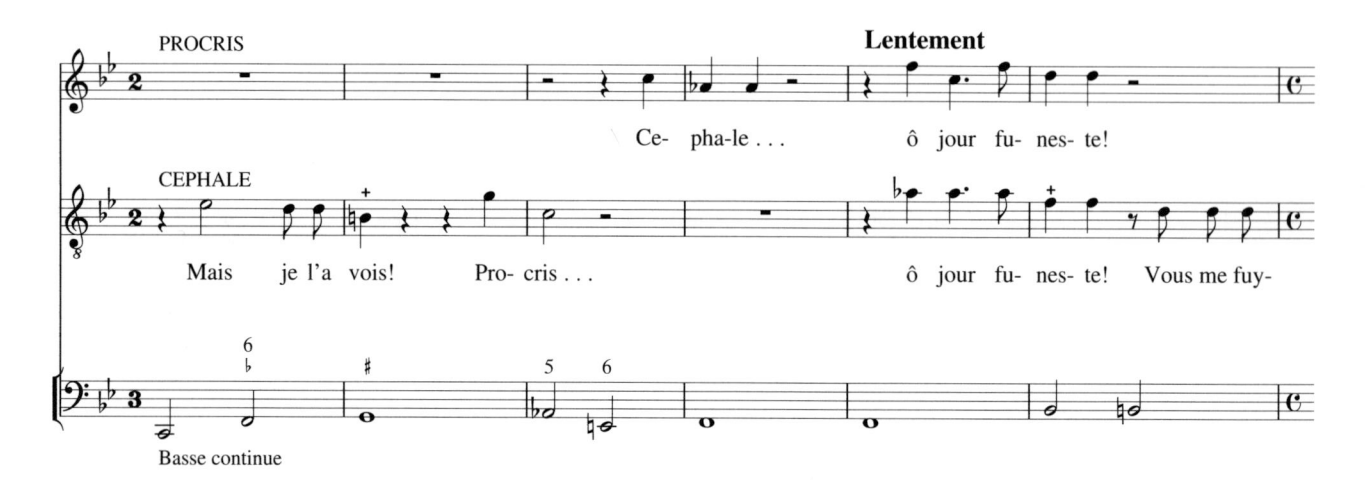

PROCRIS — **Lentement**
Ce- pha-le... ô jour fu- nes- te!

CEPHALE
Mais je l'a vois! Pro- cris... ô jour fu- nes- te! Vous me fuy-

Basse continue

ez? ah! res- tez dans ces lieux! Vou- lez- vous m'en- le- ver le seul bien qui me

res- te?

Hé bien! Ce- pha- le, hé bien! re- ce- vez mes a-

-dieux. A sui- vre vos dé- sirs mon pro- pre a- mour m'en- traî- ne; j'au- rais vou-

-lu, de peur d'aug- men- ter vo- tre pei- ne, me pri- ver du plai-

-sir de mou- rir à vos yeux.

Je vais vous sui- vre en la nuit é- ter- nel- le.

[enchaîner]

270

-nir de nos tris- tes a- mours ne trou- ble point le re- pos de vos jours, ou- bli- ez- moi plu- tôt, c'est moi qui vous l'or- don- ne. Tout mon corps s'af- fai- blit, je fré- mis, je me meurs. Dé-

30
Silence
Silence
-ja du noir séjour j'entrevois les horreurs; à mes yeux obscur-
35
-cis la lumière est ravie. Reçois ma main, Cephale, et sois sûr qu'en ce
40
jour, le dernier soupir de ma vie, est encore un soupir d'amour.

Elle tombe entre les bras de Dorine qui l'emmène.

CEPHALE
Achève, ô ciel barbare! assouvis ta colère! Ah! je sens qu'à la fin tu te rends à mes cris! Tu cesses de m'être sévère, je succombe à mes maux, rien ne m'est plus contraire, et je vais aux enfers rejoindre ma Procris.

FIN DU CINQUIEME ET DERNIER ACTE

Critical Report

Sources

This edition is based on the following four sources:

1. A set of manuscript partbooks for the complete opera housed at the Bibliothèque Nationale (Vm² 125). These partbooks serve as the principal source for this edition (hereafter "manuscript partbooks"). The partbooks contain emendations by Sébastien Brossard in some numbers of the prologue.

2. Sébastien Brossard's arrangement of the prologue, which he created for a performance at his Académie de musique in Strasbourg in 1696 (hereafter "Brossard's arrangement").

3. A printed score of *Cephale et Procris* published in 1694 by Ballard (hereafter "Ballard print"). The particular print used for this edition is owned by the University of California, Berkeley, Music Library.

4. The *livret*, as published in the eighteenth-century collection *Recueil géneral des opéra représentez par l'Académie Royale de musique, depuis son établissement* (Paris, 1703–46; reprint, (Geneva: Slatkine Reprints, 1971).

Manuscript Partbooks

The manuscript partbooks appear to have come from the Foucault shop on the Regle d'Or, the primary commercial source for acquiring partbooks in Paris in the 1690s. (For more on this shop, see Patricia Ranum, " 'Mr. de Lully en trio': Etienne Loulié, the Foucaults, and the Transcription of the Works of Jean-Baptiste Lully (1673–1702)," in *Jean-Baptiste Lully, Actes du colloque/Kongressbericht, Saint-Germain-en-Laye—Heidelberg 1987*, ed. Jérôme de La Gorce and Herbert Schneider [Laaber: Laaber-Verlag, 1990], 309–30.) These partbooks were therefore not intended for use by the professional orchestra at the Opéra, but for purchase by amateurs who wished to perform sections of an opera in their own home. This particular set of manuscript partbooks is the only one known to exist for Jacquet's opera and came to the Bibliothèque Nationale with Sébastien Brossard's collection of music and books on music, which he offered to the king in exchange for a pension around 1729.

The set includes eight partbooks: premier dessus recitante, second dessus recitante, haute-contre recitante, taille recitante, basse recitante, premier dessus de violon, second dessus de violon, and basse continue.

This edition is based on the manuscript partbooks. This source is given priority because it was intended for use by a group of musicians, albeit amateur, and because it contains information not found elsewhere (internal choral parts, ornamentation, etc.). I have not attempted to eliminate performance information added by Brossard to prologue pieces in the manuscript partbooks during the course of creating his arrangement. These have been allowed to stand, given their significance as a window on performance practice in a specific place, Strasbourg, at a specific time, 1696. Since Brossard's arrangement only contains music for the prologue, these parts have been consulted to clarify scoring, but no attempt has been made to indicate every variant note, rest, or ornament.

Brossard's Arrangement

Brossard's arrangement of the prologue includes a conductor's score bound with the following vocal and instrumental parts: haute-contre, taille (two books), basse, violino ripieno, violino 2, 3e dessus ou haute-contre de violon, basse de viole, fagotto ou basse de violon. The conductor's score, as might be expected, essentially duplicates the parts found in the manuscript partbooks and Brossard's prologue parts (the conductor's score indicates a few ornaments at different points than those found in the partbooks).

Comparing the list of manuscript partbooks with the parts in Brossard's arrangement quickly reveals that the latter does not contain sufficient parts to perform the prologue. There are no dessus recitante parts, for example. This suggests that Brossard used the set of commercially available manuscript partbooks (which he probably purchased during a trip to Paris in 1695) as the basis for his arrangement, supplementing these partbooks with parts that he himself wrote out or had copied. This hypothesis is supported by the fact that the premier dessus and basse recitante partbooks contain certain markings found only in the prologue. These markings give performance indications, such as breath marks, and performing versions of some solo and duet pieces in the basse recitante partbook, as described in "Notes on Performance." The basse continue partbook likewise has extensive figured bass indications for the prologue, but none for acts 1 through 5.

The parts in Brossard's arrangement are less complete than a straightforward listing indicates. The taille and haute-contre recitante parts, for example, contain music only for the choruses in the prologue, while the manuscript vocal partbooks each contain all the music for that voice part, solo music as well as choruses. Apparently the soloists in Brossard's performance used the appropriate manuscript partbook and the chorus members used the vocal part from his arrangement.

Brossard composed one completely new part, the 3^e dessus ou haute-contre de violon. This was perhaps because he did not have three string players available to cover the usual three internal parts: haute-contre, taille, and quinte de violon. The front page of this part contains the following description: "3e Dessus / ou haute contre de Violon / avec la quelle on se / peut passer de Taille / et de quinte / Tante dans les Simphonies / que dans les choeurs. / acommodée et composée / par SB 1696."

Both the manuscript partbooks and Brossard's arrangement contain important performance information. The choral manuscript partbooks contain internal choral parts (haute-contre and taille) for most of the choruses (although internal parts are consistently missing for the two full choruses in act 5). The manuscript partbooks also provide many ornamentation indications for both voice and instruments, many more than are found in the published score.

Ballard Print

The Ballard print is a "memorial" score, published for amateurs to purchase so that they could play and sing their favorite sections of the opera in their homes. It is published in *parties réduits* and therefore contains only the outer voices (dessus and basse), except when trio texture is present. In these cases both of the two dessus parts are present along with the lowest part, which is usually in the haute-contre range. Several copies of this score are known to have survived: RISM lists sixteen (fifteen in European libraries and one at the University of California, Berkeley). One other copy exists in the United States: Special Collections at Honnold Library of the Claremont Colleges also holds a copy of the 1694 Ballard print. (This library has not participated in the process of reporting their holdings to RISM.) The score is part of the Seymour Collection and was a gift from a donor. It has been held by the library for about twenty years.

The main contribution of the Ballard print to this edition is the figured bass indications for acts 1 through 5. As noted in the introduction, there are no figures outside of the prologue in the basse continue partbook.

Livret

The *livret* as it appears in the eighteenth-century collection cited above is the only known source for this text. (The copy of the *livret* at the Bibliothèque et Musée de l'Opéra in Paris came to my attention too late to be of use in this study.) Descriptions of the stage at the beginning of each act (or scene, if appropriate), as well as several stage directions, which do not appear in either the manuscript partbooks or the published score, are found in this source. Since Ballard only lists the characters who actually sing or dance in that scene, the list used in this edition is usually taken from the livret. Discrepancies are noted in the critical report.

The text in the *livret* does not exactly match the text in the music sources, which is not unusual for the time. There are brief passages of poetry that appear in the *livret*, but which are not set to music; likewise, there are brief passages of poetry that are set in the opera, but which do not appear in the *livret*. The *livret* also has a few scene divisions that differ slightly from those in the published score. (See below under "Editorial Methods" for discussion of how these various discrepancies are handled in the edition.)

Editorial Methods

This edition retains as much as possible the musical text as found in the manuscript partbooks, while putting this information into a useful performing edition, one in which issues of consistency must necessarily override those of retaining insignificant details. For example, the length of the final note in some pieces varies from part to part in the manuscript sources. Ballard usually shows these to be consistent, that is, all whole notes or all dotted half notes. When there was a discrepancy among the manuscript partbooks, I employed the note value that appeared most often at that point, or, if there was no clear concensus, consulted Ballard and followed its lead. The length of the final note for each part that differed from what appears in the edition is noted in the critical notes.

Parts Added to Complete the Score

As already described, the set of manuscript partbooks on which the present edition is based is not complete. Seventeenth-century French orchestral texture is essentially five-part, but the partbooks have music for only the two outer voices, dessus and basse. Since the Ballard print was published in *parties réduits,* it also contains only the two outer parts. No partbooks for the three internal instrumental parts have come to light. I have, therefore, composed the three missing string parts, haute-contre, taille, and quinte de violon. Brossard's prologue arrangement includes a 3e violon part for those pieces that would have called for full orchestra, but this was apparently a compromise measure adopted to make up for a shortage of instrumentalists. I have not transcribed this partbook in this edition, although I consulted it for appropriate rhythms and implied harmonies while preparing the internal parts. Brossard's 3^e violon part contains rhythms which differ slightly from the outer two parts. I have incorporated these deviations in the internal instrumental parts in the prologue. Brossard's 3^e violon part also occasionally crosses above the dessus de violon. These crossings appear in the haute contre de violon part in the prologue. Lacking an internal instrumental part for acts 1 to 5, I have been more conservative in both rhythm and voice crossings when realizing these internal instrumental parts.

Due to the unusual nature of the sources, the score as presented represents a balance between giving the reading of the sources and providing the minimum of editorial additions to allow for performance of the work. To this end, the following criteria have guided editorial decisions:

1. Dessus parts, both vocal and instrumental, are presented on one staff where possible, with all relevant instrument names listed at the beginning of the number. For trio textures the dessus splits into two staves. Textual cues above the staff indicate variations in the orchestral texture.

2. Except for the prologue, where it is based on Brossard's part, the basse de violon duplicates the basse continue.

3. Haute-contre, taille, and quinte de violon have been added by the editor. These parts complete the inner voices of the five-part texture in use at the time. They fill in the harmony and do not aim for independence. In choruses the instrumental parts fill in the harmony, and do not simply double the internal choral parts. The haute-contre de violon generally uses treble clef and the other two use alto clef.

The internal choral partbooks (haute-contre recitante and taille recitante) contain many alterations, both in pitch and rhythm, in the two prologue choruses. These changes were probably made by Brossard when preparing his Strasbourg performance. No attempt has been made to determine the original notes in these passages, as the original notes have been thoroughly obliterated. Internal choral parts do not appear to have been tampered with in acts 1 through 5.

Internal choral parts are missing from the chorus "Quel plaisir pour les coeurs fidèles" in act 2 and from the two choruses found in act 5, "Empressons-nous" and "Est-il de plus douce victoire." Adequate space was left in each choral partbook, and the indication "Choeur" appears at this point in both the haute-contre and the taille recitante partbooks. I have therefore created these two parts for both choruses for the present edition.

The taille recitante partbook also indicates an additional chorus for which a part was apparently called for, but never copied into the partbook: the second "Choeur de Démons" in act 4 ("Sortez, sortez d'un honteux esclavage"). This chorus appears to be a two-part chorus in Ballard with the top and bottom staves indicating alto and bass clef respectively, reflecting the nature of a *parties réduits* score. These two parts are found in the haute-contre and basse recitante partbooks. Since this chorus appears to have been originally a three-part chorus, I have also created the missing taille part for this chorus.

All of these editorially added parts are signaled in the score by the use of italic for the voice names.

Title Elements

Titles for acts, scenes, and individual pieces are based on Ballard, but spelling and accents have been modernized and periods at the end of words or lines have been omitted. Included with these titles are stage descriptions found in the livret. These are presented in italic type with modernized spellings and accents. Titles of individual pieces, which originally appeared between the staves in the manuscript partbooks and Ballard, are centered above the top staff as in modern practice. Scene designations follow the partbooks, some of which differ slightly from the *livret*. Discrepancies are noted in the critical notes. As was often the case in seventeenth-century *tragédies lyriques,* the prologue does not contain any scene divisions.

Rather than retaining the inconsistent approach present in Ballard, the words "Basse continue" appear at the beginning of each piece during which the harpsichord would probably have played. (See "Notes on Performance" in the introduction.)

Textual cues in the partbooks, such as *seul, duo,* or *choeur,* have been tacitly removed. Indications such as *accompagnement, tous,* etc., have been retained as these indications provide information about intended performing forces. In a few cases character names are missing from the manuscript sources. These are supplied in brackets from Ballard or the *livret*.

Score Elements

Tempo indications are found in the manuscript partbooks only in the prologue, with one or two exceptions. All tempo indications are placed above the winds and above the strings as in modern practice, first letters capitalized and spellings modernized (e.g., *viste = Vite).* Where one partbook indicates a French tempo and another its Italian equivalent, I have used the French term and reported the Italian designation in the critical report.

Modern score order is employed, with vocal parts immediately above the basse continue. The original part names, both choral and instrumental, have been retained, but spelling and orthography have been modernized. As in modern practice, brackets have been used to group together instrument families and braces delineate multiple staves of the same instrument.

Clefs have been modernized. The French violin clef (G1) has been transcribed throughout as a treble clef (without indication). C clefs in the haute-contre and taille vocal parts have been transcribed with a treble or tenor G clef, as appropriate. C clefs in the basse continue have been regularized. Treble clef is used for the haute-contre de violon and alto clefs for the taille and quinte de violon parts created for this edition.

Key signatures have been modernized to eliminate redundant indications. All meter signatures have been retained as in the original manuscript partbooks, with any discrepancies among the partbooks specified in the critical notes.

Repeat signs have been modernized to show first and second endings. Completion of the second ending has been added when necessary for clarification, with the original indicated in the critical notes. Repeats are sometimes inconsistent in the manuscript partbooks. One partbook, for example, contains a repeat indication where another writes out the entire passage. In these cases, the music has been written out in full if ornaments or other markings differ between first and second versions, and a comment appears in the critical notes.

The measures are numbered consecutively for each piece. Long sections of recitative are treated as a single piece. When such sections are interrupted by an air, the air is treated as a separate piece. When the texture changes from *duo* to *choeur*, for example, measure numbering starts over even though a double bar may not be indicated in the source. As in modern practice, the ends of pieces are indicated with thin-thick barlines. This should not be interpreted to indicate that a large break is appropriate, as music in the *tragédie lyrique* was essentially continuous (see "Notes on Performance" in the introduction). This is reinforced throughout the score by use of the word *enchâiner* at the ends of pieces.

Dances or other instrumental pieces repeated from earlier in the scene are reproduced in full in the present edition. Pieces to be repeated to serve as entr'actes, however, are indicated in the score by a written directive.

Notation

Stem direction follows modern practice, which does not differ greatly from what appears in the sources.

No attempt has been made to indicate passages that should be performed with *notes inégales*. The dotted eighth-sixteenth patterns found in the final section of the *ouverture* are transcribed here as they appear in the manuscript partbooks with one modification. These passages appear in the partbooks notated with simply a dot, the necessary shortening of the next note to a sixteenth being understood. I have employed modern practice, showing both the dot and the subsequent sixteenth note. In the score, only the basse de violon and basse continue have been regularized in respect to the *notes inégales*.

The seventeenth-century convention of employing dotted notes for durations that cross the barline has been modernized by dividing the note into two note values and using a tie across the barline. Whole notes occurring in measures with meter signatures such as $\frac{6}{4}$ are transcribed without comment using dotted whole notes, rather than the plain whole notes in the original. Beaming follows modern practice, making each metrical unit as clear as possible.

Very few slurs or ties have been added to those found in the manuscript partbooks. Those added editorially are shown as dashed slurs.

Breath marks which appear in the prologue in the premier dessus recitante partbook have been included as modern breath marks (an elevated comma).

A few grace notes and appoggiaturas are found in the sources. These are included in the transcription without any attempt at interpretation. Ornaments are indicated in the sources solely by a French trill (+). Those found in the present edition come from the manuscript partbooks, as relatively few ornaments are present in Ballard. Occasionally, a trill sign occurs where a singer has one syllable spread between two notes, indicated by a slur. When the ornament appears in the original to be between the two slurred notes, an attempt has been made to recreate the look of the original (see, for example, act 1, scene 4, "Pourquoi veux-tu que je m'engage," m. 22).

Neither accents nor articulations can be found in the sources, so none are included in the edition. Fermatas appear only at a few points and are placed above the top staff of each instrument family in the edition, rather than above each individual part. If a fermata appears in only one partbook, it has not been included, but its presence indicated in the critical notes.

The only dynamic indications are found in the prologue, presumably added by Brossard. In the sections where the texture alternates between full orchestra (*grand choeur*) and trio (*petit choeur*), the words "tous," "tutti," and "fort" indicate full orchestra and the words "trio" and "doux" indicate the smaller group. When present in the manuscript sources, these indications are included above the strings in the edition. Editorial additions are given in square brackets.

Accidentals have been modernized so that they apply through the end of the measure in which they appear, and so that the natural sign is used to cancel a sharp or flat. Redundant accidentals have been removed without comment. Accidentals implied in the music but missing from the score appear in brackets next to the note. Cautionary accidentals appear in parentheses in front of the note.

Figured bass indications derive from two sources: in the prologue they reflect the extensive figures found in the basse continue partbook, figures added by Brossard for his Strasbourg performance. In the prologue I have deleted Brossard's figures for the large instrumental pieces and choruses in which no trio textures occur, retaining them only for the pieces which the harpsichord would have played. The figures found in acts 1 through 5 come from Ballard, as there are no figured bass indications in the basse continue partbook beyond those in the prologue. While figures sometimes appeared above and sometimes below the basse continue line in the seventeenth century, figures in this edition are placed above the basse continue stave. Editorial figures appear in square brackets. The edition retains the practice of the source in which a sharp means a major third above the bass or cancels a flat, and a flat means a minor third above the bass. The indication 3♯ has been changed to ♯ without comment.

Lyrics

The use of an ampersand (&) in the original text has been modified throughout to the French word "et." Syllabification follows the guidelines in *The Chicago Manual of Style*, 14th ed. Orthography follows modern French practice in both spellings and accents. The *livret* as printed in the "Text and Translation" section has been made to agree with the text underlay in the edition. Deviations of individual words between the *livret* and the manuscript partbooks are noted in the critical notes.

Neither the vocal manuscript partbooks nor Ballard's arrangement attempt to underlay text so that specific syllables and notes are clearly aligned. The text underlay in the edition, therefore, reflects my understanding of how text and music fit together. Punctuation in the manuscript partbooks is haphazard or missing altogether, so punctuation in the edition largely reflects what is found in the printed *livret*.

Critical Notes

The notes below describe rejected readings of the manuscript partbooks. Pitch names are standard: c′ refers to middle C. The following abbreviations are used: D = Dessus; HC = Haute-contre; T = Taille; B = Basse; Fl. = Flûte; Hb. = Hautbois; Bn. = Basson; Tpt. = Trompette; Vn. = Violon; Hc.Vn. = Haute-contre de violon; T.Vn. = Taille de violon; Q.Vn. = Quinte de violon; B.Vn. = Basse de violon; B.c. = Basse continue.

Prologue

OUVERTURE

M. 18, B.c., Presto. Mm. 21–22, B.c., barline missing. M. 36, B.c., notes 4–6, doubled an octave below. M. 37, B.c., notes 1–4, doubled an octave below. M. 45, B.c., Adagio. Mm. 45–46, Vn. 2, both the Vn. 1 and Vn. 2 part appear after note 1. M. 47, B.Vn., notes 2–5, eighth notes. M. 49, Vn. 2, notes 1–2, eighth notes. M. 51, B.Vn., notes 2–5, eighth notes; B.c., note 1, figured bass flat. M. 54, Vn. 2, note 6 is b′. M. 55, B.Vn., notes 2–5, eighth notes. M. 56, B.Vn., notes 3–6, eighth notes. M. 57, B.Vn., notes 3–6, eighth notes. M. 58, B.Vn., notes 5–6, eighth notes.

"IL EST TEMPS"

Commentary. The indication "Mr Robert" appears in the basse recitante partbook. He was one of the singers known to have been in the employ of the Cathedral in Strasbourg where Brossard was *maître de musique*.

M. 1, B., note 1, d and g.

"RIEN NE DOIT RETARDER"

M. 1, B., ¢. M. 10, B., meter is missing. M. 11, B.c., note 1, figured bass flat.

CHOEUR: "CHANTONS, CHANTONS"

Commentary. Livret lists this piece as "Choeur de Nymphes et de Faunes" (Chorus of Nymphs and Fauns).

M. 2, B.c., note 4, figured bass flat. M. 16, T, note 5 is e′. M. 26, B.c., note 1, eighth. M. 29, Bn., T, B, B.Vn., note 1, half note. M. 58, T, half note and half rest; B.Vn., and B.c., half note.

RONDEAU

M. 40, Vn. 2, half note; B.Vn., note 1, first note of "Passe-pied pour les violons"; B.c., crossed out.

PASSE-PIED POUR LES VIOLONS

M. 1, B.c., Prestissimo; quarter note added over two eighth rests. M. 25, Vn.1, dotted quarter note.

PASSE-PIED POUR LES HAUTBOIS

M. 1, B.c., no rests. M. 15, B.c., note 1, sixteenth, note 3, eighth. M. 25, B.c., has repeat sign.

"QU'UN COEUR"

M. 6, *livret* has "Sous l'empire." M. 8, B.c., no repeat sign (passage written out).

PASSE-PIED POUR LES VIOLONS [REPRISE]

M. 1, B.Vn. and, B.c., no rests; B.c, Prestissimo.

PASSE-PIED POUR LES HAUTBOIS [REPRISE]

M. 1, B.Vn. and B.c., no rests. M. 25, B.c., dotted quarter note.

"QUELLE DIVINITÉ"

M. 7, Flore, whole note.

MARCHE POUR NERÉE

Commentary. The untranscribed Basse de violle part gives the tempo as Presto.

CHOEUR: "CHERCHONS À SATISFAIRE"

M. 6, D 1 and 2; note 2, g″. M. 20, B.c., note 2, figured bass 5; note 3, figured bass 7. M. 41, B.c., note 3, figured bass 6. M. 68, HC, fermata: B.Vn., meter signature is $\frac{6}{4}$ with dotted half note tied to half note.

LOURE

M. 12, Vn.2, notes missing.

"L'AMOUR SOUMET"

M. 20, HC (Dieu), no repeat sign

GIGUE

M. 1, B.c., Prestissimo.

"A L'ABRI DU FRACAS"

Commentary. The name "Mr Pichon" appears in the basse recitante partbook. He was one of the singers known to have been in the employ of the Cathedral in Strasbourg where Brossard was *maître de musique*.

"VOLEZ, VOLEZ"

M. 1, B.c., Presto. M. 9, HC, note 2, a♭′. M. 21, B.c., note 2, two eighth notes, c′–b. M. 58, HC and T, half note. M. 114, D 1 and 2, note 3, b.

Acte I

Scène première

Commentary. Ballard lists those on stage only as "Borée, Procris."

"UN SEUL DE VOS REGARDS"

M. 5, B.c., notes 2–4, b–a–g.

"MALHEUREX QUI RESSENT"

M. 2, *livret* has "On ne goûte." M. 48, Borée, note 2, could be c♯′.

Scène seconde

"Cephale a t'il su"

M. 19, Procris, note 1, half note followed by half rest.

Scène troisième

Commentary. Ballard lists those on stage only as "Procris, Arcas."

"Le devoir de Cephale"

M. 12, B.c., note 2, Ballard has 5♭6 in figured bass.

Scène cinquième

"Célébrons"

M. 65, B.c., bass clef missing.   M. 103, Vn. 1, beat 3, quarter note.   M. 104, Vn. 1, beat 3, two eighths.

Second Air

M. 1, B.c., quarter rest followed by dotted half note. M. 9, B.c., note 3, d.   M. 16, Vn. 1, note 3, a″.   M. 30, B.c., second ending missing.

Scène septième

"Que vois-je?"

M. 9, Prêtresse, fermata over the rest.   M. 30, Prêtresse, whole note.   M. 51, livret has "Mon rival." M. 60, Roi, dotted half note.

Acte II

Scène première

"Lieux écartés"

M. 17, B.c., note 2, Ballard has 5♭ in figured bass.   M. 70, Vn. 2 and B.c., meter signature missing.   M. 89, Vn. 1 and 2, note 3, ♮.

"Cephale vient"

M. 3, Procris, meter signature missing.

Scène seconde

"L'amour, belle Procris"

M. 10, *livret* has "Ce n'est pas."

"Le ciel m'avait flatté"

M. 2, *livret* has "d'une."   M. 12, Procris and Cephale, note 3, ♮.   M. 28, Procris, note 1, g♮′.

Scène troisième

"Dieux cruels"

M. 7, Vn. 2, note 3, half note.

Scène quatrième

"Quel plaisir" (choeur)

M. 10, Vn. 1., note 3, eighth.

"Paisibles habitants"

Mm. 1–26, Thrace, vocal music not in manuscript partbooks (transcribed from Ballard).

Scène cinquième

Les Pâtres

M. 20, B.c., note 3, B.   M. 23, Vn. 1, no repeat sign.

"Les Rossignols"

M. 1, B.c., note 3, b.   M. 25, Vn. 1, no repeat sign.

Scène sixième

Commentary. Ballard lists those on stage as "Cephale, Borée, Troupe de Thraces."

"Vous n'êtes pas"

M. 23, Cephale and B.c., meter signature change missing.   M. 30, B.c., meter signature missing.

Scène septième

Commentary. In the *livret*, the beginning of this scene is indicated at L'Aurore's entrance just before Cephale sings "Le traître me braver."

"Nous ressentons"

M. 5, B.c., note 1, figured bass has flat below the 6.

"Procris peut vous tromper"

M. 3, B.c., note 1, figured bass 6 is below the flat.   M. 9, *livret* has "à mieux le connaître."

"Quoi, l'objet charmant"

M. 1, B.c., key change missing.   M. 11, Cephale and B.c., meter signature missing.   M. 30, L'Aurore, keychange is after rest; B.c., key change missing, but present at beginning of next system (m. 34).   Mm. 30–31, B.c., double bar.   M. 39, L'Aurore, note 2, g′.   M. 44, B.c., notes 2–4 are G–F–E.

Acte III

Scène première

"Amour, que sous tes loix"

M. 20, B.c., note 2, figured bass 6.   M. 42, Vn. 2, notes missing.

Scène troisième

Commentary. The *livret* lists the characters on stage as "Cephale, Iphis, La Volupté, Troupe de Jeux, de Plaisirs, et de Suivantes de la Volupté." La Volupté is given there as singer for "Tendres amants" and "Loin de ces lieux."

SYMPHONIE

M. 41, Vn. 1, note 1, quarter.   M. 46, Vn. 2, note 2, b'. M. 49, Vn. 2, note 2, c".

"LOIN DE CES LIEUX"

Commentary. Livret lists "La Volupté" as the singer.

PASSACAILLE

M. 75, Vn. 2, notes 2–3, rests.   M. 76, Vn. 2, whole rest. M. 77, Vn. 2, note 1, rest.

"LA DOUCE FOLIE"

M. 35, Vn. 2, notes 1–2, f♯'.

"VOUS ME BRAVEZ, CRUEL"

M. 10, B.c., note 1, figured bass 9.

Scène quatrième

Commentary. The *livret* lists those present only as "L'Aurore, Iphis, Cephale."

"POUR DISSIPER VOTRE TRISTESSE"

M. 60, key signature change missing (2 sharps indicated starting on the next system, m. 62).

Acte IV

Scène première

"LE FEU DE TON AMOUR"

Mm. 18–23 left out of present edition: copyist's error that repeated mm. 12–16 with no text underneath.   M. 20, Dorine, no fermata.

"N'ESPEREZ PAS"

M. 14, B.c., note 4, figured bass sharp.

"LES MÉPRIS"

Mm. 21, Vn. 2, note 4, c".

"VIVONS TOUJOURS"

M. 3, Dorine, note 3, c".

Scène seconde

Commentary. The indication "Dorine et Arcas se retirent" appears only in Ballard, not in the *livret*. *Livret* indicates a change to scene 3 at this point. Scene numbers between *livret* and partbooks are off by one until scene 6.

"O VOUS IMPLACABLE ENNEMIE"

M. 21, Vn. 1, notes 3–7, d'.   M. 22, Vn. 1, note 3, d'. M. 26, Vn.1, note 1, dotted half note.   M. 27, Vn. 1 and Vn. 2, note 2, g'.   M. 32, Vn. 1, notes 2–3, eighths.

"SORTONS, LA JALOUSIE"

M. 10, Aurore, note 1, half note.   M. 38, B.c., note 1, figured bass sharp.

Scène troisième

"FUNESTE MORT"

Commentary. M. 38: Natural sign on second half of measure is present in Ballard but not in the basse continue partbook.

M. 32, B.c., note 1, figured bass is $\frac{6}{4}$.

Scène quatrième

Commentary. Ballard lists no characters on stage.

Scène sixième

Commentary. Ballard lists only "Choeur de Démons" at beginning of scene.

"ACCOURONS"

M. 2, Vn. 1, notes 4–7, sixteenths.

CHOEUR: "SORTEZ"

M. 5, HC, note 2, e'.   M. 7, HC, note 2, c'; B, note 2, a. M. 48, Vn. 1, note 6, a'.   M. 50, Vn. 1 and 2, notes 8–9, d"–b'.

SECOND AIR

M. 11, Vn. 1 and Vn. 2, note 4, a'.

Scène septième

Commentary. Livret lists only "Procris, Cephale" at beginning of scene.

"L'INGRAT"

M. 44, B.c., note 2, c.

Acte V

Scène première

"NE ME PARLE PLUS"

M. 69, Procris, rest, no fermata.

Scène seconde

Commentary. Livret lists characters on stage as "Procris, Borée, Dorine, Troupe de Thraces."

PRELUDE

M. 1, B.c., note 1, missing.   M. 6, Vn. 1, note 5, c".

"APRÈS DE MORTELLES PEINES"

M. 6, B.c., no repeat sign (passage written out).

"Empressons-nous"

Commentary. Problematic scoring in the sources has been changed to reflect a typical chorus with alternating *grand* and *petit choeur*. The second dessus recitante partbook simply doubles D 1 throughout, but there is a second voice stave in Ballard which has rests everywhere except in the passages which have a C clef in the B.c. There Ballard indicates notes for D 2, a third below D 1. This is typically how Ballard indicates where D 2 separates from D 1 for *petit choeur* passages, rather than setting the entire piece with two largely identical vocal lines. In the present edition, the transcription for the second dessus recitante reflects the typical scoring in which that voice doubles D 1 except in trio texture passages.

M. 12–13, Vn. 2, all notes up a third.

Air

M. 15, Vn. 2, no second ending.

"Est-il de plus douce"

M. 36, B.c., note 3, a. M. 53, Vn. 1, notes 6–8 are f″–e″–c″.

Choeur: "Est-il de plus douce"

M. 34, Vn. 1 and Vn. 2, note 3, e″.

Premier Air

M. 26, Vn. 1 and Vn. 2, meter signature is $\frac{6}{4}$, half note.

Second Air

M. 18, Vn. 1, two dotted half notes, tied.

Scène cinquième

"Que fais-je?"

M. 21, B.c., note 1, figured bass sharp.

Scène sixième

"Hé bien"

M. 3, B.c., note 1, dotted half followed by three eighths, d–c–B. M. 10, B.c., meter signature missing. Mm. 11, B.c., meter signature missing. Mm. 11–23, Iphis, key signature has one flat.

Scène septième

Commentary. Livret lists characters on stage as "Cephale, Troupe d'Atheniens."

Scène dernière

Commentary. Livret lists characters on stage as "Procris mourante, soutenue par Dorine, Cephale, Troupe d'Atheniens."

"Mais, je l'a vois"

M. 20, Procris, meter signature missing.

"Non, vivez"

M. 4, B.c, note 1, figured bass $\frac{6}{3}$. M. 44, Vn. 2, fermata over the rest.